Enriching
Business Ethics

PLENUM STUDIES IN WORK AND INDUSTRY

Series Editors:
Ivar Berg, *University of Pennsylvania, Philadelphia, Pennsylvania*
and Arne L. Kalleberg, *University of North Carolina, Chapel Hill, North Carolina*

A Continuation Order Plan is available for this series. A continuation order will bring delivery of each new volume immediately upon publication. Volumes are billed only upon actual shipment. For further information please contact the publisher.

Enriching Business Ethics

Edited by

Clarence C. Walton

The American College
Bryn Mawr, Pennsylvania

With a Foreword by
Reverend Theodore M. Hesburgh, C.S.C.

PLENUM PRESS • NEW YORK AND LONDON

Library of Congress Cataloging in Publication Data

Enriching business ethics / edited by Clarence C. Walton; with a foreword by Theodore
M. Hesburgh.
    p.   cm.—(Plenum studies in work and industry)
    Includes bibliographical references.
    ISBN 0-306-43450-4
    1. Business ethics. 2. Business ethics—United States. I. Walton, Clarence Cyril, date. II.
Series.
HF5387.E67   1990   90-34656
174 .4—dc20   CIP

© 1990 Plenum Press, New York
A Division of Plenum Publishing Corporation
233 Spring Street, New York, N.Y. 10013

Printed in the United States of America

Contributors

Ivar Berg, School of Arts & Sciences, University of Pennsylvania, Philadelphia, Pennsylvania 19104-6383

Paul Camenisch, Department of Religious Studies, DePaul University, Chicago, Illinois 60614

Dennis McCann, Department of Religious Studies, DePaul University, Chicago, Illinois 60614

Clarence J. Gibbs, Jr., Laboratory of Central Nervous System Studies, National Institute of Neurological Disorders and Stroke, National Institutes of Health, Bethesda, Maryland 20892

James R. Glenn, Jr., San Francisco State University, School of Business, San Francisco, California 94132

James W. Kuhn, Graduate School of Business, Columbia University, New York, New York 10027

Lynn Sharp Paine, Harvard Business School, Boston, Massachusetts 02173

Barry Schwartz, Department of Psychology, Swarthmore College, Swarthmore, Pennsylvania 19081

Rabbi Gordon Tucker, Jewish Theological Seminary, New York, New York 10027-4649

Clarence C. Walton, The American College, Bryn Mawr, Pennsylvania 19010

Foreword

Over thirty years ago, Alfred North Whitehead wrote: "If America is to be civilized, it has to be done (at least for the present) by the business class who are in possession of the power and the economic resources. . . . If the American universities were up to their job, they would be taking business in hand and teaching it ethics and professional standards."*

To the intellectual elites of his time, there was something of a minor heresy in Whitehead's view. Few of them saw business as a civilizing force and even fewer, feeling that business was not to be tamed, relished the role of the lion tamers. Not many today doubt Whitehead's wisdom. Organizations of wealth and power have accepted their corporate social responsibilities, and universities have launched major efforts to provide ethical instruction for business personnel.

So far as the scholars are concerned, they quickly came to realize the difficulty of an undertaking that seeks to redefine and apply moral criteria to a very complex corporate world. Philosophers, in particular, have learned (or perhaps have relearned) how their speculations on ethics must take into account the "living ethic" expressed in the American culture— and here anthropologists, sociologists, and theologians were needed to provide an expertise that the moral manuals did not. Ethicians also came to appreciate the executive's concern for efficiency and profits—and at this juncture, the lawyer and economist played their roles in defining the connection of morality to law and competition. Moralists also discovered that understanding relationships between management and labor is far more complicated than understanding only the significance of strikes or lockouts—and so the expertise of historians and labor relations scholars had to

---

*Lucien Price, Ed., *The Dialogues of Alfred North Whitehead*. New York: New American Library, 1956, pp. 56–57.

be relied on. The catalog of the philosopher's need for help from other disciplines could, of course, be extended.

Recognizing this need led Clarence Walton, himself a recognized pioneer in business ethics, to assemble a group of scholars who were asked to respond to an easily phrased but not easily answered question: "What is there in your discipline that seems to have special relevance to the field of business ethics?" Their essays are uniformly informative and provocative.

From Walton's brilliant overview to each of the contributors' essays has come a feast for the mind: Incisive commentaries on the relevance of the Judeo-Christian tradition to modern business; splendid treatments of the changing secular culture and the questions it raises for traditional values; summons to labor and management to end their century-old rivalry because their common interests demand it; and a biting critique of the paradigms used in neoclassical economics, sociobiology, and behavioral psychology. There is also an essay on the latest scientific information on the AIDS crisis and the moral questions it has raised, and another on the results of a study made of student attitudes toward ethics—a point of special interest to employers and university admissions offices.

While Clarence Walton's primary effort is to help the ethicists, the final result helps all of us—managers and media, professors and students, doctors and lawyers. It is no surprise that, with each essay a gem, the totality is sparkling.

REVEREND THEODORE M. HESBURGH

President Emeritus
University of Notre Dame

Preface

During the late nineteenth century, the field of history experienced a drastic change when great scholarly journals began to appear in Western Europe and in the United States. Their appearance encouraged university-based historians to specialize in narrow fields to the neglect of those grand-scale narratives that their early mentors had once written. As specialization intensified, historians wrote mainly for other historians and the practice of refereed journal articles became the standard route to promotion and tenure. A century later, philosophers who concentrated on management behavior and business institutions were spared the criticism leveled at the historians—and for solid reasons: Their numbers were few; their influence was meager; their readership was minimal. The first public awakening to the importance of business ethics came in the late 1950s when General Electric and Westinghouse managers were indicted for price fixing. At that time, however, the emphasis was more on the *unlawful* than the *unethical*.

Roughly a decade ago, things began to change—quickly and dramatically. In the defense industry, Lockheed, Northrop, and General Electric pleaded guilty to overcharging the government. Wall Street began to hemorrhage when Boesky, Levine, and Milken were cited for insider trading; the savings and loan industry sat on a powderkeg of incompetence and, often, corruption; the various "-gates" (Water, Contra, and Wright) grabbed headlines in American newspapers. A typical response to such shenanigans came in a 1988 survey of over 1,000 senior executives, deans of business schools, and members of Congress. The results were sobering: 99 percent of the deans, 95 percent of the corporate leaders, and 77 percent of the Congress felt deeply troubled over the unethical behavior of major figures in the country's financial and manufacturing organizations.

With a suddenness that caught most people off guard, the cry for "Mr. Clean" began. The clamorings were soon matched by contributions. The firm of Arthur Anderson and Company made available $5 million to support efforts to improve the teaching of business ethics at both the graduate and undergraduate levels; John Shad, former head of the Securities and Exchange Commission, made a splash with his pledge of over $20 million to support teaching and research in ethics at his alma mater, the Harvard Business School; centers and institutes on business ethics appeared with dizzying speed; ethical consultants were suddenly in demand; chairs in business schools went begging. Business ethics was the "in" thing.

Because philosophers of business now enjoy a relatively high profile, their immediate danger comes not from writing only for others in their own domain—the historians' problem—but from spinning sophisticated theories (moral egoism, deontology, or utilitarianism) that have not been enriched by the latest insights from the social and biological sciences, from law and religion. If ethicists face any challenge, it is to widen their lenses in order to capture and incorporate findings from other disciplines. This has become critically important because the primary reasons given in the polls for unethical activity were business' concentration on short-term earnings and decay in the nation's culture and social institutions.

The "social decay" factor is especially disturbing to church leaders, psychologists, sociologists, lawyers, and managers themselves. For this reason, representatives from these fields must be heard. To encourage the "hearing" process, the writer organized a symposium at which business philosophers themselves would not speak so much as listen, would not provoke but be provoked, would not expand the horizons of others but expand their own. It was hoped that representatives from the cognate disciplines would expose their modes of reasoning as well as some of the results of their analyses. If business economists concentrate on the bottom line and legal scholars on the boundary line, ethicists focus on the fair line and religions on the skyline. Managers walk on all lines and recognize the importance of knowing who draws the lines and why they are drawn in particular ways.

Financial support for the project came from Arthur Andersen and Company, one of the Big Eight accounting firms, and from The American College in Bryn Mawr, the oldest accredited nontraditional institution for the educational preparation of professionals in life insurance and financial counseling. Participants from all parts of the United States who attended the seminar engaged in lively dialogue. The essays that provoked such discussions have been incorporated into this volume for distribution to a wider audience of managers, professors, and students.

In preparing a book of this kind, dependence on others is particularly heavy. It follows, therefore, that although debts mount, not all can be acknowledged. However, it is important to express gratitude to special groups or people. First are the authors who have contributed to this volume. Next are the participants in the symposium, whose insights have enriched the essayists' respective works. Not to be ignored are the sponsors, the American College and Arthur Andersen and Company, whose generous financial support has made it all possible. Finally, I wish to name two individuals who have worked with me in the preparation of this volume—Mrs. Sue Turner and Mrs. Laura Turner. Not sisters, they nevertheless worked smoothly as a family team. I thank them most sincerely.

CLARENCE C. WALTON

Bryn Mawr, Pennsylvania

Contents

Chapter 8

Business Students and Ethics: Implications for Professors
and Managers 213

James R. Glenn, Jr.

Chapter 9

Acquired Immune Deficiency Syndrome: The Biological, Ethical,
    and Moral Dilemmas of This Twentieth-Century Plague 235

Clarence J. Gibbs, Jr.

Chapter 10

Clarence C. Walton

I
OVERVIEW

Business Ethics
Widening the Lens

Clarence C. Walton

When the field of business ethics is discussed, critics call it soft and muddled—even pale in the shadow-gray world it so often depicts. What critics overlook, however, is the ability of moral philosophers to help them *think through* critically important value issues. A mode of thinking that is better than other forms of moral analysis is what ethicists seek to promote. From its critics, however, ethicians hear fusillades that sound something like this: Business ethics is *useless, irrelevant, dangerous*, and *confused*. By such standards, business ethics should never have been conceived. If these descriptives were accurate, moral philosophers would find their feet in ankle-high canons of scholarship. It is well, therefore, first to address each of the charges before considering the main task, namely, learning what other social sciences can offer to business ethicists.

I. THE STATE OF BUSINESS ETHICS

A. The "Useless" Argument

Influential people like Wall Street guru Felix Rohaytn and MIT Dean Lester Thurow have stated publicly that teaching business ethics to adults makes little sense: People learn values at their mother's knee, or they never learn them. It is a comforting thought—without substance. In the light of

Clarence C. Walton • The American College, Bryn Mawr, Pennsylvania 19010.

so many corporate aberrations, parents either do not teach or cannot teach—or many of their offspring are abysmal learners. The fact is that all life is a moral journey. New experiences provide new challenges, and new responses require new insights. To say, therefore, that the moral life is lived without moral learning runs counter to reality. There is, furthermore, empirical evidence from psychologists that shows that roughly between ages 18 and 30 significant advances are made in moral understanding.[1] So it is time to dismiss the "useless argument" as useless.

B. The "Irrelevant" Argument

No one conversant with the literature on business ethics can fail to be impressed by the recurrent use of an argument made over 20 years ago in the pages of the *Harvard Business Review*.[2] The proposition was advanced by Albert Z. Carr who wrote that business, like poker, had its own rules. The trick is to learn the rules, obey the rules, and pledge total fealty to the organization. Moral codes for one's personal life were salutary but "in their office lives managers cease to be private citizens; they become game players who must be guided by a somewhat different set of ethical standards."[3] It should be noted that Carr was more circumspect than many of his followers who came to believe that the development of other rules for either market operations or for business careers might well produce ethical schizophrenics.

Here again, critics overlook an important point. Individuals do not automatically shed their moral codes the moment they enter office doors. If no effort is made to sharpen moral insights, the result is a business world peopled by moral eunuchs where a Gresham's Law of morality develops: Bad ethics drive out good ethics. The relevance of honesty, truth, and fairness to the efficient operation of the market system (and to organizations operating within it) is demonstrably true. To conclude in this fashion is not to say that there are no rules of the game in business. It is to say that without moral rules the game turns nasty.

A variant of the "irrelevant" theme has been made by economist Milton Friedman who argues that business ethics provides two criteria— and two only: (1) use resources efficiently and (2) obey the law.[4] By doing so, all other blessings will come. But efficiency and equity do collide, and laws can be ineffective or poorly administered. It is lawful to peddle pornography. It is legal to pay minimum wages to the nonunionized. It is legal to lead a takeover assault—even when the takeover artist has absolutely no interest in promoting stockholder interests. It is legal to engage in leveraged buyouts by management when the game strategy is solely to preserve the boss's job. The litany goes on. What is lawful can be unethical.

C.   The "Dangerous" Argument

Many who subscribe to high levels of morality for business are none-theless skeptical of business ethicists. They fear that philosophers are less interested in education and more in indoctrination. Business deans have been sensitive to this charge, often pointing out that courses in business ethics first flourished in church-related institutions. At this point an histor-ical footnote is worth recalling. Twenty-five years ago (when the Carnegie and Ford reports on reforming the business curricula appeared), quality faculties faced the issue of business ethics and its role in the professional curriculum. What the Columbia business faculty did was symptomatic of those times: It discussed and debated, created task forces, and heard detailed reports—but it circled the problem quite circumspectly. The near-est the faculty came to business ethics was its pioneering program, Con-ceptual Foundations of Business. A fascinating effort, the course dealt with the origins of private property and contract, the evolution of unions and corporations, and so on. But the course was overwhelmingly descriptive. Its analytical content dealt overwhelmingly with the need for economic efficiency. Questions of equity came slowly, and often indirectly.

Because senior executives generally favored a substantial component of ethics in the business curriculum, it appears in retrospect that deans and faculties missed the boat. And the one on which they are now asked to embark worries some of them. Is the vessel of ethics to be called the *Crusader*? What port will it visit? How much will the sailing cost?

D.   The "Confused" Argument

The most telling criticism of business ethicists is that they themselves neither agree on the kind of moral reasoning that is most logical nor on the criteria most relevant for specific acts or policies. Raised here is the specter of endless quibblings between the deontologists who believe with Kant that morality consists in doing one's duty according to principles estab-lished *a priori* by the mind[5] and the utilitarians who subscribe to John Stuart Mill's maxim that ethics consists of doing things that promote the greatest good of the greatest numbers.[6]

The confusion has been exacerbated by the popularity of Cambridge Professor G. E. Moore who, in 1903, startled his contemporaries by flatly denying that *good* was definable: "goodness, like yellowness, is a subjec-tive assessment [resting] on a form of perception, not on inference."[7] Moore would have us believe that practical moral principles are inaccessible to the mind and that seeking to establish them has little relevance to actual conduct. The debates continue. Stephen Toulmin recently assured us that because the truth or falsity of moral judgment can be determined by the accurate possession of facts, Moore is, therefore, wrong. One can make valid inferences that lead to valid moral judgments.[8] Whereas Toulmin concentrated on specifics, another respected philosopher, R. M. Hare, stressed universals—a command or imperative reached syllogistically on the basis of inductive analysis.

> All men are mortal
>
> Socrates was a man
>
> Socrates was mortal[9]

Hare feels that ethics has two essential features: It is prescriptive (a person should do so-and-so), and it has universability (all are obliged to follow a common norm). In sum: There is some truth in the charge that business moralists have much to do to put their house in order. But to cease seeing value in ethical inquiry is like ceasing to see value in legal or economic inquiry: Learned judges reverse other learned judges; respected economists critique other respected economists—and so on. The utility of ethical inquiry, like the value of other forms of critical investigation, is found in the way individuals learn the art of moral reasoning, an art demanding the same levels of analytical sophistication that are found in other of the nonphysical sciences.[10]

II. THE ART OF MORAL REASONING

What, then, are managers and students to make of all this? Are moral judgments the results of gut reactions? Is one person's morality as good as another's? Pleasant though an affirmative answer may be (it removes from our mental shoulders the heavy freight of hard thinking), its results are a form of moral relativism that threaten an organization's success and a government's effectiveness. Carried to extremes, moral relativism negates a basic purpose of university education, namely stimulation of the student's reasoning faculties on all aspects of reality.[11]

So managers and managed, as well as pupils and pedagogues who enter the moral thicket, sense that a word made famous by René Descartes is the name of the game: *cogito,* "I think." Critical thinking about moral issues releases people from the bondage of dogmas and ideologies. Individuals so involved may seek resources for their business philosophies in diverse places—Puritanism or Confuciousism, Judaism or Islamism, Catholicism or Protestantism, Kantianism or Benthamism.[12] The attempt is to reconcile individual and societal needs—what philosophers call the *One* and the *Many.* So a learner may find a inspiration in a single major philosopher—Aquinas or Anselm, Bentham or Kant; on the other hand, mentoring may come from many—Aquinas and Anselm, Bentham and Kant. Sorting out the best from each may be the best we can do. Whether the approach is toward synthesis or sorting, it demands the *cogito* element.

A.   The "Sidgwick Circle"

An example of the *cogito* effort can be found in Henry Sidgwick, a late nineteenth-century English philosopher whose great contribution to managers and students was a clear description of his own intellectual odyssey.[13] It was a struggle that moved from conviction to confusion and back again to conviction. Sidgwick was first attracted to the Intuitionists, a badly split group heavily influenced by Kant, who claimed that through the union of understanding and sense-acquired knowledge one could discover canons of morality.[14] Finding Intuitionism quite unsatisfactory (they were hopelessly loose in their definitions and axioms, said Sidgwick), he became a Utilitarian because Bentham and Mill struck him as having made a good case for the argument that an act was good when it promoted the greatest good of the greatest number. He then began to build his own logic for supporting Utilitarianism, but construction was halted when Sidgwick discovered flaws in Bentham's and Mills's reasoning. One that particularly upset him was the ambiguous meaning they attached to *happiness*, a key concept in their vocabulary. So Sidgwick retraced his steps to intuition via Aristotle's theory of commonsense morality (veracity and good faith are the authentic ethics) and Kant's principle of justice.[15] By combining the two he constructed Utilitarianism on different principles: "I was a Utilitarian again, but on an Intuitional basis . . . and I could find no real opposition between the two."[16]

Divorced from jargon, Sidgwick's reasoning goes something like this: A duty ethic of Kant (do no harm) is a good place to begin. However, because harm is the consequence of an action, concern for consequences cannot be dismissed. What consequences are, therefore, to be sought? Bentham, speaking for the Utilitarians, has a quick answer: the greatest good of the greatest number. So far, so good. But consequences of what sort, asks the increasingly frustrated inquirer? *Pleasure* is the utilitarians' reply. But problems persist: Is it not possible that one person's pleasure is another's pain? Is it not possible to contribute the greatest good of the greatest number while harming a minority, especially a helpless minority? Finally, is it possible to be sure that actions intended to serve the greatest number are what the greatest number will deem to be in their best interests at some future date?

Uncertain answers to one or all questions begin to dampen enthusiasm for total acceptance of Bentham's argument. So back to Kant, aware that you have already found his ethic deficient. Nevertheless, his do-no-harm ethic involves not simply action and result: It also involves the motive that precedes the act, not simply the consequence that follows the act. Motive is important. Emerging is a possible combination of criteria from Kant and Bentham, a Kan-Ben ethic that says: Will no harm and do no harm but, in addition to avoiding harm, do things that help the large majority of the community. Willing no harm eliminates casual hurting any minority. Willing a "good" means serving others effectively. What Kan-Ben ethics stresses are the rights of others. The I-Thou maxims must remain secure. Sidgwick's journey may be repeated by those who seek to sharpen their modes of moral thinking. It is likely that "cogito" managers and students will run full circle before breaking out to develop their own moral logic. In the so-called real world, they know that recipe answers to different moral questions are hard to come by. They also know that answers have to be made. In the response process, comfort comes from the fact that some logical defenses are more trustworthy than others, but they have to be discovered, ironically enough, in what are often called "self-evident" truths.[17]

B. Closing the Circle

To end with analogy: Ethical reasoning is like a tourist taking the Circle Line river tour around New York. Schedules and piers are published, and after a leisurely 2-hour cruise visitors return to the same dock. But they are not exactly the same people. Different perspectives of the skyline have resulted in different perceptions of the metropolis. The urban image becomes more complex—and more exciting. Perspective sharpens perception. Consider, for example, the story told by A. A. Achenbaum (then a senior vice president and director of marketing services at the J. Walter Thompson advertising agency) who described his experience at a meeting on general semantics and information flow.

> At that meeting, a group of twenty executives were told to sit in a circle. The group leader asked us to describe an apple, and passed one to the first person he came to. The obvious answer of the first person was to say that it was red. The next—following the color lead—said it was also yellow; another said it had green in it; the next said it was mostly red.
>
> There then followed a whole series of descriptions on its shape (some saying it couldn't be measured) until someone remarked that we were only talking about the outside. How about cutting it in half and describing the inside? Once more, someone mentioned its color and said it was white; the next person said it had pits which were brown and black. This was followed by statements that it had a peel, it felt moist, it was cold, it contained water, it was pulpy. And then someone realized that the apple's color had changed. In the half hour we handled that poor apple it turned somewhat brown and a bit grey on the inside. The dynamics of this began to play a role in the description. Now

we noticed that it was softer than before, it lost its stem, etc. It was well over an hour, after hundreds and hundreds of descriptions—this was truly a creative group, none of whom ever wrote a piece of copy to my knowledge—and not one thought of tasting the apple, or trying to describe its taste, or how it could be used or eaten.

But once that subject was brought up, another plethora of descriptions came forth until the question of nutrition was raised. And off we went on another track. The exercise, I must tell you, continued for two hours. In that time, over four thousand words or phrases were used to describe the apple, or trying to describe its taste, or how it could be used or eaten.

My point (and the point of the exercise in perception) is quite simple. Any tangible item has an almost infinite number of descriptions, and to communicate . . . all of them is virtually impossible.[18]

If difficulties mark efforts to describe a small fruit, one can imagine what difficulties attend the search for descriptions of such intangibles as truth and beauty, right and wrong, responsibilities and rights, intuitions and judgments. Like the observers of the apple and the excursionists on the Hudson tour, perceptions change with perspectives. A widened lens helps make a wiser moralist and all of us, after all, are moralists who need large perspectives.

III.   PERSPECTIVES FROM RELIGION

Unlike many European countries whose governments had formal ties to particular churches, Americans subscribe to a separation-of-church-and-state doctrine. With their utilitarian bent, however, the people—or at least their leaders—see religion as a stabilizing force in society's need for a certain moral seriousness. When Americans differ on points of doctrine they fall back on a "civil" religion to hold them together in a moral consensus. The civil religion rests on the people's belief in three things: (1) belief in a God–Creator, (2) belief in themselves as a "chosen people," and (3) belief in public schools as the primary instrument for socializing their children.[19] Because traditional churches are challenged by the civil religion, a question arises: Are they really relevant to today's world? This very question merits a response.

A.   Jewish Traditions

So accustomed are American ears to hearing that Western civilization has been shaped by Judaic-Christian beliefs we neglect to ask what father Abraham, lawgiver Moses, and Jesus the Christ really mean to our ways of thinking and behaving. Take, as a first instance, our Jewish ethical traditions: What are they? What do they signify? Not much to many Jews.

Products of an urban society where competing views claim to represent God's word and will, the Supreme Being becomes another item in a consumer culture. Articulating this view is Sherwin Wine who says that "the modern Jew is a non-theological secular Jew," having a life-style radically different from that of Moses and David, the Baal Shem Tov, and the Gaon of Vilna—in short, an individual who rejects the past, affirms the present, welcomes the future.[20] Wine wrote:

> The most interesting Jews of the last one hundred years never joined a synagogue.
> They never prayed.
> They were never disinterested in God.
> They paid no attention to the Torah lifestyle.
> They found bourgeois Reform as parochial as traditional Orthodoxy.
> They preferred writing new books to worrying about the meaning of old books.
> They had names like Albert Einstein, Sigmund Freud, and Theodore Herzl.
> They were the stars of the contemporary Jewish world. No rabbi or theologian had their power or relevance.
> Although they were not aware of the label, they represented the boldness and excitement of a new kind of Judaism. They were the non-deliberate prophets of Humanistic Judaism.
> Humanistic Judaism is less well known than Orthodoxy, Conservativism, and Reform. But on a behavioral level, it represents many more American Jews than any of these official ideologies.
> Humanistic Judaism is the philosophy of life which motivates the actions of the vast majority of contemporary Jews.[21]

But the rabbis have heard similar claims before. Depressed but not despairing, they still see in Judaism a shining city on a hill. Murmuring against tradition is part of their memories. There is, for example the "legendary reality" of the Hasidim and the story of the Zakkidim, the moral stalwarts who "stood the test" yet murmured aginst the rabbis.[22] There are, too, the earlier murmurings of their forebearers who, marching out of bondage in Egypt and scarcely 3 days removed from alien control, murmured against Moses, saying "What shall we drink?" Despite an adequate water supply, the Israelites did not consider it sufficiently sweet. More serious murmuring took place a few weeks later in the Sinai Desert (within sight of the mountain upon which they were to receive the Ten Commandments) because the Israelites were unwilling to accept food rationing. Perhaps the author of the Exodus story exaggerated their difficulties in order to dramatize the high price of freedom. Whatever his purpose, the murmuring about the "bitter water" had hardly died when the whole congregation of the people of Israel murmured against Moses and Aaron in the wilderness.

The contemporary "murmurings" come, therefore, as no surprise to the rabbis who have heard them before and know they will hear them again. But the rabbis take comfort in the fact that thousands of years of living and learning cannot be summarily dismissed by contemporary "murmurs." Although no summary can capture the richness of the Jewish tradition, certain salient points can be noted for their relevance to business:

1. Emphasis by Moses on the organic relationship between individual and community—with the implication that employers should seek to make their organizations as much a community as possible.

2. The almost imperceptible transfer of the single "thou" into the social "we" was a transfer deliberately intended "to bring home the lesson that, while the law is promulgated for society as a whole, "it is the individual who must observe it personally with a view toward the whole of society."[23] Without such mutual obligations there can be neither a moral society nor a moral individual.

3. The doctrine of individual responsibility for social righteousness so typically Deuteronomic (Mosaic) has been accepted by every social reformer in history, up to our own time. The Talmud's stress on righteousness continues to be the "heart and soul of Judaism."[24]

4. The importance of character that is tested by "suffering in a furnace of affliction" (Isaiah 48:10). Exile is one of the worst furnaces, and only steadfast belief in God and His creatures make suffering bearable. Steadfastness made steady people, and steady people made stable societies.

5. An obligation to help and protect the poor and unfortunate. The Moses of Leviticus tells his followers that "if your brother becomes poor and cannot maintain himself with you, you shall maintain him; as a stranger and a sojourner he shall live with you" (Leviticus 25:35).

6. A sense of humility, the only one of Moses' virtues that the Bible singles out for special mention.

Today that rich lode of tradition still has relevance to business, argues Gordon Tucker in the second essay: To deny Judaism's relevance is to deny historical fact.[25]

B. Catholic Traditions

Children of the same Divine Father Yaweh and of the same natural father Abraham, united in a common belief in one God, inspired by the same hope for God's coming (parousia)—it is not surprising to find Hillel, a near contemporary of Jesus, teaching maxims that were in the spirit of Christ's teaching. Even some of his words were expressed in phrases well known to Christians: "What is hateful to you, do not do to your neighbor. This is the entire Torah. All the rest is commentary. Now go forth and learn."[26]

Yet relationships between the two great religions were not without tensions. Although it is true that during the early Middle Ages the dominant Christian populations—except Visigothic Spain—"granted" (itself a loaded work) toleration to the Jews, it was because Christians thought that Jews would have to be converted eventually to Christianity in order to fulfill the biblical prophecy.[27] Theological debates between Jewish and Christian theologians were often conducted with wit, urbanity, charm, and civility. With the rise of towns and universities, the interest of Christian scholars in the *Hebraica Veritas* rose. This interest was an implicit admission that the Christian's knowledge of the Old Testament was inadequate. But the disputes turned sour in many quarters. Although there were many (Anselm of Canterbury and Chancellor Eudes of the University of Paris) who encouraged young scholars to undertake fresh and open investigations of pre-Christian religious legacy, others acted like Peter Damian who said that Christian disputants would conquer "every insanity of Jewish depravity."[28] The moment that Jews always feared—persecution and expulsion—came in the thirteenth century.

Although Catholic scholars never completely removed themselves from their Jewish predecessors, they were more skeptical of the free market, capitalism, and the drive for personal enrichment than were the rabbis. Furthermore, adaptations were made to suit the times. To illustrate: Catholic social thought was expanded by Pope Leo XIII in his pioneering encyclical, *On the Rights of Labor*, that long before the New Deal defended the legitimacy of labor unions to a world conditioned by the survival-of-the-fittest doctrine of Social Darwinism. Forty years later Pius XI issued an equally famous encyclical that went beyond his predecessor's thinking by emphasizing the duty of governments to intervene in market operations when substantial segments of society were being cruelly exploited. In these famous papal letters, Catholic social thought nevertheless remained close to the spirit of the Torah. Perhaps most novel to the nineteenth-century secular world were Catholic concepts of social justice and social charity, respectively. Justice required cooperation between management and labor, not enmity; charity required some form of partnership through industry councils organized along vertical, not horizontal, lines.

Catholics in the United States soon became aware of the ambivalent feelings exhibited toward them by the Protestant majority. On one hand,

Catholic immigrants were welcomed by business to offset labor shortages; on the other, Catholic social thought was met with such hostility that a ghetto mentality marked the behavior and attitudes of both hierarchy and laity. But there was another reason for dislike and that was found in the way Catholic social thinkers intermingled metaphysical and moral elements in their theories. The former sought to identify and explain universal principles, the latter, principles applicable to specific institutions and concrete situations. Although often difficult to distinguish between them, an illustration might help to clarify the point. The metaphysical element in the Catholic social ethic stresses work as necessary to human growth—what work is and why workers need useful employment were most recently given expression by the present Pontiff, John Paul II.[29] American bishops, too, have spelled out the meaning of social justice in such metaphysical terms as the right of everyone to be treated as an end, not a means, the right of all to private property, and the right of workers to fair wages. The moral content is found in their specific application to what they called a "preferential options" toward the poor: Human needs come before human wants, necessities before luxuries. The "preferential option" was deliberately designed to give a particular expression to a metaphysical constant, namely social justice.[30]

God as a common Father, justice and love for the oppressed, government intervention when necessary, the individual's obligations to the community—these Catholic ideas resonate to early Jewish thought. That Catholic theory—evolving steadily, systematized incompletely and articulated unevenly—needs to be reassessed and restated is more compelling now than it was a century ago when an immigrant church responded instinctively to Leo XIII's defense of labor unions. Perhaps the most remarkable difference between metaphysical and moral elements in Catholic social thought is the slow movement from hostility toward capitalism to broad accommodation of its concrete expression in the United States. The work of management is now viewed in positive terms; market competition is accepted as necessary for economic growth; even plant closings, though unpalatable, are accepted as often necessary adjustments to changing economic circumstances.

C. Protestant Traditions

Protestant theology toward American business found early inspiration in the Puritan concept of work as a vocation, the belief that the rich have special obligations toward the poor, and a generally more favorable attitude toward market competition. Unlike the Catholic bishops who saw early a great need for institutional reordering, the Protestants called for individual reformation. Institutions themselves, however, came under critical review during the late nineteenth century when the so-called "Social Gospel" of Washington Gladden and Walter Rauschenbusch captured much of the Protestant imagination. Their views on the necessity for economic reform received formal assent in 1908 when the Federal Council of Churches in America adopted a "social creed" that defended the worker's right to a living wage, an end to child labor, a day free from work in each week, and better working conditions, especially for women. Aside from specifics, the importance of the Social Gospel is found in its rebuke to traditional Protestant emphasis on the individual's behavior and its recognition that there was much truth in charges by labor leaders and socialists that Protestantism had become too much of an ally of the propertied class. Although much of its appeal was eroded by the rise of labor organizations, its philosophy was not lost and remained congenial to Catholic social thought.[31]

One cannot speak of Protestantism without taking note of the famous "Protestant Ethic."[32] Ever since the appearance of Max Weber's classic definition of this ethic, scholars have wrestled with two problems: (1) the accuracy of Weber's diagnosis and (2) the practical implications of his hypothesis. Did Protestantism spur a particular form of individualism that brought a special dynamism to capitalist societies?[33] Was work defined in terms initially neglected by Catholic moralists? Did interest taking survive Catholic denunciation of it because Protestantism recognized the importance of capital to economic growth? Did its apologia for American free enterprise save it from Catholic skeptics like the influential Amintore Fanfani who savaged capitalism in Europe?[34] Through point and counterpoint, the Weberian thesis has survived as a persistent force in Protestant–Catholic dialogue. The result is that a robust sector of scholars believe strongly that religious thought has, in fact, influenced (if not shaped) the roots and rise of capitalism, and that a "pure" form of the Protestant ethic should continue to influence management morality.[35]

A final point: Just as there are similarities and differences between Jewish and Christian religious teachings, so are there similarities and differences between Catholic and Protestant tenets. Catholics (at least those who came as immigrants to America) did not place as much stock on worldly success as did Protestants; preferring the security of their own ghettos, they did not move into the mainstream as did Protestants; by adopting a defensive strategy, their leaders made less contributions to the economic life of the nation. One of the most influential Protestant theologians, Reinhold Niebuhr (who incidentally was critical of the political program of the Social Gospel), said that the Protestant theology of love and law as part of *one* commandment differs from Catholic thought that is based on multiple sources—the Bible, revelation, and the Magisterium.[36]

D. A Common Challenge

Divisions among the churches have often weakened church influence in America. To some this is a good thing. To others it is a sorrow. If, however, matters of faith are more and more privatized, religious leaders confront a formidable task, namely, to help provide moral guidelines for policymakers in both the public and private sector while, at the same time, attending to individual needs. Clearly the common challenge to both Jews and Christians is found in these words of Jacob Neusner who wrote:

> The ancient rabbis look out upon a world destroyed and still smoking in the aftermath of calamity, but they speak of rebirth and renewal. The holy Temple lay in ruins, but they ask about sanctification. The old history was over, but they look forward to future history. Theirs, as we see, is a message that what is true and real is the opposite of what people perceive. God stands for paradox. Strength comes through weakness, salvation through acceptance and obedience, sanctification through the ordinary and profane, which can be made holy. Now to informed Christians, the mode of thought must prove remarkably familiar. For the cross that stands for weakness yields salvation, and the crucified criminal is king and savior. That is the foolishness to which the apostle Paul makes reference. Yet the greater the "nonsense"—life out of the grave, eternity from death—the deeper the truth, the richer the paradox! So here we have these old Jews, one group speaking of sanctification of Israel and the people, the other of salvation of Israel and the world. Separately, they are thinking along the same lines, coming to conclusions remarkably congruent to one another, affirming the paradox of God in the world, of humanity in God's image in the rabbinical framework; of God in the flesh in the Christian. Is it not time for the joint heirs of ancient Israel's Scripture and hope to meet once more, in humility, before the living God? Along with all humanity, facing backward toward Auschwitz and total destruction, and forward toward complete annihilation of the world as we know it—is it not time?[37]

Accepting the invitation to speak together on specific issues will not be easy. The privitization of faith commitments makes people reluctant to support anything that smacks of a public religious crusade. Young professionals recoil from calls for sacrifice—especially when the "callers" have themselves achieved material comfort in the society they wish to transform; intermural suspicions of others' motives continue to exist; and, finally, there is the ever-present skepticism of corporate leaders who worry that rabbis and pastors are impractical idealists. Nevertheless, the original assumption that religions have practical things to say to practical people remains unshaken. Because ethics is a practical discipline, philosophers cannot close their lens on theologians—that is, unless the former is prepared to argue that what ethics teaches as fundamental human values differs markedly from what religion teaches as fundamental human values.[38] In addition to religion, law and other societal values profoundly reflect and form those values—and to these topics attention is turned.

IV. PERSPECTIVES FROM LAW, SOCIOLOGY, AND LABOR

A. Law

Although accepting economist Milton Friedman's first premise (leaders of business behave morally when they make efficient use of scarce resources), ethicists strongly resist his second, namely, that the rest of business morality consists in simply obeying the law.[39] Because Friedman's voice is heard in many places of power, it follows that the interplay between law and morals is always of interest to moralists. Although admitting that law and morality are interrelated, ethicists deny they are identical. One reason for denial is that philosophers and lawyers exist in a different subculture. The difference recalls C. P. Snow's thesis that understanding reality is made difficult by the different vocabularies used by scientists and humanists, respectively.[40] In similar ways, when lawyers use certain words as the special "tools of their trade," philosophers may use the same words to mean quite different things.[41] "Hearsay evidence," for example, is generally taboo in law, whereas philosophers would give it due weight if both the alleged teller and hearer are persons of rectitude. Philosophers also wonder why evidence on industry standards relating to product design and widespread use of that product is sometimes inadmissible when, in the search for truth, all evidence seems relevant in ethics.[42] The same phenomenon exists in their respective understanding of the words "business competition," and neither moralist nor lawyer may be getting quite right what the other means by the word. If there is any truth in what some anthropologists call "Whorf's law": (that *language shapes thought and culture*), it is very important indeed to get words right.[43]

Competition is a word of different meanings for managers, judges, and moralists. To managers, it means outthinking the rival—even if the thinking is done on the rival's noncopyrighted database. To judges, the legal meaning is spelled out in the ambiguously written Sherman Antitrust Act of 1890. To courts the meaning has shifted over time. To moralists, competition should be consistently held to be fair in all respects and at all times. A new element in competition is intelligence gathering. When—and how—does it promote efficiency and equity? Are there unexamined ethical norms that corporations and courts should apply to make competition economically more viable and ethically more acceptable? Are markets beginning to drift further and further away from their moral moorings? If so, what are the consequences? The ethicist's lens must see what managers, judges, and economists have to say on a matter of great interest to society.[44]

Related to court decisions (because they so often succeed in shaping them and are always affected by them) are special interest groups. There are two helpful ways to approach the problem created by their existence: through political and sociological analysis. Because the latter is treated in detail in Berg's essay, it is useful to concentrate on political science perspectives.

B. The Political Science–Sociology Nexus

To recall the fateful days of September of 1787—when relatively few men, working in secrecy, drafted the American Constitution—is to relive political drama at its fullest. Reason told them that an untested theory called consent-of-the-governed was a good thing, even though trusting the people was heresy to European minds. But colonial experience had also taught the framers the limits of such trust. People and their leaders could have hallucinations, legislate wild schemes, succumb to the political snake oil of mean slicksters. So they crafted into the document another revolutionary idea—checks and balances. If any branch of government showed signs of running too fast and too far down a slippery slope, a carefully placed check could stop—or at least slow—the dizzy ride. The check gave ruler and ruled a chance to regain balance.

Now suppose there had been no such institutional arrangement. Would Americans have had experiences similar to the French people who had so generously befriended them during the Revolution? Even if the question is hypothetical, it is worth pursuing. French revolutionary leaders had, with great originality, redesigned concepts of time and space yet they were not nearly so original politically as the Americans. There were no real checks on the political passions of the French youth who cavorted in the gardens of the Palais Royal and paraded on streets of Paris carrying poles on which were spiked the heads of the guillotined. From 1791 to 1795 the guillotine's swish of death was heard again and again. In one chilling sentence, historian Robert Darnton wrote: "In all of them the crowds cried for bread and blood, and the bloodshed passes the historian's understanding."[45] French writers—from Montaigne in the sixteenth century to Pascal and Descartes in the seventeenth—had spent considerable time discussing, in theoretical terms, the meaning of the "passions."[46] The eighteenth century French showed the practical meaning of political passion.

Ordinary decencies did not, of course, entirely vanish. Recently one American poet even found a bond of courtesy between executioner and victim when he wrote:

Our sainted great-great
Grandmothers
Used to sit and knit
Under the gallows.

No one asks what
It is they were knitting
And what happened when the ball of yarn
Rolled away
And had to be retrieved.

One imagines the hooded executioner
And his pasty-faced victim
Interrupting their grim business
To come smiling to their aid.

Confirmed pessimists
And other party-poopers
Categorically reject
Such far-fetched notions
Of gallows etiquette.[47]

Compared to the French, Americans had no remembrances of real or imagined "gallows etiquette" or of real or imagined massacres. However, the fact that it happened *there* and did not happen *here* should not obscure the fact that it could have happened here. Checks and balances reduced the likelihood of such aberrations and although they sometimes kept the engines of government from being efficient, they also insulated the engineers from total insanity. What American political innovators did not do was to establish check-and-balance techniques to control outside power blocs. That they would be checked, however, was argued by James Madison in his famous Essay Number 10 of the *Federalist Papers*. Madison knew that factions would appear to advance their special interests—sometimes at the expense of the larger community. Such factors might consist of debtors or creditors, landed gentry or manufacturing tycoons. How, then, were the "passions" of such private groups to be restrained? Madison's answer was explicit: In a country as large as the United States, one faction would be offset by the power of another. Contemporaries call this "countervailing power."

Today's question, however, is whether a formula adequate for the late eighteenth century is effective in the late twentieth when a single corporation is richer than many nation states. In the present environment, does Madison's observation fit corporate practices? Over a decade ago, Ivar Berg joined fellow investigator Mayer Zald to hypothesize that business interests are so differentiated they "find it difficult to weld themselves into a solidified group."[48] Yet, class theorists (often of Marxist persuasion) are less ready to accept the Berg–Zald pluralist view. Using *graph theory*, these

sociologists identify important cliques that make up the graph and conclude that there are enough contacts among various business units that,
despite differences, one clique is able to speak for the others.[49]

Certainly, one technique—influencing the courts—was never anticipated by Madison who assumed that the Supreme Court would not be
terribly powerful and that, if power came, nonelected judges would stand
above partisan pressures. The reality is quite different. Interest groups
have hit upon a device that works, namely, the use of amicus curiae briefs
filed prior to a Supreme Court decision to hear a case. Each year the Court
sets its agenda and determines new winners and losers—a fact of life not
lost upon interest groups. It makes no sense for one "faction" to be passive
if hundreds of decisions by lower courts go unchallenged and theirs is
called into question. Loss in a lower court galvanizes the defeated party
into action designed to bring its case to the Supreme Court. And the
justices listen. Like other mortals, different justices subscribe to different
ideologies, have heavy work loads, and are under stringent time schedules.
Dependence on knowledgeable outsiders is the result. Amicus curiae
participation by organized interests provides information and signals,
often otherwise unavailable, about the political, social, and economic significance of cases on the Court's docket. Although the Justices make every
effort to remain independent, their dependence on outside specialists is
evident.

Because courts really depend so often on help from outside groups,
business moralists might assume that judges would be driven to test
"outside" information against all other available evidence—to search for
the full truth. Absent such search, judges are suspect. However, much of
this criticism rests on an assumption, that the purpose of a trial is to
determine the truth and to settle legal rights and obligations in accordance
with it. An examination of the legal process reveals rather convincingly that
seeking truth is only one function, and sometimes not the most important
function, of conflict resolution. The law's stated purpose to seek the truth,
the whole truth, and nothing but the truth is a myth: Justice involves many
elements of which the truth is only one.[50]

Despite the court's approach to competition and conflict, truth is vital
to a firm's success: Truth about its own research and development potential, truth about consumer wants and, of course, truth about the competition. The last item always becomes a priority in business when competition
intensifies. That is why inferences about the potential impact of their
decisions can be made by observing the extent of amicus activity. Consequently, the mere presence or absence of an amicus curiae brief may even
weigh more than the substantive arguments.[51]

If, as appears to be the case, a nonelected Court responds to organized interest groups when choosing its plenary docket, it may be inferred that elected officials are very vulnerable when important pieces of legislation are being considered. Is Aristotle's idea of the common good, or Bentham's notion of the greatest good of the greatest number, endangered by organized groups who see only their trees and not society's forest? In his essay, Professor Berg feels that there is great danger.[52] This conclusion is important to ethicists when they examine the morality of government and business operations. One may speculate whether the old biblical notions of "thou" and "we" are about to be interred at a funeral where no one weeps—except the corpse.

If the old fear was worry over factions, the present one is over fractionings. The Vietnamese in America not only want to maintain their own culture, they also want their children to remain true to their Asian heritage. The graying of America had led to a fractioning of the age groups. Feminists do not want assimilation into the work culture—they seek to change that culture. Individuals often want children but not spouses. Homosexuals demand a right to marry. Many black youngsters simply drop out of American society. The nation has had long experiences dealing with "factioning." It has limited experience dealing with "fractioning." In the past, America's future-oriented philosophy practically guaranteed that the nation would internally change itself. For the future the nation will change because of failures external to the indigenous culture.

C.   Labor

Relations between management and labor have not made for a happy story in the United States. Often, the so-called "captains of industry" were skippers of pirate ships who recruited hungry immigrants to work in the steamy unsafe engine rooms they called factories. Competitors were enemy ships to be sunk on sight; judges became their lackeys, licking the captain's boots; ministers of mainline churches often extolled the virtues of the self-made men. Exaggeration? A resurrected statement of Ida Tarbell and her muckraking associates? Possibly so. But no one can survey post-Civil War America without recognizing how Social Darwinism had distorted the moral vision.[53]

In such a climate, it was not surprising that factory hands (recruited largely from Europe's poor) should be ambivalent toward their employers. Gratitude for employment, their first reaction, turned to hatred of greedy bosses as their second. In the absence of real choice, workers had only unreal options: quit or organize. The first was impossible, the second improbable. And it was improbable because their powerlessness was pitted against combinations of political and corporate power. Throughout the first half of the nineteenth century, lawyers and judges fashioned a double standard: Corporations became persons under the Fourteenth Amendment. And unions become quasi-conspirators. The Sherman Antitrust Act of 1890 provided further weaponry: Picketing was deemed a violation of the corporation's property rights, and the very act of organizing was seen as subversion of the social order.

When workers turned to violence, the strategy backfired. Before the New Deal, union organizing recorded a few successes and some astonishing defeats. Formed in 1867, the National Labor Union collapsed in 1872; the Knights of Labor began a spectacular rise in 1879 (enrolling over 700,000 workers in less than a decade), but by 1893 the Knights were, for all practical purposes, dead; the International Workers of the World (IWW) (a radical group dedicated to the overthrow of the capitalist system) burned out in a relatively short career that lasted from 1897 to 1920. In such circumstances, unions scored few successes: Steel workers lost their bloody Homestead strike in 1889; Pullman Company employees lost in 1895 when the government intervened on behalf of management; leaders of the Molly Maguires in coal-mining towns were jailed or hanged.

Alone it its long-term success was the American Federation of Labor (AFL). Its achievements were due largely to two factors—the power of skilled workers and a philosophy of restraint. A strike by skilled employees could cripple a plant, and management knew it; the conservative leadership of Samuel Gompers emphasized bread-and-butter issues, not social revolution. Yet even within the relatively narrow range of issues the AFL put on the bargaining table, both management and labor saw in the other an adversary who must be kept at bay. Suspicion has never left chieftains of the American Manufacturing Association or the AFL/CIO. But are old suspicions appropriate to a corporate world threatened by home-grown takeover sharks and by foreign competitors from Pacific Rim countries and from Western Europe?[54]

D. Future Needs

Today both managers *and* workers are at risk. More and more frequently white collars join blue collars in exit lines when firms are merged and factories closed. Salary freezes accompany wage concessions; retirement benefits for both supervisors and supervised are endangered. This unexpected and uncomfortable experience should induce management and unions to consider new strategies of cooperation and new alignments for the common defense. Will they? The answer is mixed, but the story of their responses to the Civil Rights movement suggest caution.

It is a story worthy of a brief retelling. In the early 1940s, over 2 million blacks left Southern farms for job opportunities in the industrialized urban North, and another million moved into Southern cities. For the first time, American blacks were becoming proletarianized.[55] The CIO responded initially with enthusiastic welcomes to black workers and, relatively soon, a half million of them were enrolled in the Congress of Industrial Organizations (CIO), a union open to unskilled workers. Further the *Brown v. the Board of Education* decision in 1954 (voiding the separate-but-equal doctrine in public school education) legitimated much of the social struggle. It remained hobbled, however, until given political force by a growing protest movement. The appearance of industrial unions during the New Deal had offered working-class blacks a legal standard to legitimate their demands; the one-man, one-vote policy implemented in thousands of National Labor Relations Board (NLRB) elections endorsed equality in suffrage; the industrial citizenship that union contracts offered once marginal elements of the working class granted dignity to the hitherto demeaned; and the patriotic egalitarianism of the government's war-time propaganda generated a rights consciousness that gave working-class black militancy a moral justification in ways similar to that evoked a generation later by the Baptist spirituality of Martin Luther King, Jr.[56]

How did segments of management and labor respond? Was there a unified voice to protest injustice? To begin with business is to encounter at the local level ineptitude and insensitivity. When black workers sought to organize a CIO union affiliate in the R. J. Reynolds Tobacco Company in Winston-Salem, North Carolina, the white business community organized an Emergency Citizens Committee in an unsuccessful attempt to block the effort, claiming that "self-serving representatives of the CIO were destroying a satisfactory race relationship and would likely lead to riots and bloodshed."[57] And what might be said of unions? The initial reaction was loud and clear: The United Auto Workers (UAW) put their substantial resources behind efforts to have automobile management and government organize to advance black job rights. Ten thousand people rallied in Detroit's Cadillac Square in 1943 to show their support for racial justice; large delegations lobbied before state legislators in Lansing and before congressmen in Washington. Yet when automobile management sought to transfer three blacks into an all-white department, 25,000 whites left their jobs, despite UAW's Walter Reuther's stern rebukes to the striking whites.

Although the crisis for civil rights leaders was slow in building, the two elements that precipitated it were management and union. Management intensified its efforts to weaken CIO locals that enrolled large numbers of blacks, and big unions showed less and less interest in promoting the blacks' cause. By 1960 blacks had formed opposition movements in several old CIO unions, but they now encountered resistance to their demands not only from much of the white rank-and-file but also from union leaders who presided over institutions that had accommodated themselves to much of the industrial status quo.

In the light of that history, what expectations can be generated for future cooperation? The present challenge, flowing from takeovers and foreign competition, lacks the dramatic quality of the Civil Rights movement. Burnings and bloodshed will, hopefully, be absent. However, the crisis of the 1990s is a real one and when the year 2000 arrives, Americans will know—with joy or with sadness—whether hatchets have been buried. This time, jobs for managers and workers are on the line. A unified front might appear, and a spirit of cooperation just might dislodge a conflict mentality. But cooperation may not turn out to be an unalloyed blessing. Third parties—consumers and governments—could be hurt. The development bears watching.[58]

V.   PERSPECTIVES FROM HIGHER EDUCATION: DISCIPLINES AND DISCIPLES

A.   The Disciplines

A cursory review of the history of the social sciences reveals a common trend: efforts by their founders to lend credibility to the disciplines by appeals to "laws of nature." Adam Smith's famous metaphor, the invisible hand, offered a quasi-mechanical and impersonal interpretation of the market because it operated like an automatic system on laws fairly similar to those found in classical physics. Karl Marx saw in the economic formation of society a clear "process of natural history."[59] August Compte, who "invented" sociology in 1838, offered a secular religion based on "natural laws" governing human behavior in social contexts.[60] Phenomena are explained, wrote Compte, through observation, hypotheses, and experiments—the style used by the physical scientist. And when Compte's views appeared to falter, Herbert Spencer stepped forward with the view that all phenomena are to be understood according to the "law of evolutionary progress."[61]

Attempts to rest the social sciences on physical-science principles has a beguiling appeal: A "law," after all, is preferable to an hypothesis when explanations of social phenomena are sought; physics is more attractive than theology when the cosmos is analyzed; behavioral psychology is more reliable than moral philosophy when human actions are discussed;

the "invisible hand" seems sturdier than God's invisible hand when the economy is studied. And so it goes. But there are voices of discontent. Assumptions and claims made for such social sciences as economics, experimental psychology, and sociobiology are under increasing attack.

Perhaps the quickest way to get a "fix" on the problem of the disciplines is to ressurect an old definition of certitude—the goal toward which social theorists of the "scientific" persuasion seek to move their inquiries. Three forms of certitude are commonly defined: (1) *metaphysical* (propositions cannot be and not be at one and the same time); (2) *physical* certitude that comes from observation of certain physical laws like gravity; and (3) *moral* certitude that is often like, albeit not identical to, probability theory. The last form of certitude holds that predictions can be made regarding people's behavior under known sets of circumstances—drivers generally stop at red lights, employees normally come to work on schedule, and so on. However, social scientists are aware that moral certitude is "shakier" than the other two. People do ignore red lights, and healthy employees do call in ill. With these general observations in mind, it is appropriate to comment on the current state of economics, sociobiology, and experimental psychology as each seeks to provide a high degree of certitude in its own domain.

1. Economics

Long the butt of ridicule because of their abysmally inaccurate predictions of the market's future performance, economists are in a defensive posture. But their performance as prophets is no better or worse than other social scientists: Prediction is easy when the future is not involved. More important for economics itself, however, as well as for business students following prescribed courses in economics, is not so much its track record in prophecy but the reliability of some of its basic assumptions—the so-called paradigms. Skepticism toward the neoclassical paradigms is not new. Seventy years ago Thorstein Veblen launched a spirited attack—one that John Kenneth Galbraith recently, and joyously, revived:

> Veblen established himself, first of all, as a critic of the classical system; this he did in a series of short papers published just before and just after the turn of the century. In these he held that the central ideas of the classical system did not reflect a search for truth and reality; rather they were and are a celebration of approved belief. Any society has a system of thought founded not on what is actual but on what is agreeable and convenient to the influential interest. The carefully calculating, pleasure-maximizing economic man in classical economics is an artificial construct; human motivation is far more diverse. Economic theory is an exercise in "ceremonial adequacy," timeless, static in tendency and universally and continuously valid, as is religion, but economic life—

a familiar point—is evolutionary. Economic institutions change; so does or should economic subject matter; there can be understanding only if one is in tune with change.[62]

Particularly under siege are the following "maxims" in economic theory:

1. The model of "economic man" as a rational, utility-maximizing individual operating in a morally neutral social vacuum.
2. Prices come through a reconciliation between supply and demand, a Cartesian paradise, when as "every businessman knows, this is not the way the world turns. Supply and demand are determined by price, not the other way round."[63]
3. Humans as pleasure-seeking animals reach pleasure and joy by following their instincts when in reality the two are not commensurable.[64]
4. General welfare is best explained by the principle of Pareto Optimality (a value-neutral concept that says allocations should be adjusted to benefit some people only so long as they do not hurt others. (However, not all preferences [heroin vs. food] are on an equal moral level.)[65]

The current criticism, however, is spurred by fears that fallacious paradigms have spread to other social sciences that figure heavily in the education of managers and business students. Two deserve specific mention: sociobiology and Skinnerian psychology.

2. Sociobiology

A contemporary philosopher, Thomas Hill Greene, put his dilemma in a question: "Can we find scientific warrant for believing in a process by which, out of susceptibility to pleasures incidental to the merely animal life, there have grown those capacities for enjoyment which we consider essential to general well-being? If we can, it would seem that we have given to our rational system of ethics—the ethics of moral sentiment—the solid foundation of a natural science."[66] He continued:

It is no wonder that the evolutionists of our day should claim to have given a wholly new character to ethical enquiries. In Hume's time a philosopher who denied the innateness of the moral sentiment, and held that they must have a natural history, had only the limits of the individual life within which to trace this history. These limits did not give room enough for even a plausible derivation of moral interests from animal wants. It is otherwise when the history may be supposed to range over an indefinite number of generations. The doctrine of hereditary transmission, it is held, explains to us how susceptibilities of pleasure and pain, of desire and aversion, of hope and fear, may be handed down with gradually accumulated modifications which in time attain the full measure

of the difference between the moral man and the greater ape. Man will then have
ascertained his place in nature as perhaps the noblest of all animals, but an
animal still.[67]

Harvard's Edmund Wilson feels he can answer the philosopher's questions. In the decade following the 1975 publication of his book on sociobiology, Wilson has won acclaim and condemnation in almost equal amounts.[68]
Pushing the frontiers of evolution beyond what Herbert Spencer had been
able to demonstrate (and even beyond what August Compte dreamed),
Wilson linked ethics and evolution in very exciting and profoundly troublesome ways. To Wilson morality is the story of genes: Good and evil are
found not in conscience but in the hypothalmic-limbic system of the brain;
survival of the gene pool is more important than survival of the individual;
moral canons come not from philosophers or preachers but from evolutionary biologists. Wilson's imperialistic claims have not gone unchallenged.
When sociobiologists insist that behavior is genetically determined, critics
respond that the "morals of genetics" are of little value in promoting
understanding of the varieties of human behavior.[69] Closely related to
biology is the study of psychology and hypotheses recently advanced in
that discipline merit comment.

3. Skinnerian Psychology

The history of psychology (derived from a combination of two Greek
words meaning *soul* and *concept*) falls roughly into two time periods: a long
one of 2,000 years dating back to the Greeks and a short span starting
roughly in the 1850s.[70] Aristotle usually gets credit for fathering psychology and his book, *De Anima*, served as a fundamental text until the modern
period began. The study of living things was part of the science of nature,
and the study of humans was a special part of that science. In the thirteenth
century Aquinas introduced important refinements, to wit, the need for
clinical observations and controlled experiments.

The modern period may be said to begin with a philosopher–physicist
named Gustav Fechner (1801–1887), who published the results of his findings in a work called *Elements of Psychophysics*. The title itself is intriguing.
By joining soul and matter, Fechner put himself in the vanguard of those
who saw the social sciences in terms of a physical science orientation.
Various schools of thought followed Fechner. Gestalt's psychology was
based on the notion that perception arises from seeing organized wholes.
Behaviorist J. B. Watson saw merit in the Pavlovian idea of conditioning:
Certain stimuli (S) will generate predictable responses (R).

From the behavioralist tradition emerged B. F. Skinner, widely acclaimed as the most influential living psychologist.[71] Experimental results

convinced Skinner that the traditional stimulus and response (SR) premises of behaviorism needed refinement. Real learning, he said, consisted not in a stimulus to get a desired result but in reinforcements for actions people normally do that bring the desired result. Such reinforcements come from what Skinner called "operant conditioning." With operant conditioning, employees would work harder, morale would rise as a consequence, and productivity would increase. It all sounds like a management dream fulfilled. But is it? We are left pondering the conclusion of Edward S. Reed, a psychologist who, though lacking formal training in the field, was highly respected: "Scientific psychology seems to me ill-founded. At any time the whole psychological applecart might be upset. Let them [psychologists] beware."[72] That Skinnerian psychology, Wilsonian sociobiology, and neoclassical economics require critical reexamination is the theme of Barry Schwartz's essay.[73] And because the results have significant effects on what value business students learn in their professional education, it has relevance to business ethics. If the "learned" are wrong, what happens to the learners?

B. The Disciples

Heard so repetitiously that it has become almost a maxim is the statement that today's university students are selfish, materialistic, badly educated, and, possibly, morally crippled. Prominent corporate lawyer and author, Louis Auchincloss, asked if there were any rules now? "Do people care about anything except being caught? Not from where I sit."[74] But people in businesses are the products of our schools and, if a problem exists, it surely cannot be disconnected from the community of scholars. Time spent in the university and college is part of the young adult's critical years—the period when a capacity for self-awareness changes perceptively and the role of the mentor increases.[75] Two critics, from quite different perspectives, have launched serious charges against academe. One is Philosopher Allan Bloom whose blistering attack in 1987 has stirred up a hornet's nest of controversy; the other is Sociologist Amitai Etzioni who entered the fray in 1989. What each says is worth pondering.

In defining the problem, Bloom said there was

> one thing a professor can be absolutely certain of: almost every student entering the university believes, or says he believes, that truth is relative. If this belief is put to the test, one can count on the students' reaction; they will be uncomprehending. That anyone should regard the proposition as not self-evident astonishes them, as though he were calling into question 2 + 2 = 4. These are things you don't think about. Openness and the relativism that make it the only plausible stance in the face of various claims to truth, and various ways of life and kinds of human beings—is the great insight of our times. The

true believer is the real danger. The study of history and of culture teaches that all the world was mad in the past; men always thought they were right, and that led to wars, persecutions, slavery, xenophobia, racism, and chauvinism. The point is not to correct the mistakes and really be right; rather it is not to think you are right at all.

He continues:

The students, of course, cannot defend their opinions. It is something with which they have been indoctrinated. The best they can do is point out all the opinions and cultures there are and have been. What right, they ask, do I or anyone else have to say one is better than the other? If I pose the routine questions designed to confute them and make them think, such as, "If you had been a British administrator in India, would you have let the natives under your governance burn the widow at the funeral of a man who had died?," they either remain silent or reply that the British should never have been there in the first place. It is not that they know very much about other nations, or about their own. The purpose of their education is not to make them scholars but to provide them with a moral virtue—openness.[76]

To Bloom, openness is emptiness—the classic copout justified on grounds of toleration. Full-scale openness is full-scale mindlessness. To challenge the morality of an act is boorish. The freshman's relativism is the senior's shallowness.

Coming from a different perspective, Sociologist Amitai Etzioni, concluding his critique of the neoclassical paradigm in the social sciences (man as a calculating, self-seeking, pleasure-driven creature), warned that its continued acceptance would have disabling effects on students and on the general public. Each year millions of high-school and college students are exposed to assumptions that downplay the significance of ethical judgments in policymaking, as well as in personal and organizational decision making. For example: The neoclassical paradigm allows respected economists like Gary Becker to speak of children as durable consumer goods. Marriage is secularized through cost benefit analysis; human parts will be sold to the highest bidder; auctioning a "right" to pollute implies moral acceptability of an evil act. Students should know certain things are questionable, but if their own moorings are questionable their only alternative is to play by the secular rules of the game.

Not only are the affects devastating for individuals, they are devastating for the world of business in which the students will carve out careers. Etzioni makes this point vividly:

A paradox arises to the extent that it is true that the market is dependent on normative underpinning (to provide the pre-contractual foundation such as trust, cooperation, and honesty) which all contractual relations require. The more people accept the neoclassical paradigm as a guide for their behavior, the more the ability to sustain a market economy is undermined. This holds for all those who engage in transactions without ever-present inspectors, auditors, lawyers, and police: if they do not limit themselves to legitimate [i.e., normative] means of competition out of internalized values, the system will collapse, because the transaction costs of a fully or even highly "policed" system are prohibitive. This holds even more so for the regulators that every market require. If those whose duty it is to set and to enforce the rules of the game are out to maximize their own profits, a la-Public Choice, there is no hope for the system. It is our position that they are not so inclined, but neoclassical education may push them in the amoral, anarchic direction.

In short, because the neoclassical paradigm is part of the modern mentality, and not merely an academic field, it affects the way people see their world and themselves, and the way they behave.[77]

The concerns do not ruffle the claimants. One of America's most distinguished economists, George Stigler, of Chicago, said that the theoretical supremacy of economics over other social sciences allows him and his colleagues to apply price-auction markets to explain phenomena not only in business but in politics and law, marriage and children, crime and urban renewal. What makes the claim important is that the Chicago School, of which Stigler is a part, has influenced business schools and political science departments, White House policy, and the Congress.

Are affairs so out of hand that redemption is impossible? Are students themselves content with paradigms that paralyze? Although in no way denying the charges made by scholars like Bloom and Etzioni, James Glenn has concluded on the basis of his empirical research that there is hope. Business students, by an admittedly slim margin, want more training in ethics. Seeing the evils perpetrated by the Boeskys and Levines, they know that something is rotten on Wall Street. They read of corporate overcharges in the defense industry. Scams multiply daily. So it is not surprising that business students express an interest in ethics education. What may come as a surprise is the amount of chicanery in their own world where certain practices (paid surrogates taking examinations for others, paid outsiders preparing term papers, plagiarism, and stolen library books) are not uncommon.[78] Needed are empirical data on which to base our own judgments, and Glenn offers a good beginning.

VI. A SPECIAL PERSPECTIVE: THE AIDS CRISIS

Whenever science and industry are mentioned, people instinctively think of research and development, words closely linked as if research always means development. During the present decade, however, science means delayed salvation for thousands of people afflicted by AIDS. Medical researchers have labored in vain to find a cure. Corporate managers have labored in vain to find satisfactory policy for employees. Government bureaucrats scurry to develop a united front. And behind all the scramblings lurk profound moral issues. Employees are frightened by their stricken co-workers; managers are confused by demands by healthy employees for protection; victims say compassion is more important than justice in resource allocation policies; government agencies have yet to get their act together; the health care field has moved slowly in developing guidelines for its members. The suddenness of its appearance, the ferocity of its attack, and the fear it has engendered make AIDS a special problem for business ethicists.

A.   Background

In admittedly oversimplified terms, the history of employers' concerns for their employees' health and safety is a chiaroscuro. A century ago, legal theory supported the dominant philosophy that held that on-site accidents were usually the fault of the individual worker—or the worker's colleagues. The "logic" was straightforward. People want work. Work involves risk. Risk-taking individuals pay for their own misfortunes. Tuberculosis (black lung) struck down coal miners in Pennsylvania; limbs were severed by machines in New England textile mills; immigrants froze to death building transcontinental railroads during savage winter storms; steel workers were burned at smelting mills. Injury and death were part of the game.

By and large the early workers' organizations were ineffective in forcing employers to share responsibility. However, as noted, the New Deal changed matters; gradually, if unevenly, unions began to extract concessions: the 8-hour day, extra compensation for overtime work, paid vacations, and a grudging admission by corporations of a responsibility for workers' safety and health. However, unresolved questions remain. To what degree, if any, are employers responsible for accidents due to an employee's behavior off the job? To what degree, if any, are employers responsible to employees who engage in activities known to be health threatening? To what degree, if any, are employers responsible for the health and safety of those in the work force who are—or feel they are—endangered by the illnesses of fellow workers?

The AIDS pandemic raises all these questions. How prepared are Americans to tackle the problem? "Not very," according to Admiral James Watkins, former Chief of Naval Operations, who headed a presidential commission appointed by Ronald Reagan to investigate and make recommendations. Following completion of the study Watkins wrote:

> What we discovered is a nation not ready for an epidemic of this type. As we crisscrossed the country and listened to almost 600 witnesses in 43 hearings, we realized that the virus could not be attacked in isolation from a host of related issues. The nation is almost bankrupt in its ability to deal with interrelated social, economic, health and *ethical* issues.
>
> As we viewed contemporary American society through the HIV lens, we learned that discriminatory practices against persons afflicted with the disease are the rule rather than the exception. I didn't expect to find that in our country.
>
> We saw firsthand the frightening specter of drug abuse and its relation to the spread of the virus. We found an increasingly litigious and adversarial relationship between consumers and providers of health care. We discovered a drug development system unresponsive to the fast-changing unknowns surrounding this epidemic. This country has only two pharmaceutical companies working to develop an AIDS vaccine because the threat of liability has scared others away.
>
> We discovered that the Food and Drug Administration is totally out of budgetary synchronism with the National Institutes of Health, the premier drug development agency in the world. And we found that while we are pumping up resources dedicated to AIDS at FDA, the agency's total resources remain nearly constant. Therefore, work is delayed on attacking other terminal diseases that affect more people than AIDS.
>
> Every rock we turned over exposed the flaws in society's programs and in educational programs. Looking at these broader issues transformed my thinking to the view that it's time to change the way we do business among ourselves. . . . Why are we so ineffective? Consider the many departments and agencies that play roles in formulating policies for dealing with the epidemic. There is the Attorney General's office, the White House, Congress, the departments of Education and Health and Human Services. The Department of Commerce is worried about the AIDS threat to the future of international competition, and a very big issue at the Department of Labor is the effect of AIDS in the workplace.
>
> When we try to coordinate these agencies' work on the HIV virus with more than twenty drug enforcement entities, the question is: "Who's in charge?" The Commission found no one in charge and concluded that that is at the heart of the fragmentation and confusion.[79]

B. Ethical Implications

If the history of the war against smoking is an example, change will come at a snail's pace: too little and too late for too many. Over a quarter century has passed since the Surgeon General reported publicly that "smoking far outweighs all other factors" as the cause of lung cancer and that the health hazard was of sufficient importance to warrant "appropriate remedial action."[80] Despite evidence that 300,000 people die annually from diseases linked to smoking, a million persons join the ranks of the smoking brigade each year. Fifty million Americans continue to puff away.

In one sense, the smoking problem is replicated by AIDS: initial skepticism toward claims regarding the cause-and-effect relationship between habit and disease; a slow development in coordinating the work of government agencies; confusion among employers in response to workers' complaints. But important dissimilarities cannot be overlooked. There are no doubts today about the relationship of homosexual promiscuity or the addict's use of dirty needles to the deadly virus. Nor in the past was the public asked to support public funding for the victims (and possible victims) on a massive scale. Nor was there worry over invasions of privacy. Smoking carried no badge of dishonor, whereas homosexuals had to come "out of the closet." And, finally, there was recognition that doctors who smoked would not likely infect their patients. This may not be true about AIDS.

The last comment deserves elaboration. By fall of 1988, 3,182 health care workers with AIDS (including 356 physicians), had been reported to the Center for Disease Control (CDC) in Atlanta. Although there is not one documented case of a patient catching the dread disease from a doctor or nurse, the medical community itself is unsure how to proceed. Uncertainty among the doctors will certainly bring the courts into action. A harbinger of things to come appeared in California when James S. Gordon, a gynecologist, was barred from treating patients by his two partners when he told them he had AIDS. In 1988 Gordon sued for breach of contract. Any number of scenarios could be written about the issue. Suppose the California court upholds Gordon's claims and he resumes practice with his two partners. Suppose, further, one of his patients gets AIDS. Is Gordon personally responsible? Is the partnership responsible? Is the American Medical Association responsible for not having developed a policy for its doctors? Is the federal government responsible? Is California at fault?

The public expressed its views on the doctor–patient relationship in a 1987 Gallup poll: 86 percent said they had a right to know if a health care worker treating them had AIDS. In no sense does it seem to Lorraine J. Day, Chief of Orthopedic Surgery at San Francisco General Hospital, that the patient is invading the privacy of the provider: "An individual's rights shouldn't supersede everybody else's right to stay alive. . . . Telling surgeons not to cut themselves is like telling a carpenter to go the rest of his life and not get injured."[81] But the issue remains clouded. When, for example, a Cook County Hospital in Chicago refused to allow Dr. Alan Bouffard, a physician with AIDS, to perform operations in its facilities, the American Civil Liberties Union sued the hospital in federal court for violating federal antidiscrimination laws. The ACLU won on grounds that AIDS is a physical handicap protected under federal and state antidiscrimination laws. Would ethical reasoning support legal reasoning in the Bouffard case? Not likely. So, at a minimum, disclosure is necessary in cases represented by the Gordon and Bouffard incidents.

The AIDS pandemic has also raised the problem of health care *rationing*. Exploding health needs are pressing against relatively constant resources. Rationing became part of the policy debate in 1984 when H. J. Aron and W. B. Schwartz published a book called *The Painful Prescription: Rationing Hospital Care*.[82] The two hypothesized an American system based on Great Britain's National Health Service, which accepts budgetary limits on what a nation can do for its ill. Use of the word *rationing* has been criticized, however, on grounds that to accept a reduction in services for purely financial reasons would place on patients and their physicians the entire burden of choice when, as a matter of fact, all Americans are collectively responsible through the political process. To call what we are now doing rationing in health care, say the critics, is to dignify what is really discrimination based on income.[83] For business, however, rationing is a reality. Financial resources—and the suitable allocation thereof—are on the minds of corporate managers when policy decisions are made toward employees. Special help for one stakeholder (the ill employee) affects allocations to other stakeholders, notably healthy and productive workers and sophisticated stockholders.

Nevertheless, AIDS raises issues of compassion, of individual privacy and others' rights to know, of the market's effectiveness and the market's inadequacies, of shared obligations between the professions (medical *and* legal), and between private industry and government. Meeting the AIDS problem raises the question of how justice can be linked to charity. Planted securely in common law was the principle that charity could not sit at the corporate table. That it will sit there in the future is now a sustainable thesis.[84]

VII. SUMMARY

From the foregoing may be drawn certain conclusions that provide a general thematic framework for the separate essays. These include the following:

1. Traditional religions have more to say about matters important to business (commitment, loyalty, contract, property, justice, and equality) than does the civil religion that limits itself to broad generalizations about God, the country's mission, and the like. To

say this is not to denigrate the civil religion, but to note only that its utility may sometimes blind Americans to the significance of those older and more comprehensive visions offered through Judaism and Christianity. (See the Tucker, Camenisch, and McCann essays in this volume.)

2. Legal concepts, although related to ethical concepts, are not identical. The law's notion of fair competition can be illumined by ethics to the benefit of business and society. (Relevant is the Paine essay in this volume.)

3. The relevance on James Madison's idea of countervailing power is not well suited to control factions today. Special interest groups have demonstrated a capacity to influence not only elected officials but nonelected judges on the Supreme Court.

4. Sociologists, possibly even more than political scientists, may have more to say to ethicists when they warn that *fractioning* is a greater threat to the common good than *factioning*. (Ivar Berg examines this problem in this volume.)

5. Union and business leaders who retain their historic adversarial stances toward one another are myopic; continuance of past management–labor relations will not address rapidly coming problems. (James Kuhn develops this theme.)

6. Institutional arrangements in business, government, and the health services field for handling the health crisis posed by AIDS are inadequate. (Clarence Gibbs has used his vast research experience to offer a solid explanation of what AIDS is and what it means in moral terms.)

7. Certain trends in the social sciences, especially the effort to universalize some of their assumptions, pose an intellectual and moral threat to students and society. (This is the proposition offered by Barry Schwartz.)

8. Hard data on student attitudes toward education in business ethics suggest that a slim majority feel that their needs are not being met. The fact that only a slim majority shares this view cannot be dismissed as relatively unimportant because their mentors are professors who themselves are often hostile or indifferent to the need for business ethics in professional schools of management. (From extensive data derived from his empirical studies, James Glenn defines the contours of the problem.)

9. Given the foregoing, the need for continued dialogue between business ethicists and scholars in the functional fields of business—as well as in other disciplines—has intensified.

NOTES

1. See James R. Rest, "A Psychologist Looks at the Teaching of Ethics," *Hastings Center Report*, 12 (Feb. 1982), pp. 29–30.
2. Albert Z. Carr, "Is Business Bluffing Ethical?" *Ethics for Executives, Reprints from the Harvard Business Review*, No. 21075 (n.d.), pp. 127–134.
3. Ibid., p. 129.
4. Milton Friedman, *Capitalism and Freedom* (Chicago: University of Chicago Press, 1962), Chapter 1.
5. Immanuel Kant, *The Metaphysics of Morals* (New York: Harper and Row, 1964). For a clear exposition of the deontologist view from a contemporary philosopher, one could read with profit Charles Fried, *Right and Wrong* (Cambridge: Harvard University Press, 1978).
6. John Stuart Mill, *Utilitarianism* (Indianapolis, IN: Bobbs-Merrill, 1971).
7. G. E. Moore, *Principia Ethica* (Cambridge: Cambridge University Press, 1903), pp. 5–8, 15.
8. Stephen Toulmin, "The Recovery of Practical Philosophy," *The American Scholar* (Summer, 1988), pp. 337–352.
9. R. M. Hare, *The Language of Morals* (Oxford: Clarendon Press, 1952), p. 33.
10. For an old but still important critical review of some leading twentieth-century moral philosophers, see George Kerner, *The Revolution in Ethical Theory* (Oxford: The Clarendon Press, 1966).
11. Allan Bloom, *The Closing of the American Mind: How Higher Education Has Failed Democracy and Impoverished the Souls of Today's Students* (New York: Simon and Schuster, 1987), p. 14
12. Robert Cummings, a professional philosopher teaching at SUNY in Albany, did this in his intriguing book, *The Puritan Smile* (Albany: New York State University of New York Press, 1987).
13. Henry Sidgwick, *The Methods of Ethics* (Chicago: University of Chicago Press, 1907), 7th ed.
14. Immanuel Kant, *Critique of Practical Reason* (London: Longmans, Green, 1963), tr. by T. K. Abbott.
15. For a contemporary view of the workings of intuition, see Bernard Lonergan, *Insight: A Study of Human Understanding* (New York: Philosophical Library, 1988).
16. Sidgwick, p. 45.
17. William Edward Hartpole Lecky, *History of European Morals from Augustine to Charlemagne* (New York: Appleton and Company, 1898), 2 vols. Lecky stressed the importance of having both clear perspectives and clear perceptions, I, pp. 92–93.
18. Francesco M. Nicosia, *Advertising, Management, and Society: A Business Point of View* (New York: McGraw-Hill, Inc., 1974), pp. 258–259.
19. John F. Wilson, *Public Religion in American Culture* (Philadelphia: Temple University Press, 1979).
20. Sherwin T. Wine, *Humanistic Judaism* (Buffalo, NY: Prometheus Books, 1978), pp. 10–11.
21. Ibid., p. 1.
22. Martin Buber, *Tales of the Hasidim: The Early Masters* (New York: Schocken Books, 1975), Vol. 2, p. 1. See also Ayre H. Rubenstein, *Hasidism* (New York: Leon Amiel Publisher, 1975). As a movement, Hasidimism appeared some three centuries before Christ to resist the inroads being made by Greek infidels; it reappeared in Germany during the twelfth and thirteenth centuries when a group of Jews insisted that God's will required justice in all things, economic and social equality, and even acceptance of martyrdom at the hands of the crusaders. In eighteenth-century Poland arose a movement called Hasidimism. Critical of the Jewish men of learning who, in their view, ignored the poor, Hasidim

stressed the Creator's mercy more than His judgments, God's joyousness more than His annoyance with His creatures. This resulted in the *perud*, or a radical separation between the learned class and the people, so much so, that the Talmudists, in 1781, condemned the movement as heretical.

23. Rabbi David Goldberg, *The Leaven of Judaism* (New York: Twayne Publishers, 1979), p. 36

24. *Ibid.*, p. 37.

25. Rabbi Gordon Tucker, Chapter 2, this volume.

26. Jacob Neusner, *Judaism in the Beginning of Christianity* (Philadelphia: Fortress Press, 1984), p. 64

27. David Berger, "Mission to the Jews and Jewish-Christian Contacts in the Polemical Literature of the High Middle Ages," *The American Historical Review*, Vol. 91 (June 1986), p. 577.

28. Jeremy Cohen, "Scholarship and Intolerance in the Medieval Academy: The Study and Evolution of Judaism in European Amsterdam," *The American Historical Review*, Vol. 91 (June 1986), p. 596.

29. John Paul II, *Laborem Exercens* (Washington: National Conference of Catholic Bishops, 1984). For background, see Clarence Walton, "The Connected Vessels: Economics, Ethics, and Society," *Review of Social Economy*, Vol. 40 (Dec. 1982), pp. 251–291.

30. "Economic Justice for All" (Washington: National Conference of Bishops, Nov. 18, 1986).

31. See Paul Camenisch and Dennis McCann, Chapter 3.

32. Max Weber, *The Protestant Ethic and the Spirit of Capitalism* (New York: Charles Scribner, 1930), Tr. by Talcott Parsons.

33. Ibid, pp. 179–193.

34. Amintore Fanfani, *Catholicism, Protestantism and Capitalism* (London: Sheed & Ward, 1935).

35. R. H. Tawney, *Religions and the Rise of Capitalism* (New York: Harcourt-Brace, 1954). Relevant, of course, is Ernest Troeltsch, *The Social Teachings of the Christian Churches* (London: 1928).

36. Reinhold Niebuhr, *Christian Realism and Political Power* (New York: Scribner's, 1953), p. 149.

37. Neusner, p. 101.

38. Paul Camenisch and Dennis McCann, Chapter 3.

39. Milton Friedman, *Capitalism and Freedom* (Chicago: University of Chicago Press, 1962), Chapter 1.

40. C. P. Snow, *The Two Cultures* (New York: Cambridge University Press, 1969).

41. Lord Denny, *The Discipline of Law* (London: Buttersworth, 1979), p. 5. See also Clifford Geertz, *The Interpretation of Cultures* (New York: Basic Books, 1973), especially Chapters 1 and 4.

42. The nice distinction made by judges between strict liability and negligence sometimes is lost upon the philosopher. See the *Pennsylvania Bar Association Quarterly*, Vol. 59 (October 1988) p. 202, for an example.

43. Named after Benjamin Lee Whorf (1897–1941), an anthropologist who investigated the Hopi Indians. See Michael Cole and Sylvia Scribner, "Culture of Language," in David W. McCurdy and James P. Spradley, eds., *Issues in Cultural Anthropology* (Boston: Little, Brown, 1979), pp. 78–92.

44. Lynn Sharp Paine, Chapter 4, this volume.

45. Robert Darnton, "What was Revolutionary about the French Revolution?" *The New York Review of Books* (January 19, 1989), p. 6.

46. Anthony Levi, S. J., *French Morality: The Theory of the Passions* (Oxford: Clarendon Press, 1964), pp. 7–26.

47. Charles Simic, "Ancestry," *Weather Forecasts for Utopia and Vicinity* (Barrytown, NY: Station Hill, 1983), p. 23.

48. Ivar Berg and Mayer Zald, "Business and Society," *Annual Review of Sociology*, Vol. 4 (1978), p. 137.

49. Alan Neustadtl and Dan Clawson, "Corporate Political Groupings: Does Ideology Unify Business Political Behaviors?" *American Sociological Review*, Vol. 53 (April 1988), pp. 172–190.

50. Relevant is Frank Easterbrook's essay, "The Influence of Judicial Review on Constitutional Theory," in Burke Marshall, ed., *A Workable Government: The Constitution after 200 Years* (New York: W. W. Norton, 1987), Chapter 7.

51. Gregory A. Caldeira and John R. Wright, "Organized Interests and Agenda Setting in the U.S. Supreme Court," *American Political Science Review*, Vol. 82 (December 1988), pp. 1109–1128.

52. Ivar Berg, Chapter 5, this volume.

53. Richard Hofstadter, *Social Darwinism in American Thought* (New York: Beacon, 1955), rev. ed.

54. Martin K. Starr, ed., *Global Competitiveness* (New York: W. W. Norton, 1988).

55. See Allen J. Matusow, *The Unraveling of America* (Harper & Row, 1984) for a good overview of the times.

56. Robert Korstad and Nelson Lichtenstein, "Opportunities Found and Lost: Labor, Radicals, and the Early Civil Rights Movement," *The Journal of American History*, Vol. 75 (December 1988), p. 787.

57. Ibid., p. 790.

58. James W. Kuhn, Chapter 6, this volume.

59. Karl Marx, *Capital* (New York: Modern Library, n.d.), p. 15.

60. August Compte, *The Catechism of Positive Religion* (Clifton, NJ: A. M. Kelley, Inc., 1973), 3rd rev. ed., tr. by R. Congreve.

61. Herbert Spencer, *First Principles: The Study of Sociology* (New York: Appleton, 1882), p. 418.

62. John Kenneth Galbraith, *Economics in Perspective: A Critical History* (Boston: Houghton Mifflin, 1987), p. 171.

63. George P. Brockway, "The Future of Business Ethics," in Oliver Williams, Frank Reilly, and John Houck, eds., *Ethics and the Investment Industry* (Savage, MD: Rowman and Littlefield, 1984), p. 179.

64. Tibor Scitovsky, *The Joyless Economy* (New York: Oxford Press, 1976). See also Mark Lutz and Kenneth Lux, *Humanistic Economics: The New Challenge* (New York: Bootstrap Press, 1988).

65. Amitai Etzioni, *The Moral Dimension: Toward a New Economics* (New York: The Free Press, 1988), pp. 244–248.

66. Thomas Hill Greene, *Prolegemena to Ethics* (Oxford: Clarendon Press, 1969), 5th ed., p. 7.

67. Ibid., pp. 7–8.

68. Edmund O. Wilson, *Sociobiology: The New Synthesis* (Cambridge: Harvard University Belknap Press, 1975).

69. Alan R. Rogers, "Does Biology Constrain Culture," *American Anthropologist*, Vol. 90 (December, 1988), pp. 819–831.

70. Specialists will be annoyed by significant omissions in the author's review. Not all can be mentioned, but it is appropriate to note the experimental studies by Wilhelm Wundt (1830–1920) who founded the first laboratory for experimental research in 1879 at the University of Leipzig. Soon thereafter others opened laboratories at Columbia, Clark, Catholic University, and Cornell. Gestalt psychology and behaviorism came later.

71. Especially relevant are B. F. Skinner's two books, *The Behavior of Organizations* (New York: Appleton Century, 1938), and *Beyond Freedom and Dignity* (New York: Alfred Knopf, 1972).

72. James S. Reed, *James J. Gibson and the Psychology of Perception* (New Haven: Yale University Press, 1988). Reviewed by E. H. Gombrich in *The New York Review of Books* (January 19, 1989), p. 13.

73. See Barry Schwartz, Chapter 7, this volume.

74. *New York Times* (October 28, 1988), p. D4.

75. Sharon Parks, *The Critical Years: The Young Adult Search for a Faith to Live By* (New York: Harper & Row, 1986).

76. Allan Bloom, *The Closing of the American Mind: How Higher Education Has Failed Democracy and Impoverished the Souls of Today's Students* (New York: Simon and Schuster, 1987), pp. 25–26.

77. Amitai Etzioni, *The Moral Dimension*, p. 250. Asking students to read George Stigler, *Memoirs of an Unregulated Economist* (New York: Basic Books, 1988) would be a powerful incentive for them to develop sharp insights into the differences between morally neutral and morally laden approaches.

78. See James Glenn's essay, Chapter 8, this volume.

79. James D. Watkins, "Tracking AIDS," *Catholic University Magazine*, Vol. 1 (Winter 1989), p. 13.

80. *The Wall Street Journal* (January 6, 1989), p. B-3.

81. *The Wall Street Journal* (January 4, 1989), p. B-21.

82. H. J. Aron and W. B. Schwartz, *The Painful Prescription: Rationing Hospital Care* (Washington, DC: The Brookings Institute, 1984).

83. Michael D. Reagan, "Health Care Rationing: What Does It Mean?" *The New England Journal of Medicine*, Vol. 319 (October 27, 1988), p. 1151.

84. See Clarence Gibb, Chapter 9, this volume.

II
PERSPECTIVES FROM RELIGION

The calendar developed in the sixth century by Dionysius Exiguus has recorded stories of peace and war, growth and decline, innovation and inertia, glory and infamy. A decade hence that calendar leads the world into a new millennium. It is interesting to compare what will happen 10 years from now with what happened 10 years ago. A decade ago, Americans were exuberantly celebrating the birth of their Constitution, and the rhetoric abounded with references to liberty. A few years hence religious leaders will emphasize responsibility—to ourselves and to others. In reality, liberty, and responsibility are two sides of the same coin. What, then, explains the difference in emphasis? One answer is that religious leaders see liberty being turned into licentiousness to justify the headlong rush toward hedonism. The second reason is that if church influence in the life of American society declines, the power of the state will increase.

What is striking about this new momentum toward hedonism and statism requires a comment or two. So far as the first is concerned, the conventional secular wisdom holds that God is dead and the Church is his mortuary. Why, then, follow a code of loyalty to the dead? Behind the claim is the belief that Americans are indifferent toward religions and, therefore, see churches as a superfluity. The findings of major surveys over the half-century, however, suggest that there is more stability than decline in religion in America. "Contrary to the recent wisdom in the social sciences and the mass media," two sociologists said they "could find no evidence for religious secularization as measured by attendance at church services."[1] Andrew Greeley accused those who take a pessimistic view of religion as people who have often broken with the religion of their youth and who have a need to believe that their break is a reflection of the unalterable course of the history of progress.[2] Using a 10-point scale to indicate the importance of God in their lives, Greeley reported that Americans scored 8.2, the Irish 8.0, the Italians 6.9, the Spaniards 6.4, and the Germans and English 5.7. Lowest on the scale were the Swedes who scored less than 4. Another sociologist, Peter Berger, commenting that the level of religious belief on behavior in the United States is roughly comparable to

*India, made the acerbic observation that, religiously speaking, America is a nation
of Indians governed by an elite of Swedes.*

*The second concern of the churches is that when religion declines in influence,
governments step in to take their place. Governments decide on the child's educational need. Governments establish curricula. Governments define responsibilities
of the spouses and govern divorces. Governments approve or disapprove life-styles.
Because the American "elite Swedes" are palatable to those who hold that the state
surpasses the Church in terms of importance, it is not surprising to find striking
defenses of the government's power. Lawrence Tribe, of the Harvard Law School, for
example, has argued that the Constitution's establishment clause provides the only
permissible accommodation of religious interests. In Tribe's interpretation, the state
permits. In the Church's view, God commands. It is the kind of command that Ted
Koppel, the well-known television commentator, outlined at a Duke University
graduation when he said that we have spent*

> 5,000 years as a race of rational human beings trying to drag ourselves out of the
> primeval slime by searching for truth and moral absolutes. In the place of truth,
> we have discovered facts; for moral absolutes, we have substituted moral ambi-
> guity; we now communicate with everyone and say absolutely nothing. We have
> reconstructed the Tower of Babel and it is the television antenna, a thousand
> voices producing a daily parody of democracy in which everyone's opinion is
> afforded equal weight regardless of substance or merit. In short, religious
> indifferentism finds truth too indigestible: in its purist form truth is not a polite
> tap on the shoulder; it is a howling reproach. What Moses brought down from
> Mt. Sinai were not the Ten Suggestions; they are commandments—*are* not *were*.
> The sure beauty of the Commandments is that they codify in a handful of words
> acceptable human behavior, not just for then or now, but for all times.[3]

*Koppel's words come from a tradition that church leaders hold sacred. They
insist that any community of moral significance must be a political and social reality
able to answer the quo warranto question: By what right? And they answer the
question by an answer derived from a belief in God's existence, God's creative act
and God's Providence. As a consequence, all moral institutions are benefitted by
theological insights.[4] Since the appearance of capitalism in the United States and
socialism in many European states, adherents of each have sought to find support
from one or other of the religions. The record suggests that the Judaic ethic has been
neutral toward capitalism and socialism,[5] the Protestant (Calvinist) view more
inclined toward capitalism, and the Catholic heritage more favorable, until very
recent times, toward Christian socialism.*

*It is perhaps of great significance that in addition to individual morality the
churches are addressing problems of what may be called public morality—the
reasons for certain governmental policies, the importance of the rights and duties of
corporate executives, the claims and responsibilities of unionized and nonunionized
workers, and so on. These issues are discussed by three theologians from the Jewish,*

Protestant, and Catholic traditions, respectively: Gordon Tucker, Paul Camenisch, and Dennis McCann. Sifting through the various propositions offered by the three results in a certain commonality:

- Work is a calling or a vocation to be followed according to the individual's perception of the Divine will.
- Social institutions rest on trust.
- Responsible persons use their gifts not only for personal fulfillment but also for the common good.
- Reaching the common good is a venture on which the vitality of the communal life exists.
- Viable organizations are caring organizations that, in turn, contribute to a caring community.
- The leader is a servant.
- It is every person's responsibility to be genuinely productive.

From a sociological viewpoint, an interesting difference between Jews and Catholics may have developed. The very similative processes expressed in the melting pot theory of American growth has generated concern among the rabbis over the public identity of the Jews.[6] Catholics, on the other hand, have moved easily into the American mainstream since World War II and seem unconcerned about their identity. Whatever concerns or nonconcerns exist, adherents of the three major churches participate in large numbers in the life of the commercial republic. Because what they believe is important to what they do, it is salutary to learn what their churches have taught.

NOTES

1. Michael Hout and Andrew Greeley, "The Center Doesn't Hold: Church Attendance in the United States, 1940–1984," *The American Sociologal Review*, Vol. 52 (June 1987), p. 325–345.
2. Andrew Greeley, *Religious Indicators, 1945–1980* (Cambridge: Harvard University Press, 1989).
3. Ted Koppel, "The Last Word," *American Governance Board Reports*, Vol. 29 (July-August, 1987), p. 47.
4. Robert Gordis, *Judaic Ethics for a Lawless World* (New York: Jewish Theological Seminary, 1986).
5. Meir Tamari, *With All Your Possessions: Jewish Ethics in Economic Life* (New York: The Free Press, 1987).
6. Walter Kaufmann, "The Future of Jewish Identity," *Conservative Judaism*, Vol. 24 (Winter 1970), pp. 2–14.

2

Jewish Ethical Perspectives toward Business

Rabbi Gordon Tucker

I. INTRODUCTION

This chapter is intended to be a preliminary foray into the territory where the concerns of the Jewish ethical tradition and the world of modern commerce intersect. It will focus on two particular sorts of activities—one associated primarily with corporations and the other associated principally with individuals. But it is hoped that much of what will be said will be applicable to more general problems and settings in the business world and, perhaps, even beyond.

Because the ethical problems that confront businesspersons have received lengthy treatments in recent years (in both business and philosophical journals), it may not immediately be clear what the realm of Jewish ethics can contribute to this field. In this context, it should perhaps be noted at the outset that the Jewish tradition is extraordinarily rich in material relating to the conduct of business. Indeed, fully one-fourth of the massive legal literature of the Jews is devoted to various aspects of commercial law, contracts, torts, and related areas. Because that literature includes not only codified law but also case law (called *responsa*) that spans more than a millennium and scores of locales and cultures, it stands to reason that there may well be experience and insights stored in this corpus that can be appropriated for our time. More important, however, is the exercise of

---

Rabbi Gordon Tucker • Jewish Theological Seminary, New York, New York 10027-4649.

viewing the prescriptions of a particular tradition in its own context; that is, even if a norm of Jewish ethics for the businessperson duplicates that which we have come to accept in another way, there is still much to be learned from examining how that norm flows from—and coheres with—the most general foundational assumptions of Jewish ethics. This we shall only be able to do in a fragmentary way here, but it is worth the effort.

Another observation called for at this point is that the legal claims of the Jewish tradition have long not been enforceable, even on Jews. Real political autonomy among Jews (apart from very fleeting and localized episodes) came to an end in 63 B.C.E., and even the legal system of the modern Jewish state in the Land of Israel is not based primarily on Jewish religious law. Although legal autonomy in a variety of areas of life lingered on in parts of the Jewish world through the Middle Ages and beyond, the so-called "emancipation of European Jewry," which began in Western Europe in the late eighteenth century, put that to rest for good. Thus for some hundreds of years Jewish legal norms have had to rely on *voluntary* compliance: Self-motivation and communal reinforcement have had to fill the gap left by the demise of agencies and powers of enforcement. Whatever advantages such a state of affairs may have, it takes but a moment of reflection to realize that the availability of the option to disobey or disregard a legal system's norms effectively stifles refinement and development of those norms. Why struggle with refining problematic laws when no sanction attaches to ignoring them? This is a pervasive problem faced by those who choose to live by the prescriptions of Jewish law, and it is a fact that must be noted by anyone who studies Jewish legal literature, particularly in its modern period.

One final preliminary note: We have been referring primarily to Jewish law, for it is largely through legal literature that the Jewish tradition expresses its prescriptions. How does one identify that within the Jewish tradition which can be called, "Jewish ethics"? Often, when we speak of "ethics" as opposed to "law," we have in mind something like the following: Law in a given society is the minimum that that society demands of all, whereas ethics is that which the history, ethos, and self-image of the society would seem to require but which it is not practical or possible to demand. The Jewish legal tradition, however, claims to encompass virtually all of human activity (even the most private of matters), and it might thus appear that law and ethics would be indistinguishable in Judaism.

Nevertheless, there is in the Jewish tradition a clearly articulated notion that even the totality of the law is not a complete blueprint for the moral and religious life. It is possible, in the tradition's own words, to be "a scoundrel within the boundaries of the law." And, indeed, it is possible, through induction, generalization, and sensitive reading between the lines, to derive general principles from the law that can serve as ethical guides in other situations where the law may be silent or ambiguous. For example, Exodus 21:26–27 prescribes that a slave whose eye or tooth has been destroyed by his or her master is entitled to immediate manumission. It is reasonable to infer from this that in the hierarchy of values, that of human life and limb ranks higher than the protection of private property (i.e., the slave). This inference would, of course, need further corroboration from other sources. It is, in fact, far from a valid deduction (for example, would it be just for the state to confiscate thousands of my dollars to pay for a life-saving operation on a complete stranger?). That, of course, shows that this pursuit of ethical principles can never be as precise or exact as the identification of legal norms. Nevertheless, some such principles may well, in a broad range of situations, serve as guides for the resolution of moral dilemmas. At any rate, that is roughly how the realm of Jewish ethics can be explored and mined, and in this respect, it differs little from other ethical traditions.

On the most fundamental level, the Jewish tradition sees the conduct of business as a human activity that must proceed, as much as possible, within an atmosphere of trust, fairness, and justice. The pursuit of wealth and profit is not in any way illegitimate in Judaism, as long as it rests on such foundations. It will suffice to cite a few sources in order to bolster this general observation. Leviticus 19:14 reads: "You shall not insult the deaf, or place a stumbling block before the blind. You shall fear your God; I am the Lord." The rabbinic tradition has long interpreted this biblical verse to mean that we may not mislead someone who, although not physically blind, is in some situation dependent on us for information and advice. And much of rabbinic law that forbids false and misleading advertising, for example, proceeds from this basic axiom about market conduct.

Another verse in Leviticus contains the following exhortation: "When you sell property to your neighbor, or buy any from your neighbor, you shall not wrong one another" (Leviticus 25:14). This biblical prohibition has been taken in Jewish law as the basis for a whole range of enactments that forbid overcharging for merchandise, willfully misleading another with respect to one's intentions to buy or sell, and a host of other practices that violate the baseline insistence on the pursuit of profit within an atmosphere of honesty and trust. The most extreme expression of this expectation appears in an eighth-century rabbinic work, which claims that a Jew has at least a moral obligation to follow through on a deal that he or she intended to transact, even if no contract, written or oral, were executed.[1] In other words, the ideal standard is that there be such implicit trust among all actors in the marketplace that one would not even mislead another person through *silence*, by failing to articulate one's true intentions.

These are, of course, very broad and general postulates. We now turn to two specific issues in the conduct of business in our day, with the intention of doing some beginning analysis and exploring how principles of Jewish business ethics might apply to them.

II. BRIBERY ABROAD

A corporate business practice that lies in both a legal and moral penumbra and that is thus of particular interest for ethical analysis, is the bribery of foreign officials in the course of doing business abroad. Although the Foreign Corrupt Practices Act of 1977 sought to outlaw this practice unequivocally, amendments to the law, and intense debates and disagreements over the law's original intentions, have continued ever since among businesspersons, legislators, government officials, and concerned citizens. It is therefore of interest to consider what traditional Jewish sources, and their implications, might have to offer to that debate.

Before that can be done, however, it is necessary to give a brief conspectus of the history of the issue in this country, as well as of some of the arguments that have been made for and against the practices in question. That is the subject of the subsequent sections.

A. History of the Foreign Bribery Issue

The exposure of a pattern of bribery of foreign government officials and political leaders on the part of American corporations doing business abroad was one of the legacies of Watergate. The disclosure of questionable or illegal payments made to political parties and elected officials in the United States inevitably led to a widening of the investigation by prosecutors, and especially the press, into the area of bribery overseas. What was uncovered by these investigations led the *Wall Street Journal* to observe that

> not . . . since the robber baron era and certainly not since the 1930's—when New York Stock Exchange president Richard Whitney was convicted of stock theft and utility mogul Samuel Insull escaped prosecution by fleeing abroad dressed as a woman—has America witnessed such an epidemic of corporate corruption.[2]

The kinds of activities that eventually came to light are exemplified by the following:

1. Lockheed Corporation paid officials and political organizations in Japan some $22 million over 5½ years in order to obtain lucrative contracts. This figure included $2 million to Japanese politicians in connection with

the planned sale of L-1011 aircraft to All Nippon Airways, and $7 million to the leader of a militaristic political faction for similar purposes.

2. United Brands paid a bribe of over $1 million to a government official of Honduras in order to reduce considerably the amount of export tax due on its bananas, and it falsified its corporate records in order to conceal that fact. It also made a substantial payment to an official in Italy in order to avoid delay in the unloading of approximately 15,000 tons of bananas.

3. Gulf Oil Company agreed to requests for $3 million in payments to the ruling party in South Korea to prevent interference with Gulf's activities in that country.

4. Esso Italiana (a subsidiary of Exxon Corporation) made payments totaling $46 million—the largest known payments overseas—to Italian political parties in order to "help bring about a political environment favorable to Esso Italiana's business interests."[3]

As the sampling suggests, there are several reasons why a corporation would make a payment of questionable propriety abroad:

1. To obtain new business or maintain existing corporate activities
2. To avoid or minimize the payments of taxes or duties
3. To prevent interference with legitimate corporate activities
4. To expedite specific matters at lower levels of government (e.g., customs officials)

Of these four general motivations for questionable payments, some seem to be more problematic than others. For example, reason 2 would undoubt-edly elicit fairly universal condemnation (though even here, there could be grossly inequitable or discriminatory tax rates imposed by foreign coun-tries for political purposes).[4] Avoidance of taxes imposed by the foreign country *ipso facto* indicates that the laws of that country are being violated, and surely that should not be tolerated in the American business commu-nity. Reason 4 is perhaps a bit more problematic because there is a great deal of difficulty in drawing a line between a bribe and a payment to facilitate some action to which the corporation is clearly entitled without the payment. One can, for example, certainly sympathize to a large extent with United Brands contemplating the fact that a payment to a customs official is what stands between a large sales volume and 30 million pounds of rotting bananas!

Reason 3 gets even trickier, for here we are dealing with the very thin line separating bribery from extortion. Many corporations in fact disclosed payments they made overseas and attempted to portray these payments as responses to extortionary demands made by government officials. Though this cannot be ruled out, some degree of skepticism is probably called for as well. That brings us to the most problematic of all the categories, to wit, number 1. What about those payments to obtain new business or to maintain old arrangements? How are they to be viewed, assuming that they are legal in the foreign country in question (a critical question of fact that must also be considered)? Are they bribes made necessary by the need for American companies to compete within the established rules and mores of the market they are courting, or are they a perversion of the free market system? These questions will be addressed next.

B. The Arguments for Leniency

No one, of course, simply comes out and supports bribery, even if it is done far away from home. However, a number of arguments have been advanced that suggest that distinctions must be made between what all would agree are corrupt payments with no redeeming value and other payments that are more in the nature of a gratuity, or a "value added tax" imposed by the mores of a particular foreign culture. Given the difficulty of distinguishing between these two categories of payments (so goes the argument) and given the aggregate effect on the American economy and balance of payments if significant foreign markets must be foregone, it is preferable to err on the side of tolerance and perhaps wink at some of the practices for the sake of the national interest. The most interesting arguments in the overseas payments debate were those that appealed not only to facts but to political or economic philosophies as well.

1. The Hardball Argument

This argument began with the observation that the "greasing" of foreign officials is a way of life in many parts of the world and thus can be considered an essential, inseparable part of the routine process of doing business. Everyone is doing it and has been for a long, long time. Because everyone is doing it, anyone who does *not* do it will lose out in the end; any attempt to live by a standard of morality by which no one else intends to live results in a slow death by suicide in the international market. The invocation of the suicide taboo was particularly effective in this case, for the comatose patient was not simply the individual corporation—nor even its many shareholders—but the American economy in its entirety, which could ill afford a further deterioration in its trade balance.

The hardball argument did not, however, simply point out the rather uncontroversial fact that bribery is a common practice. It went on to argue that the data indicated that in the years following the outlawing of these payments, American corporations doing business abroad *in fact* lost a considerable amount of ground to their competitors. A 1979 estimate, for example, indicated that a total of some $10 billion per year in contracts were lost by American firms as a result of antibribery provisions in law.[5] Another study also reported that among the hardest hit industries were the aircraft and construction industries. Construction companies complained that "entry fees" were required in many countries simply to get on the bidding lists. As a result, the industry claimed that from 1977 to 1979 the United States dropped from fourth to seventh place in worldwide construction.[6]

2. The Don't-Invade-Their-Culture Argument

This argument noted that it is a form of cultural imperialism to seek to impose our own standards of business propriety, no matter how attached we may be to them at home, on a situation occurring in, and under, the jurisdiction of another sovereign country. This line of reasoning began with the assertion that in many countries and societies, there is simply not the judgment that certain inducements to do business are either improper or illegal. Indeed, the experiences of American corporations suggested to some that some payments that are frowned upon in the United States are all but *required* in other countries. Not only does a business refraining from such payments lose out in the competition, but the tacit message given by that restraint, namely that there is something immoral about the way business is done in the foreign land, constitutes an embarrassment and an insult to the people and society of that land. Anecdotes were often cited to support this argument.

3. The Laissez-Faire Argument

This was an argument both in political-economic theory and in ethics. Its political-economic side was the quite familiar one invoked by all proponents of free market ideology. The main point was that the proper role of government with respect to the economic institutions of society is one of "hands off as much as possible." Because businesses operating overseas are presumably competing within the rules set down by the marketplace in which they are operating, they are doing what is required of them by their nature. For the government to determine the rules of the marketplace is, at best, dubious at home; when it attempts to interfere in that way abroad, it has crossed the boundaries of futility and absurdity. Businesses should be allowed to be guided by market forces and only market forces and have their successes or failures determined by them.

But there is an ethical theory lurking here as well, one that has to do with the meaning of the words *ethics* or *morality* when applied to a business corporation. It is a theory that holds that corporations, and even individuals in their capacities as corporate representatives, are not subject to the same set of moral standards that govern individuals acting on their own behalf. Thus, even if we might believe (as undoubtedly most, if not all, free market ideologues do) that offering a bribe for personal advantage is morally wrong, those standards do not apply when we are dealing with *corporate* action. The special morality to which corporations are subject may include some such prohibition as a secondary or tertiary derivative, but only as it can be shown to follow from its primary precept, which is that the corporation exists in order to be a productive and profit-making actor in the economic arena. Milton Friedman has expressed this principle many times in his words, "the social responsibility of business is to increase its profits." Because those responsible for the well-being of the corporation (and their own careers!) have assuredly taken possible adverse effects on the corporation into account when making the decision to engage in questionable payments overseas, it is simply wrong for the government to inject an extraneous and irrelevant new constraint into the system.

4.   The Libertarian Argument

This argument concedes that overseas bribes might be a moral issue. The real point is that it does not matter whether they are or not. The government has no business legislating morality for anyone, including corporations, when the so-called moral infractions amount to victimless crimes. The government's responsibility is to protect its own citizenry and virtually nothing else. Indeed, according to this philosophy, it would be no business of the U.S. government, for example, if an American company did business overseas in such a way that it grossly endangered the lives of foreign citizens, even if it would be admitted that the government would have a right to prohibit such practices in the United States. Because it seems fairly clear that the payment victimizes no American citizen, the government (indeed *anyone* but the corporation's shareholders) has no right to interfere in such practices.

Although these four arguments do not exhaust the spectrum of those brought forward to support relative inaction on the matter of foreign bribes, they do cover most of the factual and philosophical bases; other arguments were to a great extent variations or derivatives of those given here.

C.   The Arguments for Stricter Regulation

In addition to some ambiguity concerning the data on business loss appealed to by the hardball argument, that argument was weakened by yet another obvious, but often overlooked, consideration: Behind the legislative action prohibiting bribes lay a judgment that it was better to forego a certain amount of business rather than have to secure it in ways that were deemed contrary to the American public interest. The legislative history made that abundantly clear. George Ball, in testifying before the Senate Banking Committee in April 1976, noted that:

> To be sure, for a limited time span, some American companies might lose certain business opportunities, but that is an expense we should be able to tolerate for the good health of our political and economic system.[7]

In other words, the demonstration that business had been lost overseas could not *by itself* be an argument against criminalizing overseas bribery.

1. The Whom-Are-You-Kidding Argument

This argument aimed certain facts at a crucial part of the hardball argument. The latter attempted to show that restraining American corporations from paying bribes overseas could and did result in significant loss of business for those corporations. But the figures that were presented as proof of that proposition only indicated that contracts had been lost to competitors. They did not say anything about who the company's competitors would be *were the bribes to be legalized again*. The tacit assumption was that the American corporation would compete successfully against foreign corporations by means including bribes and bring home the business to where it belongs.

The whom-are-you-kidding argument simply pointed out that this was not generally true, but rather that markets that attract one American company often attract many other American companies and that there were many, many instances of questionable payments in which one American company was seeking to outdo another American company. The Lockheed payments made in Japan to help promote the sale of its L-1011 jumbo jets, for example, could only have been made for the purpose of outdoing American competitors. The only other aircraft manufacturers interested in that contract were based in the United States.[8] Or, to take another example, the General Tire and Rubber Company reportedly made a payment to an agent in order to persuade a French bank not to make a loan to an American competitor planning to build a plant in Chile.[9] Other arguments and appeals to various facts and figures also appeared on the scene. But the real centerpiece of the case for strict regulation in this area was directed at the assumption, articulated in the libertarian argument and unchallenged until this point, that foreign bribery is a "victimless crime" (if it is a moral infraction at all). The next, and final, argument of this section makes that challenge:

2. The Unfair Competition Argument

It need only be recalled that the laissez-faire argument made a number of claims. One of these was that yardsticks of individual responsibility cannot be legitimately applied to corporate entities, particularly economic ones. Were this claim to go unchallenged, it would present a formidable obstacle to the assigning of any noneconomic responsibility to corporations acting abroad. Although it is not our main purpose to refute that claim here, it should be noted that effective rebuttals have been made in the literature and what follows relies on them.[10] Another claim of the laissez-faire argument was that free market forces should be the only determinants of corporate behavior. But certainly it cannot be claimed that the overseas markets in which bribes are paid are free; indeed, it is the height of disingenuousness for those who seek to describe bribes as *extortion* payments to argue, on other occasions, that the government should not interfere with market determinants. Yet the real point of the present argument concerns the coercion that *follows* the payment of a bribe, that is, the unfair pressures that these payments exert on would-be competitors (and many of these, of course, are American firms). In short, a good case can be made for the claim that foreign bribery is destructive of fair competition and is for that reason not a victimless crime at all.

These observations were first made by Charles McManis more than a year prior to the passage of The Foreign Corrupt Practices Act when legislative solutions were being sought.[11] His argument can be summarized as follows:

1. Bribery of foreign officials or improper payments to agents are instances of anticompetitive conduct that tend to restrain trade and put competitors at a disadvantage through means extraneous to the economic factors that should determine the creation of contracts. These extraneous means are, of course, creating special arrangements with powerful officials or the manipulation of regulations enacted by the foreign government.

2. The subornation of foreign officials, even if it does not remove competitors from the marketplace, has the effect of subjecting them to demands and expectations that they otherwise might not face, thus making it more difficult for them to compete. In a real sense, this method of doing business deprives competitors unjustly of something to which they should have a "right" (certainly according to laissez-faire argument proponents), namely the freedom to seek a share of the market through competitive pricing, superior quality, and reliability.

3. A good number of parties are, in fact, injured by such practices. Among them are direct competitors of the bribing corporation, shareholders of the competitors that are put at a disadvantage by these practices,

and other corporations doing business in the foreign country, even if they are not competitors:

> If, for example, a corporation induces a foreign government to expend certain resources on "guns" rather than "butter," not only competitive manufacturers of armaments but also producers of non-military goods may be injured. Or, if one major American firm in a foreign country makes payments to government officials as a matter of course, other American firms in the country, regardless of the goods or services they produce, may be more likely than otherwise to find themselves importuned to make similar payments. [12]

These reflections suggest the conclusion that, whatever else these payments have been, they were practices that either restrained trade or that constituted methods of competition that were grossly unfair. In either case, they were inconsistent with the free market system to which American society is devoted. This is a crucial argument, which puts a definite and identifiable face on the problem of questionable payments abroad. And having thus defined the nature of the issue, we can now proceed to a consideration of how the Jewish ethical tradition can corroborate or augment the suggestions already made.

III. JEWISH VIEWS ON A PERENNIAL PROBLEM IN MODERN GARB

The title of this section is intended to suggest that doing business abroad through payoffs and bribery is not an entirely new phenomenon, but rather an instance of a general pattern of anticompetitive behavior that afflicts all ages and societies. Once it is recognized that the issue of foreign bribery is not *sui generis*, it becomes possible to evaluate it by applying the legal and ethical yardsticks of a long-standing and well-developed tradition such as Judaism. It will be our conclusion that there is sufficient reason not only to take a dim view of foreign bribery but to believe it to be incompatible with the Jewish tradition.

First, it should be noted that if bribes are in fact *illegal* in nearly all foreign countries (a matter of some dispute), then we need go no further. In such a case, Jewish law would certainly require that the law be obeyed (provided it is fairly and indiscriminately applied) on the principle that in commercial matters, Jewish law respects the legal sovereignty of nations. We are thus left to deal with the cases (if they exist) where corporations "compete" in overseas markets by yielding to requests for "facilitating payments" or kickbacks, or by voluntary bribery of officials at various levels, where such payments are not illegal in the host country. Can we extract from the Jewish tradition an ethical perspective on this issue?

There are two general areas of Jewish law and ethics that are applicable here: (1) the concern for the preservation of the freedom to compete and (2) the concern for the protection of businesses from predatory competition. Although the two sometimes lead in opposite directions, they can, and should, be understood as being based on a fundamental desire to promote fairness and forestall overreaching.

1. *The freedom to compete.* There is a clear and unmistakable concern within the Jewish tradition, other things being equal, for the preservation of a free marketplace and of competition unfettered by extraneous factors:

> In the Talmudic period the tendency of most of the Sages was to support free competition in business and trades, and we find only a moral derogation of one who competed too aggressively; moreover, it was a derogation devoid of any legal sanction.[13]

The fourth chapter of the Mishnah *Tractate Baba Metzia*, for example, includes a variety of laws clearly intended to preserve competition from noneconomic determinants, such as unfair inducements to children, misleading advertising, and predatory pricing. This attitude, as Elon asserts, persisted as the normative one. There were, to be sure, exceptions. Some were of significant scope and duration, but it is important to understand what the bases of those exceptions were. Principally, tolerance for—and even insistence on—lessened competition going as far as monopoly became a feature of Ashkenazic communities in the latter part of the Middle Ages. The matter essentially arose out of the fact that occupations were progressively closed to Jews, so that the range of their allowable business activities was narrow indeed. In such an environment, a Jew who had a commercial relationship (as financial underwriter or otherwise) with a Gentile had a considerable investment and stake in that relationship; were he to lose the clientele he had painstakingly developed, he did not have before him a wide field of "new careers." Because of this exigency, there arose various safeguards, by community consent, that tended away from unfettered competition. The most common of these was the *maarufia*, a grant of exclusive rights to Gentile customers, enforced by the community at large via threat of the ban. The theory was really simple: Because the compensation provided by a really free market, that is, the ability to compete in other fields, was not available to Jews in those communities, they could not equitably be subjected to the potential ravages of the free market at the same time.

Once this is understood, it becomes obvious that even deviations from the ideal of free, economically determined competition, clearly favored by the Mishnah, and by the Talmud as well,[14] were themselves based on a free competition calculus. That is, exceptions became necessary when—and only when—circumstances beyond the control of the community prevented free competition from being realized in all of its aspects. There is no virtue in insisting on a partial realization of market freedom if that severely jeopardizes the security of the participants. The reverse side of this observation is that when the exigencies do not exist, then competition should be maximized. And indeed, the *maarufia* was far from universally applied, even among Ashkenazic communities, but rather varied from place to place and from time to time.[15]

On the positive side, there were community enactments that actively encouraged and mandated the maintenance of an open market and clearly enjoined concentration and monopoly. One example, cited by Elon, appears in the collection of communal enactments of the Jews of Fez in the sixteenth century[16]:

> therefore we again decree . . . that among those in any trade or occupation . . . those who form combinations of more than two parties . . . will be duly punished by the court and community leader. And this applies *a fortiori* to those trades which have few practitioners, and a combination of several of them [would close the market]. . .

In any event, it should be clear that the "original" position of the Jewish tradition, *ceteris paribus*, favors maximized competition. Departures from that norm appear only in times and places that required "emergency" enactments (to prevent victimization of those whom the free market ideal was designed to protect). It then follows quite naturally that, in a case where foreign bribery minimizes competition and where no exigencies comparable to the restricted economic activities of medieval Jewry exist, that the Jewish tradition would have to prohibit it on the grounds that it restricts the freedom to compete.

2. *Unfair competition.* Corrupt payments overseas do not always result in a restraint of trade in the obvious sense of preventing competitors from even having a shot at the market. As it has already been suggested, the payments may simply be part of a general atmosphere in which there are apparently many competitors, all making the same sorts of payments, to a greater or lesser extent, and all accepting the rules of the game. But although competition *per se* may perhaps (it is a big "perhaps") be said to be compatible with such an atmosphere, it does not follow that it is *fair* competition that is thriving.

Fair competition in the Jewish tradition is a value that is closely related to free access to the market. But as was the case with some of the "emergency regulations" that were invoked from time to time to control competition, the demands of fairness in competition sometimes led Jewish authorities to impose some control (through legal means or moral suasion) on the acceptable methods of competition. There is, of course, nothing particularly special about the Jewish tradition in this respect; none but the most fanatic devotees of the free market model believe that any method of competing is legitimate. Differences among legal and ethical traditions on this issue are rather to be sought in the degree of regulation imposed.

The *locus classicus* on predatory competition in Jewish sources is found in the *Babylonian Talmud* (*Tractate Qiddushin* 59a):

> Rav Giddal was negotiating for a parcel of land when Rabbi Abba went and purchased it. Rav Giddal complained to Rabbi Zaira, who transmitted the complaint to Rav Yitzhak Nafha. The latter said, "Wait until he arrives for the festival." When he [Rabbi Abba] came, he met him and said, "A poor man waits by a stack of grain (to gather up the forgotten sheaf intended for the poor), and another comes and takes the sheaf from him. What is your ruling in such a case?" He answered: "He is called 'wicked.'" "Then why, sir, did you do what you did?" He answered, "I didn't know (that Rav Giddal was negotiating for the land)." "Then return it to him (to Rav Giddal)." He answered, "I shall not sell it, since it is my first land purchase, and that would be a bad omen. He can have it as a gift." Rav Giddal, however, would not take possession of it, for it is written (Proverbs 15), "He who spurns gifts will live long." Rabbi Abba wouldn't take possession of the land since Rav Giddal had negotiated for it. Since neither would take it, it became communal land of the rabbis.

A great deal has been written about this talmudic passage, and one of the reasons for that is the difficulty in extracting from the narrative exactly what the operative principles of law and ethics are here. Does the passage invite us to conclude that any contact between buyer and seller effectively precludes any further negotiation with a third party, as long as the interest of the first customer is still alive? Surely not, for that would open the door to the most destructive kinds of preemption in the marketplace and lead to victimization of both vendors and buyers that would far outstrip whatever evils might be averted by this prohibition. We must conclude that the passage in *Qiddushin* does not intend to limit competition but rather to restrain certain kinds of competition in certain circumstances.

But what are we then to make of the metaphor of the poor man watching the stack of grain: Just what kind of competition is its invocation intended to stifle? The answer that best fits the metaphor itself—as well as the discussions and later interpretations embellishing it—is related to what was noted earlier in connection with the unfair competition argument. In that context, we observed that competition involving the subornation of foreign officials can often deprive competitors of their expectation of winning or losing business solely on the economic grounds of quality, pricing, and so on. That expectation of reward for superior economic performance was described as a "right" that the competitor has, from the perspective of market ethics. Here, in the Jewish sources, we now find that the expectation of gain is also viewed as conferring a "right" on the primary actor, a right that can be strong enough to preclude others from depriving him of that expected gain, even when that is accomplished by what would otherwise be normal and appropriate methods of competition. That is what the metaphor of the poor man means—because the forgotten sheaf is something to which the poor man is legally entitled, the stack need only be removed for the poor man to acquire his expected gain. Because he is standing right there (having arrived first) and the expected gain is so close to being his, even if someone were to prove, at the last minute, to be quicker in bending down and picking it up, that person would be morally culpable for his act.

What does this translate into in the normal arena of economic activity? It means that if someone who has negotiated a deal with which all parties are satisfied and where the only missing element is the formal instrument that legally solemnizes it, then that person has a right to expect others to refrain from scuttling the transaction for their own benefit. This is the correct generalization of the metaphor, and it is, in fact, the position taken by the vast majority of later Jewish codifiers and decisors.[17] It is important for our purposes because it reflects clearly the notion that anticipation of economic reward can sometimes constitute an economic right. Before proceeding further from this apparently strong position, however, three qualifications must be noted.

1. The anticipated gain must be one that is genuinely *imminent*. Absent this qualification, the principle we have generalized from the *Qiddushin* passage would lead us to the grotesque monopolistic consequences that we have already pointed out. That is why the episode involving Rav Giddal had to be interpreted as referring to a situation where Rav Giddal had already completed negotiations and was simply (like the hypothetical poor man) lacking the final, *pro forma* consummation of the deal. After all, the competitive techniques used by Rabbi Abba were not intrinsically improper. They were only so in this case, where the anticipated gain for Rav Giddal was truly imminent.
2. The anticipated gain must be the result of economic factors. Someone about to consummate a transaction that he himself negotiated through extortion or other noneconomic means is certainly not entitled to protection under this principle.
3. The protection accorded to the primary negotiator here is not generally recognized as legally enforceable. It carries with it a strong ethical sanction, but one who violates it cannot ordinarily be forced to relinquish his ill-gotten gain. He is, of course, subject

to other pressures, and even ostracism, appropriate for one who has contravened a communal norm and acted "wickedly."

The recognition of expected reward as a right worthy of protection appears in Jewish sources in various contexts, apart from the episode of Rav Giddal and his land transaction. Two of these are instructive.

The *Babylonian Talmud* (*Tractate Baba Batra* 21b), in a much-cited passage, speaks of the rights that neighborhood associations have to limit the activity of competitors from the outside. One of the accepted regulations discussed in that context is the requirement that fishnets must be set up at least as far from existing nets as the normal swimming range of the fish. The commentator Rashi (Solomon ben Yitzhak—eleventh century Alsace) noted there that the reason for the fishnet regulation is that once the original net has been placed and baited, its owner can virtually assume that the fish in swimming range will be caught. Rashi thus concludes that the fish have virtually come into the possession of the first fisherman, thereby precluding the second from infringing on his rights.

Commenting on the same talmudic passage concerning neighborhood associations, the twelfth-century legal work *Aviasaf*, of Eliezer ben Joel Halevi,[18] states that, notwithstanding other opinions on competitive protection, there is one case where a shopkeeper must be protected: When an alleyway is closed off on three sides, and Reuben lives (and does business) at the far end, he should be able to prevent Simeon from coming to set up shop at the open end so that no Gentile (i.e., an impartial customer) can reach Reuben without passing Simeon's shop first. And *Aviasaf* compares this kind of regulation to the sanction of the poor man invoked in favor of Rav Giddal in *Qiddushin* 59a.

What do the statements of Rashi and *Aviasaf* have in common? Simply this: They both assert that competitors who have entered a market have the right to expect that their profit or loss will be determined by how well they produce, price, choose location, and pursue clientele. That expectation is itself a "good" that is theirs and that others must not deprive them of. In the case of the fisherman, his bait may not be the best, nor his nets, nor even his chosen location. But having set up shop, so to speak, having entered the economic game intent on playing by its rules, he has a right to reap the economic consequences of his efforts. Other fishermen miles away may be more adept, or have better locations, and thus far outstrip him. But, according to Rashi, Jewish law recognizes his right to those fish that he has virtually acquired by staking out his area of operation. In the case of the cul-de-sac discussed by *Aviasaf*, the end of the alley might be a poor location, and the goods offered for sale there may be of poor quality, or uncompetitively priced, but *Aviasaf* insists that the narrow alleyway must not be used by a competitor to forestall potential customers from ever making their choice. (This kind of competition attempted by the hypothetical Simeon cannot be justified as simply choosing a more felicitous location; the physical characteristics of the alleys to which *Aviasaf* referred make it much more analogous [as is the fish example] to the more modern instance of a chemical corporation locating upstream from a competitor and physically diverting and preempting the latter's supply of water. Such behavior, like the examples addressed by Rashi and *Aviasaf*, constitutes noneconomic competition.)

It thus appears that many authoritative Jewish sources consider it unethical, and perhaps even illegal, to compete in the marketplace in such a way as to create pressures and handicaps on others that transcend the line that divides the normal forces of the market from forces extraneous to the economic calculations that businesspersons expect to make. (It cannot, of course, be suggested that this line is a clear or uncontroversial one. That is one of the factors that makes this issue so subtle and knotty. On the other hand, the existence of gray areas does not negate the fact that there are clearly black, and clearly white ones as well.) And if the examples of Rav Giddal, or of the fishnets and cul-de-sac, called forth the reaction they did from the legal authorities, despite the fact that they at least superficially appear to involve common, if aggressive, modes of competition, we can safely assume that Jewish law and ethics would take at least as dim a view of more blatant introductions of extraneous factors, such as bribery, into the marketplace.

All of the sources we have looked at, for all of their diversity, have in common the principle that a person who competes in the marketplace must do so within the accepted rules of *economic* competition, and by doing so acquires the right to expect others to be enjoined, legally or morally, to do the same. Despite all the exigencies of Jewish economic and social history, there was never any serious retreat from the high value placed on fair competition as an ideal. And fair competition, as the foregoing analysis makes clear, can roughly be equated with the avoidance, to the greatest extent possible, of resort to methods that exploit factors extraneous to economics. Because one of the crucial arguments against the practice of foreign bribery was precisely the one that exposed it as competition that is unfair in the preceding sense, the evidence from the Jewish tradition adduced here, though certainly not exhaustive, is more than enough to support the conclusion that the corporate practices that so exercised American legislators in the late 1970s are in fact incompatible with Judaism's fundamental ethical postulates of the marketplace.

IV.   A FEW WORDS ABOUT INSIDER TRADING

We have been dealing, in the bulk of this chapter, with practices associated with corporations. What we have learned thus far can now be used for the purpose of a brief reflection on an even more contemporary issue, associated with individuals and corporations alike. The recent scandals involving insider trading in corporate securities have called forth widespread condemnation. The condemnation, however, has not been universal, and even in this case, some arguments similar to the arguments for leniency on foreign bribery have been heard. For example, it has been argued that insider trading laws, although they indubitably make many of the practices in question illegal, are nothing more than arbitrary, conventional restrictions on entrepreneurial activity and that there is no real purpose behind those laws. Indeed, it has also been suggested that insider trading serves a salutary social and economic function, in that it facilitates swift and profitable takeovers of companies that have suffered from lethargic and uncreative management. Virtually all of the other arguments (e.g., the laissez-faire and libertarian arguments) have been made as well, in a form appropriate to the insider trading issue. However, our much more lengthy analysis of the foreign bribery issue gives us a different perspective here as well, for the unfair competition argument that loomed large previously sheds its own light on the insider trading scandals as well. Indeed, I would suggest that the unfair competition approach accords best with our common sense feeling that there is, in fact, something intrinsically wrong with insider trading.

The point is, essentially, this: Just as we should be legitimately concerned with the introduction of extraneous factors that determine the "winners" in the economic arena, just as we should legitimately be concerned with whether Simeon is choking off Reuven's business in the alleyway, there are here serious questions concerning the choking off, or "hoarding" of information. In the financial markets, information is a critical commodity, indeed *the* critical commodity. We have a Securities and Exchange Commission precisely for that reason. It is there to guarantee to the public that its access to the financial markets is based on the premise that information that is available to anyone is available in principle to everyone, fairly. Without that guarantee, the markets would hardly be able to work and to generate profits for the "big winners." The supply of capital is there to be won because investors act on these implicit assurances. What insider traders do is to misappropriate that critical commodity. They often gain access to information they should not have in the first place, and once in possession of it, they buy and sell it and generally orchestrate who will have access to it and who will not.

Any variation of the libertarian argument here that would claim that insider trading is a technical violation or a victimless crime thus misses the crucial point. Were the manipulation of information to become widely known and acknowledged and if there were a sense that violators would not be found out and punished, the markets would be profoundly affected. To the extent that any investor has a legitimate expectation that his or her analyses, choices, or hunches will result in gains or losses according to economic rules and forces, insider trading frustrates those expectations. And thus it is inevitable that we conceive of this practice also under the rubric of unfair competition.

The Jewish tradition has never been particularly fond of gambling. One view expressed in rabbinic literature is that the problem with gambling is that, psychologically, no gambler ever really expects to lose, and thus the winner has taken money that the loser has not willingly parted with. That way of looking at gambling gives it at least the faint aroma of theft, though it certainly is not actual theft. But if winning money from someone psychologically unprepared to lose in an honest game of chance is morally suspect, how much more so is making a fortune in what is supposed to be a fairly regulated market, when in fact the fortune has been made by "loading the dice," as it were? There seems to be no doubt about the Jewish ethical perspective on this business practice, and this ethical verdict, too, flows ultimately from the fundamental principles relating to trust, honesty, free competition, and fair competition.

At some point every society and every tradition must confront new phenomena. Foreign bribery was once a new practice, and insider trading was as well. There will be a constant stream of new and exotic twists on business deals as long as human beings compete with one another for livelihoods. It is, however, possible, whether in secular or religious ethical thinking, to identify those features of the new phenomena that have appeared before in other guises, and carefully to apply the postulates on which we build our markets to the situations at hand. When that is done with a critical eye and with caution, a good deal of wisdom and guidance can in fact be recovered from the past.

NOTES

1. *She'eltot* of Rav Ahai Gaon (a Babylonian rabbi of the eighth century), Parashat Vayyehi No. 36.
2. *The Wall Street Journal*, March 12, 1976, p. 8, column 4.
3. Ibid.
4. For a particularly colorful example of an "unorthodox" government approach to taxes, see Arthur L. Kelly, "Case Study—Italian Tax Mores," in Thomas Donaldson and Patricia

H. Werhane (eds.), *Ethical Issues in Business: A Philosophical Approach* (Englewood Cliffs, NJ: Prentice-Hall, 1979), pp. 37–39.

5. Shelly O'Neill, "The FCPA: Problems of Extraterritorial Application," in *Vanderbilt Journal of International Law*, Volume 12 (1979), p. 704.

6. United States General Accounting Office, *Impact of Foreign Corrupt Practices Act on U.S. Business*, March 4, 1981, p. 15.

7. *Foreign and Corporate Bribes: Hearings on S. 3133 before the Senate Committee on Banking, Housing, and Urban Affairs*, 94th Congress, second session (April 1976), p. 41.

8. Ibid., p. 39.

9. Charles J. McManis, "Questionable Corporate Payments Abroad: An Antitrust Approach," *Yale Law Journal*, Volume 86, p. 219.

10. Two good articles on the subject are (1) Peter A. French, "Corporate Moral Agency," reprinted in Tom Beauchamp and Norman Bowie (eds.), *Ethical Theory and Business* (Englewood Cliffs: Prentice-Hall, 1979), pp. 175–186, and (2) Alan H. Goldman, "Business Ethics: Profits, Utilities, and Moral Rights," in *Philosophy and Public Affairs*, Vol. 9 (Spring 1980), pp. 260–286.

11. McManis, pp. 215–257.

12. Ibid., p. 252.

13. Menahem Elon, *Hamishpat Ha-ivri* [Jewish Jurisprudence], 3 volumes (Jerusalem: Magnes Press, 1973), pp. 329–330.

14. See *Babylonian Talmud, Tractate Baba Batra* 21b, where the Talmud seems to accept (as do the later authorities) the opinion of Rav Huna b. Rav Joshua, who permitted any taxpaying member of the community to set up shop next to an existing business of the same type.

15. See, for example, the article entitled "Maarufia" in the *Encyclopedia Judaica*.

16. Printed in Kerem Hemar, part II of Rabbi Abraham Ankawa, who lived in the nineteenth century. Elon quotes this in Part III of *Hamishpat Ha-ivri* (see note 13), p. II 663.

17. Aaron Levine, *Free Enterprise and Jewish Law* (New York: Yeshiva University Press, 1980), pp. 124–128 (and notes)

18. Quoted in *Mordekhai* (Mordekhai ben Hillel Hakohen—thirteenth-century Germany), Baba Batra, Chapter 2, No. 516.

3

Christian Religious Traditions

Paul Camenisch and Dennis McCann

I. INTRODUCTION

Simply to specify, much less to assess the religious dimensions of business ethics, or of business activity in this country, is to undertake a complex task that can only be sketched here. Given the currently dominant approaches to business ethics that are based on cases and philosophically articulated modes of analysis and reasoning, one is tempted to say that *the shift to religious dimensions is, among other things, a shift of focus from ethics to ethos.* The difficulty of isolating an ethos, especially in a pluralistic society such as ours, helps explain the complexity of our task.

Religious insights and convictions can be used to analyze cases and can generate patterns of analysis and reasoning analogous to philosophical ones. However, the variety of ways in which religion is embodied in a culture—institutions, sacred writings, sacramental practices and rituals, worship, the formation of character, religious proclamation and education, theological reflection and moral instruction, community life, and the like means that an almost equally varied and complex set of approaches or tools would be needed to capture its impact. At the very least, we will need to draw on currently available historical/cultural studies and perhaps even conduct additional such studies focused on economic activity and business practices, if we are to make clear that we do not face the problems of contemporary business in a vacuum, that we do not reason them out from some pristine vantage point that permits us to ignore their history, ignore

Paul Camenisch and Dennis McCann • Department of Religious Studies, DePaul University, Chicago, Illinois 60614.

ourselves, and others, and the culture in which we reason and act. Americans are heirs to multiple moral traditions, shaped as moral agents by a variety of forces, and both perpetuate and modify the patterns of response already established in the culture.[1] As should be clear to any observer of the American scene (from de Tocqueville to Bellah and colleagues[2]), a significant portion of those shaping traditions, forces, and patterns are religious.

Although this approach may seem to be significantly removed from current debates about ethical problems to be solved and corporate policies to be hammered out, it is an essential acknowledgment that morally we are not self-made agents created *ex nihilo* and that the culture—both business and otherwise in which we act—is not entirely of our own, nor of our immediate predecessors' making, but has a longer more complex history whose influences we do not escape simply by being ignorant of them.

In fact, similar insights already seem to be at work as corporations turn to questions of corporate culture and the pursuit of excellence in order to see ethical issues they face in the context of their own culture and orientation. Given that corporate culture is at most a subculture, being both subordinate to and a specification of the larger culture in which it is set, even this concern with corporate culture, intelligently pursued, requires more careful studies of the larger cultural setting of business in all its significant dimensions, including, of course, the religious dimensions.

II. FOUNDATIONAL PROTESTANT CONTRIBUTIONS

Although the Protestant Reformation of the sixteenth century may seem exceedingly remote from the reality of contemporary business, key insights and commitments from that time continue to influence our participation in, and response to, business and related activities. Much of this is generally familiar through the discussion begun by Max Weber in his now classic *The Protestant Ethic and the Spirit of Capitalism*.[3] The continuing importance of this material, at least as a topic for debate, is attested to by Robert Jackall's statement:

> A grasp of the moral significance of work in business today begins, in fact, with an understanding of the original Protestant ethic, Max Weber's term to describe the comprehensive worldview of the rising middle class that spearheaded the emergence of capitalism.[4]

Perhaps the most fundamental contribution of the Protestant Reformation in general, and of Calvinism in particular in this area, was a transformation of the attitude toward the physical universe or, more accurately, toward this world of time and space that is simultaneously the basic stuff of economic activity and the arena in which it occurs. Whatever importance this life and this world had borne in the medieval Christian world view—and that of course varied among the various strands of that synthesis—for most of Protestantism this world's significance as an arena of God's continuing activity for the salvation of the race, and therefore of humans' possible activity to glorify God and to which, along with more immediate impacts such as Calvin's qualified acceptance of the taking of interest, tended to legitimize capitalism.[5]

But what must not be forgotten is that all these beliefs were part of a religious world view, of a theologically shaped vision of the universe that located these beliefs as well as the practices and attitudes they generated in a divine economy into a plan of salvation. The Calvinist doctrine of predestination—by which the sovereign God determined even before an individual's birth whether that person was among the elect or the damned and insulated that decision from any and all influence of the one subject to it—generated in later Calvinism a disturbing uncertainty about salvation. This placing of the individual alone before the divine decree tended to accentuate the emerging individualism.[6]

Once there emerged a general, if often tacit, agreement that divine approval in this life, of which one important sign was economic success, was as good a indicator as was available for the divine disposition toward the person's next life, an intense activism in the economic life was a predictable outcome. But this was not a glorification of work, or of financial success itself, but a focusing on them only because of their relation to this much larger, and for the Calvinist, infinitely more urgent question.

Although this Calvinist perspective on economic activity currently is seldom found intact, various ghostly remnants haunt us under such labels as the *Protestant ethic*, the *Protestant work ethic*, or just the *work ethic*. Most frequently these have lost all theological grounding or content and end up simply as the endorsement, even the glorification, of work for its own sake that is often difficult to distinguish from the workaholism that currently plagues many achievers, or as the worship of the financial success such dedication to work is expected to yield. Thus there are continuities between what A. Whitney Griswold called the *Puritan ethic* of the seventeenth century and the philosophy of success of the early twentieth century as well as significant discontinuities.[7]

It is not always easy to determine what is a secularized, even bastardized offspring of the Protestant work ethic and what is the product of other seemingly similar, but often quite different ideas or ideologies. John Cawelti argues that the "conservative tradition of the middle-class Protestant ethic" was only one of three major strands forming the idea of the self-made man in America. A second strand stressed the individual's getting ahead and understood that primarily in economic terms. Cawelti says about the origins of this strand only that it emerged early in the nineteenth century as many Americans responded to signs of rapid economic expansion. The third strand related success to "individual fulfillment and social progress rather than to wealth or status" and finds its roots in Franklin, Jefferson, and Emerson.[8] Although these three strands may be kin, it is important, both for historical accuracy and for analytical clarity, that we observe the difference among them, especially those between the Protestant work ethic and the success ethic that has largely displaced it. For example, not only are these two quite different in their foundations and ultimate rationale—the one being theological and religious, the other secular and probably materialistic—but they also differ in the sorts of character traits they encourage. As Cawelti wrote,

> Where the religious tradition stressed industry, frugality, honesty, and piety—the self-disciplinary and religious virtues—the second strand indorsed [sic] such secular qualities as initiative, aggressiveness, competitiveness, and forcefulness. Moreover, where the Protestant tradition assumed a stable social order, proponents of the second version of success were sympathetic to social change and enthusiastic about the progress of industrialism.[9]

At the same time, it must be admitted that these strands sometimes came together in ways that made it difficult to distinguish between them. The gospel of wealth that flourished during the first decades of this century sometimes in its extreme praise of success ran a serious risk of muting the larger causes it was to serve. For example, the often-cited statement of Russell Conwell, a Baptist minister, that "if you can honestly attain unto riches in Philadelphia, it is your Christian and godly duty to do so,"[10] apparently often circulated without benefit of Conwell's insistence that such wealth as was accumulated should be used for various philanthropic enterprises, as Conwell himself used much of the $8 million received for 6,000 deliveries of his "Acres of Diamonds" speech.[11]

In fact, to many modern eyes it will seem that individual financial success was clearly the tail that wagged the dog of religious faith for many Christians. Self-improvement movements, popular in the United States for decades, had urged a balance of various values (political, moral, religious, and economic) that was thought to be beneficial for society as well as for the individual. But in the hands of some, they became a single-minded, sharply focused pursuit of economic success dressed in an extensively religiously toned garb[12] that in many cases virtually identified success and salvation. The difficulty of separating the economic from the religious is well illustrated in the extremely popular 1924 work by advertising executive Bruce Barton, *The Man Nobody Knows.* Barton's chapter headings, organized around Jesus' primary characteristics, clearly indicate the thrust of the work: The Executive; The Outdoor Man; The Sociable Man; His Method; His Advertisements; The Founder of Modern Business; the Master.[13]

Finally, of course, it must also be acknowledged that not all the failings of this religious endorsement of wealth and success resulted from distortions and abbreviations it underwent. Some were inherent in the stance itself. From a contemporary point of view, it was largely individualistic and socially conservative so that its adherents failed to see that individual success and even individual charity and philanthropy were not adequate to meet the systemic problems of the emerging industrial age. Concerned Protestants began and supported social and moral reforms in considerable number—the temperance movement, child labor reform, prison reform, the improvement of factory conditions, and the founding of schools at various levels. Even the Sunday School movement, the YMCA, and the YWCA, which are often seen as strictly religious enterprises, frequently had social reform agendas. But such reforms left fundamentally untouched the economic system and the various abuses its rapid and often unrestrained growth spawned.[14]

The fact that mainline Protestant churches and their frequently well-placed members generally accepted, even explicitly endorsed, the existing economic system was not missed by other less well-placed segments of the society. In 1898 Samuel Gompers took note of the general absence of workers from the churches:

> My associates have come to look upon the church and the ministry as the apologists and defenders of the wrong committed against the interests of the people, simply because the perpetrators are possessors of wealth . . . whose real God is the almighty dollar, and who contribute a few of their idols to suborn the intellect and eloquence of the divines.[15]

However, just as the prophets of the Hebrew Bible challenged the political and economic systems they confronted, so the Christian Gospel, as read by some of its followers, generated tension with the emerging economic system that led to similar challenges to change. The failings and abuses of industrial capitalism that were fueling the protests of the labor movement, and the even more fundamental Marxist critique, did not entirely fail to rouse some in the churches to an awareness of what was systemically wrong with the then-current situation.

The most important form of this Protestant response to the emerging economic order was the Social Gospel that flourished between the Civil War and World War I and had Washington Gladden (1836–1918) and Walter Rauschenbusch (1861–1918) among its major leaders. Rauschenbusch summed up much of the rationale of the movement when he wrote:

> The social gospel is the old message of salvation, but enlarged and intensified.
> The individualistic gospel has taught us to see the sinfulness of every human
> heart and has inspired us with faith in the willingness and the power of God to
> save every soul that comes to him. But it has not given us an adequate under-
> standing of the sinfulness of the social order and its share in the sins of all
> individuals within it. It has not evoked faith in the will and power of God to
> redeem the permanent institutions of human society from their inherited guilt
> of oppression and extortion.[16]

Thus the Kingdom of God, too easily identified in an individualistic reading of scripture, with the future life either of individuals following their deaths, or of all the saved after the eschaton, now meant (or at least also included) economic, social, and political achievements here on earth. The significance of such a transformation of the present order was height-ened by the liberal understanding of the importance and sacredness of each person, and the extent to which the person is shaped by the social/cultural setting in which she or he lives.[17] Many proponents of the Social Gospel believed that the business/economic sector of this setting lagged behind the educational and political sectors in the march toward a more humane society. Thus the harsher and more competitive elements of busi-ness were major targets of criticism and reform efforts.[18]

Although this was largely a social reform movement, it was not iso-lated from more traditional concerns of the church, such as worship and the formation of character. Its concerns were brought right into the heart of worship through such still popular hymns as "Where Cross the Crowded Ways of Life," "Turn Back, O Man," and Gladden's own "O Master Let Me Walk with Thee." And a number of social Gospel novels popularized the ideals of the movement. Charles M. Sheldon's *In His Steps: What Would Jesus Do?* sold 23 million copies in English and was translated into 21 other languages in the generation following its publication in 1896.[19]

World War I and, later, the collapse of the stock market did much to deflate the optimism behind the individualistic gospels of success and wealth and the myth of virtually inevitable progress on which they fed. Certainly we are heirs to these ideas in more ways than we usually ac-knowledge, and an increasing number of media evangelists, whether knowingly or not, seem to be vying to prove themselves their most direct descendants. But that gospel seems unlikely to return in its most flagrant and naive form except for a limited number of devotees. At the same time, however, such unrestrained endorsements of business activity and eco-nomic success have not for most Protestants been replaced by a general alienation from contemporary economic realities.

What does continue apace for most of the mainline Protestant churches is the concern for economic justice and a humane economic system that was so prominent in the Social Gospel movement. Even a brief charting of this development would have to include the 1948 Amsterdam meeting of the World Council of Churches around the theme, "Man's Disorder and God's Design," that argued that "the Christian churches should reject the ideologies of both communism and laissez-faire capitalism, and should seek to draw men away from the false assumption that these extremes are the only alternatives."[20] The theme of the "responsible society" developed at the Amsterdam meeting and the Evanston (1954) meeting and that of the "just, participatory, and sustainable society" articulated at the Fifth Assembly in Nairobi (1975) were also heavily economic in their thrust.[21]

And, finally, one would have to mention the major statements on the economy and Christian faith recently issued by several mainline denominations, which parallel in many ways, the pastoral letter of the National Council of Catholic Bishops. Such documents have been published by the Lutheran Church in America (1980), the Presbyterian Church (U.S.A.) (1984 and 1985), and the United Church of Christ (1987). These discussions are grounded in several of the theological themes already noted—the divine sovereignty that encompasses also the economy as God's way of caring for the one human family, our standing as trustees or stewards of the resources basic to the economy, the positive, humanizing dimensions of work and of participation in the economy. On such starting points these documents address various issues in contemporary business ethics, including distributive justice, hunger and malnutrition, unemployment, and poverty, racial and sexual discrimination, meaningful work. Although none of these documents call for the replacement of our current economic system with some alternative system—in fact some explicitly reject that as part of their agenda—they do see that the problems faced are frequently systemic in nature and are not caused by—nor to be solved by—individual moral choices alone.[22]

III.   THE PRESENT CONDITION OF PROTESTANTISM

This survey of some of the dominant interactions between Protestant Christianity and American business is of more than historical significance. It is also potentially informative with regard to the current discussion of the moral and ethical dimensions of business. Some few brave souls may still hope to sustain or revive the ideas of stewardship and vocation with their full religious/theological meanings. But the general absence of the religious foundations necessary to such a revival make this a futile effort except for some very limited communities. More illuminating is to try to discern in contemporary concerns and attitudes reflections or correlates of some of the religious concepts noted. To do this is not necessarily to credit the religious tradition for any positive elements so identified nor to blame it for the negative. It is simply to try to illuminate both the traditional religious element and the contemporary phenomenon by seeing each in the light of the other.

For example, debates about corporate social responsibility can often be illuminated by the idea of stewardship, seen in this context, of course, as a corporate rather than an individual issue. To call corporations to social responsibility is to ask them to see their activities not as self-contained, self-justifying undertakings but as activities that must be conducted in light of—and perhaps even directed toward—larger goods and goals that transcend those activities and their most immediate consequences of increasing market share, enhancing stockholder value, or generating a profit. It is to say that the resources, the accumulated capital, the labor, and the infrastructure that make corporate activities possible are not owned by the corporation in some absolute sense that cuts them free of all ties to the larger society. It is to argue that these elements are trusts *from* the society that has helped generate them and that they are to be used with an eye toward the moral claims of this larger constituency. Clearly this is an enlargement of vision similar to that experienced by the individual Christian who came to see that his or her labor was not just for the support of oneself and one's dependents but that it had ramifications, both positive and negative, for larger circles and for the society itself that should be adverted to, even cultivated. The same is true of the idea of vocation or calling, and the contemporary discussions about the meaningfulness of work. Of course one dimension of calling or vocation was even identical with the matter of stewardship just noted. A person's calling was, among other things, to serve others, including in one's workplace, to be a good steward of personal possessions and what one could generate on behalf of others. But another dimension of calling was a sense of the particularity of each person, for whom God therefore had a distinctive and unique place in the divine economy. Humans were not seen as faceless and interchangeable elements but as unique individuals called by name and having distinctive talents to use and distinctive contributions to make. Similarly the movement toward work enrichment is also motivated in part by the determination of workers not to be taken as nameless, faceless interchangeable factors of production, but to be seen as distinctive individuals who have a variety of needs and a variety of gifts to offer.

Another dimension of the religious perception of work is the meaning people derived from being related to something larger and beyond themselves; in the most explicitly Protestant context, that larger something was the fate of a person's soul here and hereafter. Again, this specific content holds little promise of resolving current problems. But to see the concern about meaningful work as a kind of secular analog focusing in some cases on such matters as the development, expression, and fulfillment of the self might give a sense of the scope and complexity of the issue met here.

A final dynamic to be noted is that of the justification of and by work. It must be remembered that the Calvinist never thought, at least when thinking clearly and Calvinistically, that his or her work itself saved. It was rather that work and success in it were presumptive evidence of a salvation already effected by God's otherwise inscrutable will. The fact that work could provide this sort of assurance served to justify commitment to work. So work was simultaneously evidence of justification and itself justified. Contemporary work seems also to be caught in this dual relation to justification. It is itself justifying or is evidence of justification. For example, contemporary business persons often cite the economic success of their corporations as one of the best moral justifications of the corporation and its practices: "How could we be doing so well, if we're not also doing good?" Of course the judge that currently issues the verdict on salvation or moral justification is not Calvin's sovereign God but Smith's sovereign-free market, this latter, however, in Smith's mind, not being entirely unrelated to the former.

On the other side of the dynamic, many persons seek a way to justify work itself as deserving a major portion of their time and energy. It is probably hopeless to try to answer these questions within the traditional content. Nevertheless, the ways in which those traditional answers functioned, primarily by locating work in a larger universe of meaning, may be instructive about how the issues might be resolved now, as long as we also remember that universes of meaning cannot be generated on demand simply to meet specific felt needs.

IV.   CATHOLIC ADAPTATIONS

The analysis of American character presented in *Habits of the Heart*, in particular, its interpretation of the conflicted interplay of the biblical and Republican tradition with the more recent "strands" of "expressive and utilitarian individualism" is noteworthy for its failure to identify any foundational contribution from American Catholicism. This should not be regarded as a sin of omission but as an accurate reflection of the historical record. The fact is that the Roman Catholic response to this nation's foundational Protestant ethos was primarily that of an immigrant church, desperately trying to cope with the social dislocations encountered by its breathtakingly diverse range of ethnic constituencies. It differed considerably from the older form of American Catholicism (a legacy of the Catholic planters of Maryland and their descendants' wholehearted support for the aims of the Revolution) so that by the second quarter of the nineteenth century a tiny, but well-established Catholic minority had been anchored firmly to this nation's biblical and Republican traditions.

By the turn of the century, however, this older form of Catholicism was in rapid decline. In attempting to understand the range of Catholic contributions to the American character, we must therefore appreciate not only the early Republican form but also the "devotional Catholicism" typical of the immigrant church. The tension between the two, and the contributions each has made, helps explain the new approach to the American economy in general and, by implication, business ethics in particular, as evidenced by the recent pastoral letter of the National Conference of Catholic Bishops, *Justice for All: Catholic Social Teaching and the U.S. Economy* (1986).

This discussion of American Catholicism is best situated once again vis-à-vis Max Weber's interpretation, *The Protestant Ethic and the Spirit of Capitalism*. Weber's thesis has always posed problems for Catholic apologists and intellectuals, and continues to do so, if Michael Novak's *The Spirit of Democratic Capitalism*[23] is any indication. For the thesis does imply that the ethos typically generated by Catholic faith and practice is developmentally unsound. In order to become a good capitalist, one must cease being a faithful Catholic. Yet this inference is laughably at odds with the evidence of unusual levels of upward social mobility achieved by self-identified American Catholics, as demonstrated by Sociologist Andrew Greeley[24] and confirmed by pollsters George Gallup, Jr. and Jim Castelli.[25] The "spirit" of capitalism, democratic or otherwise, may thus be a vexing theoretical question, but in practice ordinary lay Catholics for the most part have embraced it enthusiastically and have achieved more than their share of economic success at least over the past generation.

In light of evidence of increasing Catholic affluence, arguably, the economic consequences of Protestantism's "intraworldly" asceticism are just as attributable to the emphatically "other-worldly" asceticism of Medieval Catholicism. The noted Benedictine scholar, David Knowles, for example, pointed out how, ironically enough, the Cistercian reform movement of the High Middle Ages triggered an "agrarian revolution of some magnitude," by organizing the labor, notably, of lay brothers, in order to bring previously marginal lands under systematic cultivation.[26] Given a Rule that enforced poverty, chastity, and above all, obedience, it is not surprising that Cistercian austerity succeeded in creating the kind of wealth that may have been the ultimate undoing of the monastic system. Though this Catholic "work ethic" was geared primarily to an agrarian society, governed by relatively closed hierarchies defined by kinship, status, and religious patronage, within communities whose economic aspirations aimed no higher than self-sufficiency, it remained a formative influence on the peasant cultures that spawned the waves of Catholic immigration to nineteenth-century America.

This Catholic "work ethic," no doubt, could not have given birth to the "spirit" of capitalism, for it lacked the one thing necessary, namely a reverential attitude toward the dynamic workings of a free market system. But once that system was in place, as most surely it was by the time of the immigration, the Catholic "work ethic" provided a baseline of values and attitudes that made the immigrants ripe for exploitation as modern industrial laborers: Though uprooted from their peasant origins, they remained for the most part hard working, loyal, and submissive to authority. It is not surprising, then, that American industrialists, fearing the European specter of labor unrest and Communism, were remarkably lavish in their support of the immigrant church. For the church's "shepherds" responded to the massive social dislocation experienced by their teeming "flocks" by organizing various forms of social "charity" and preaching the virtues of temperance, self-sacrifice, and other-worldly endurance. But like the Cistercian reform, the immigrant church's pastoral strategy had generated its own economic ironies: It ensured that in an America believed to be the land of opportunity, the immigrant laborers would not long remain mere laborers.

As foreign as it may have been to the biblical and Republican traditions characteristic of the Protestant mainline, the pastoral strategy referred to here as "devotional Catholicism" provided, in Eugene Kennedy's words, "a tight, intellectually narrow, . . . and largely impermeable membrane" that enabled immigrant Catholics to quietly prosper even as they "resisted social osmosis with the rest of the country."[27] This "devotional Catholicism," which was virtually the only Catholicism available to the vast majority of lay Catholics during the period from the end of World War I until Vatican II, has been characterized in terms of four central traits: "authority, sin, ritual, and the miraculous."[28] Each represents a form of continuity with the religious presuppositions of the Medieval Catholic "work ethic" but with a difference: Each has been subtly transformed by the great dislocation of Christianity generally from the center to the periphery of modern industrial society.

Submission to authority, for example, is clearly traditional; but the tightening of internal controls dramatized by the heightening of Papal supremacy was itself a symptom of the Church's all too typically modern sense of alienation from the larger society. Furthermore, the emphasis on sin, particularly on personal sins of "drunkenness and impurity," appears to be an innovation in Catholic practice directly related to the opportunities or temptations afforded by the new urban, industrial way of life. The pervasiveness of such sin, of course, heightens the need for the church's remedies, namely increased participation in sacramental rituals, especially frequent confession and holy communion. Even Catholic fascination with the miraculous should not be dismissed as merely a residue of agrarian folkways, for it provided a popular and, apparently, effective means of escape from the tyranny of the modern marketplace, on the same level as, say, today's quest for a winning lottery ticket.

In short, the signals of transcendence generated by "devotional Catholicism" consistently offered a salvation defined in private and highly individualistic terms. Like the religious individualism customarily attributed to the dominant forms of Protestantism, "devotional Catholicism" thus helped facilitate the division of public life into various compartmentalized spheres. Hence American Catholics came to share the common misconception that religion and economics or politics are like oil and water: They do not mix and never should they be made to mix. On the other hand, this Catholic form of religious individualism also had a similarly positive impact, however limited, on personal character formation. It, too, was not only compatible with, but actually helped support the "middle-class" Calvinist virtues of sobriety, frugality, industry, and honesty that are just as indispensable to the successful maintenance of a disciplined work force.

In modern industrial America, however, "devotional Catholicism" successfully performed the additional role of preserving the immigrants' distinctive patterns of social identity, even as it was subtly transforming them. As described in Will Herberg's classic study, *Protestant, Catholic, Jew*, the intergenerational conflict within immigrant communities embarked upon the process of more or less rapid Americanization, was certainly eased by "devotional Catholicism."[29] It kept the family, and often the neighborhood, together. Yet this achievement, resting as it did on a tacit acceptance of the modern compartmentalization of public life, ironically may have made it easier for Catholics to embrace the "success ethic" characteristic of morally uninhibited business activity. For once the Catholic "work ethic" had enabled the immigrants or their children to move up from blue-collar to middle-class, managerial status—as many of them did with increasing frequency after the 1920s—there was little for these upwardly mobile Catholics to embrace in their "secular" occupations but the prevailing American norms of success.

V.   AMERICANIST CATHOLICISM

"Devotional Catholicism," as previously asserted, represents only half the story of the Catholic experience in America. In order to understand the current state of Catholic opinion on questions of business ethics and economics, it is necessary to recall in broad outline the fate of the earlier form of Catholic identification with the biblical and Republican tradition: Americanist Catholicism.[30] During the period of industrialization that began after the Civil War, Americanist Catholicism represented an elitist movement of second and third generation Irish–Americans who unsuccessfully tried to bring order to the chaos of immigration by aggressively, and perhaps uncritically, promoting the Americanization of Catholic institutions, including the parochial schools. Inspired by the vision of a Catholic America proclaimed by the convert, Father Isaac Hecker, the founder of the Paulist Fathers, Americanist Catholics, led by James Cardinal Gibbons and Bishops Ireland, Spalding, and Keane, advocated an openness toward mainstream American institutions and cultural values, including democracy and the virtues of self-reliance, that eventually clashed with Papal teaching.

At the climax of some rather complicated ecclesiastical maneuvering, Pope Leo XIII condemned the so-called "Americanist heresy" in the encyclical letter of 1899, *Testem benevolentiae*. The forward movement of Americanist Catholicism was stalled, and its spiritual and intellectual leadership placed under a cloud of suspicion that persisted until after Vatican II. The vacuum thus created was filled, of course, by the triumph of "devotional Catholicism" and the Romanizing bishops who promoted it. Yet before the movement was halted, it had set in motion two processes that are important here: The first is American Catholicism's historic identification with the labor movement; the second, the creation of a superstructure by which the Church could act as a national organization. Although both of these achievements were more or less fortuitous, their impact is decisive for understanding the current posture of American Catholicism.

That the church was already identified with immigrant workers and their families should already be obvious; but how that involvement was transformed into a close association with the aspirations of organized labor bears explaining. For the supporters of organized labor, at that time represented prominently by Terence Powderly's Knights of Labor, had to overcome not only the clergy's fear of Communist anarchy but also the traditional supposition that the moral exhortation and charitable good works were a sufficient response to society's problems. The controversy over the Knights of Labor erupted in 1886 when conservative bishops, claiming that this labor organization was a "secret society" no different from the Masons, requested that the Papal ban against Catholic participation in "secret societies" be applied equally to the Knights as well. Were it not for the impressive intervention of Cardinal Gibbons, it is likely that the Knights of Labor would have been so condemned.[31]

But having personally investigated Terence Powderly's Catholic background and mindful of the fact that perhaps two-thirds of the Knights' membership was Irish–Catholic, Gibbons skillfully blended moral principle with pastoral expediency: He eloquently defended the rights of working people to organize for collective bargaining, but he also reminded the Vatican of the losses the Church would suffer were it to be perceived as indifferent to the interests of the working class in America. A year later, the Vatican agreed to tolerate Catholic participation "on the condition that the Knights revise their constitution in order to omit any references 'which seem to savor of socialism and communism.'"[32] Though hardly a ringing endorsement, the Vatican's decision was perceived as a victory for organized labor and the forging of an enduring bond between labor and the Catholic church in America.

The Americanist Catholic appreciation for the social practices of democracy had a variety of manifestations, but none so evidently useful to the bishops themselves as their custom of meeting nationally at regular intervals for consultation, often with some degree of lay participation. Though the Papal condemnation of Americanism put a damper on such councils and congresses, the Church's need to develop a national response to the general mobilization for World War I occasioned the formation of a national organization, which after the war took on a life of its own as The National Catholic Welfare Conference (NCWC). With the Vatican's reluctant approval, this organization, the forerunner of the National Conference of Catholic Bishops (NCCB) helped coordinate and orchestrate Catholic action for social justice on a national level.

Having achieved the organizational means for addressing public policy questions, the work of the NCWC also provided the basis for a coherent ideological perspective on them. Particularly important was its sponsorship of "The Bishops' Program of Social Reconstruction" (1919) that although eschewing Socialism, advocated a package of such social reforms as "minimum wage legislation, a minimum working age, public housing, laws enforcing labor's right to organize, insurance against old age, sickness, and unemployment, the regulation of public utility rates, control of monopolies, and a partnership between labor and management through cooperative enterprises and worker ownership of the stock of corporations."[33] It is this package of reforms, many of which were enacted into law during the New Deal, that forms the basis for Catholic social teaching's reputation as a positive force for progressive social change. Though authored by the celebrated ("Right Reverend New Dealer") John A. Ryan, the "program," when compared to the writings of earlier Americanist Catholics or to the recent NCCB pastoral letter, is striking for its absence of theological argument. Such play-it-safe pragmatism, at once both socially progressive and religiously conservative, may be indirect testimony to the effectiveness of the Vatican's condemnation of the Americanist heresy.[34]

VI. CONTEMPORARY AMERICAN CATHOLICISM

To turn from these formative moments to the current situation in American Catholicism is to step into a different world. The immigrant church is dead; "devotional Catholicism" is mostly a literary monument, a ghost occasionally conjured by the likes of Mary Gordon for purposes of her own. The Catholic church, for better or for worse, is now regarded as part of the allegedly marginalized "mainline" of American Christianity. The most striking division within contemporary American Catholicism is no longer ethnically based, but ideological: a split between neoconservative and liberal intellectuals that carries into religious and theological questions the same antagonism that these perspectives represent in matters of public policy.[35] In a sense, both camps have inherited the aspirations of Americanist Catholicism, while exhibiting conflicted signs of bereavement over the death of the immigrant church. Perhaps the most significant indication of the demise of that "largely impermeable membrane" is that neither camp can offer much more than a "selective Catholicism," reflecting a range of trends within the larger society.

Justice for All, the recent bishops pastoral letter on the U.S. economy, represents an attempt to move beyond this division. Though the process of formulating and revising the letter did become a major battleground for Catholic liberals and neoconservatives, the drafting committee's bias in favor of consensus ensured that the letter yields both something more and something less than either group advocated. The religious and ethical values espoused in the letter, in this context, may be read as an attempt to synthesize the traditional Catholic "work ethic" with a critical discernment of the institutional resources and limitations of America's ongoing attempt to make modern industrial capitalism more responsive to the needs and aspirations of the nation as a whole. The letter's perspective is deeply informed by American Catholicism's historic commitment to organized labor, but it is not reducible to it. The Church has changed and so has labor; but more important so has the nature of Catholic participation in both movements. Here are some important elements of the new synthesis.

Unlike the tradition of Catholic social teaching from which much of its theology stems, the letter has quietly but emphatically abandoned the legacy of *Tercerismo*, that is, the assumption that the Church possessed an alternative blueprint for a modern industrial society and therefore was radically and evenhandedly critical of both capitalism and Communism. Deliberately, the pastoral letter is not a critique of capitalism in the abstract, but a theological and moral assessment of "the U.S. economy," as it concretely exists, embedded as it is in an historical matrix of cultural values, regulatory agencies, and institutional imperatives. American Catholicism recognizes itself as already having had a significant role in shaping this matrix, even as it adapted itself to it. The letter's basic posture, therefore, is one of ongoing reform, particularly in the direction of further democratization of the economy and, most especially, in opening greater access to full participation by all groups represented within the nation.

The Catholic "work ethic," rooted as it is in the agrarian civilization of Medieval Europe, is given a modern interpretation by identifying the Christian virtue of love with social "solidarity" and justice with "participation." These themes are meant to provide a strong counterweight to the modern strands of individualism that managed to assert themselves in American Catholicism just as tellingly as in the larger society. Indeed, "solidarity" and "participation" form the basis for discovering a new emphasis in the traditional Catholic definition of social justice: "Social justice implies that persons have an obligation to be active and productive participants in the life of society and that society has a duty to enable them to participate in this way."[36] Increasing "productivity," in this perspective, becomes a moral imperative for a renewed Catholic "work ethic."

Furthermore, the pastoral letter takes some significant steps in the direction of reconciling the Catholic "work ethic" with the Protestant ethic described by Max Weber. Though the letter avoids any identification of Providence with the dynamisms of the marketplace, it comes very close to discerning a religious "vocation" in any form of socially productive activity. Following the theological leads given in Pope John Paul II's encyclical, *Laborem Exercens* (1981), the bishops see "industriousness" as "an expression of human dignity and solidarity with others"[37]; they mean to "encourage and support a renewed sense of vocation in the business community" insofar as business serves "the common good."[38] Remarkably absent from the letter is Catholic social teaching's traditional antipathy toward business. The bishops explain their remarks on business' vocation of service by observing that "the way business people serve society is governed and limited by the incentives which flow from tax policies, the availability of credit, and other public policies."[39]

But instead of using this observation as a pretext for trundling out Catholic social teaching's traditional denunciations of "greed," the bishops sympathetically assert businesses' "right to an institutional framework that does not penalize enterprises that act responsibly."[40] Consistent with the overall tenor of the letter, they commend the matrix of regulatory agencies that are the legacy of the Progressive Era, the New Deal and beyond, not for its adversarial posture toward American business but as an indispensable element in its continued growth and proper development. The Catholic "work ethic" clearly is no longer narrowly concerned with protecting immigrant laborers.

Finally, perhaps the most telling evidence of the pastoral letter's new approach is its unstated, yet pervasive tendency to address those who exercise managerial responsibility, whether in business, government, or organized labor, as peers or moral equals. The letter is the result of a long process of dialogue, after which it has become impossible for the Catholic clergy to talk down to laypersons engaged in the range of secular occupations that contribute to the common good. The bishops on the drafting committee came to recognize that the challenge facing managers in our society is not that different from what any bishop must face in managing a diocese, or any pastor a parish.

The best evidence of this shift in basic moral attitude is apparent in a section of the letter's conclusion, outlining the responsibilities of the Church as economic actor.[41] This statement, without significant precedent in the history of Catholic social teaching, admits that "all the moral principles that govern the just operation of any economic endeavor apply to the Church and its agencies and institutions; indeed the Church should be exemplary."[42] Nor is this just a platitude, for they go on to discuss in some detail five areas of managerial responsibility within the church: wages and salaries, employee rights, investments and property management, works of charity, and their relationship to social action for justice.[43] Catholicism's impact on the attitudes and practices of American businesspeople would be all the more impressive, we believe, were pastors and bishops to open up genuine dialogue at the local level on each of these areas of shared concern.

In order to grasp the significance of the moral posture reflected in *Justice for All*, one should recall Theodore Maynard's remarks on the economic and social question in his minor classic, *The Story of American Catholicism*.[44] In two chapters, "'The Public Be Damned'" and "The Lost Land," he takes up the issues discussed here; but his characterization of those issues is vastly different from that of the pastoral letter. Maynard is well aware of the significance of the industrialization of the American economy after the Civil War, but his basic moral attitude is reflected in his choice of Commodore Vanderbilt's maxim for the "robber barons" that introduces his chapter. He finds it impossible to attribute anything good to those architects of the era of Big Business—the Rockefellers, the Carnegies, and the Morgans. Theirs was a "plutocracy" that systematically exploited the immigrant working class and cynically supported the Catholic church in order to keep them pacified. Though the reforms of the Progressive Era and beyond are welcomed for the temporary relief they may afford, Maynard's attitude remains unflinchingly radical, if not reactionary: "The truth is that a healthy Catholic life is hardly possible under capitalism."[45] The clearest evidence for this contention is capitalism's necessary connection with birth control, that is, that the harsh realities of urban life under industrial capitalism make large families unconscionable.[46] Rather than reform capitalism, Maynard's real hope is to lead some sort of exodus from the cities to rural America. His chapter, "The Lost Land," makes much of Catholic efforts to settle the immigrants in farming communities, at considerable distances from the metropolises where they actually came to live. The fate of American Catholicism, in short, depended on the success of the Rural Life movement.

Maynard's attitude is admirable for its consistency. If the modern industrial economy were nothing more than the latest and most pernicious offspring of a callous Protestant ethic, then, given a pre-Vatican II contempt for Protestantism like Maynard's, the appropriate Catholic response would be to withdraw from such a society rather than collaborate with Protestants and others in reforming it. Ironically, the elements that make up the Catholic adaptations of the American ethos have not been strong enough to permit more than a few extraordinary individuals from following Maynard's path. The compartmentalization of life tacitly supported by "devotional Catholicism" enervates the will to resist either the temptations or the opportunities of modern industrial capitalism, whereas the openness to mainstream values and practices advocated by Americanist Catholicism undermines whatever inclination Catholic social teaching may harbor toward a systematic and principled rejection of the system as a whole. These weaknesses, however, may also be a source of strength: For each in its own way has facilitated the emergence of a more or less coherent reformism, the promise of which is given in *Justice for All*. If that promise is fulfilled, American Catholicism's contribution could turn out to be a style of public moral engagement that can remain authentically Christian without becoming self-defeatingly adversarial.

VII. CONCLUSION

The conclusions that interest us here have less to do with the specific historical judgments and interpretations offered than they do with the larger implications of this entire history for the understanding of American business and for the discipline of business ethics. Our first conclusion—or was it our starting assumption?—is that one cannot ignore the religious dynamics and theological beliefs that have helped make America and Americans who and what they are and expect to understand American business and the attitudes of Americans toward it.

A second conclusion, made necessary in part by the career of the Protestant work ethic and its various offspring/competitors, is that in looking at the historical religious influences that have shaped us, we need to be careful not to take possibly superficial similarities as establishing fundamental agreement between different strains of thought. For example, we would here endorse and support major elements of the Protestant work ethic and its Catholic variant as both theologically sound and morally and humanly appropriate, but we would have much greater hesitation about endorsing the seemingly similar success ethic.

A third conclusion is that although there have been significant differences between Protestant and Catholic experience of—and attitudes toward—business and economics, currently the most interesting sets of distinctions cut across rather than between these two Christian bodies. Both have within them a devotional/pietistic side that tends to support religious individualism, and a socially oriented, activist side that challenges such individualism. Both experience tensions between neoconservatism and fundamentalism on the one side, and more liberal segments on the other; both try to remain true to social justice concerns while working realistically and sympathetically within America's existing mixed capitalist economy. Virtually any currently significant distinction made between Protestant and Catholic in the area of business and economics can at the same time be found within either of the two. Although some might mourn this loss of distinctiveness to the American melting pot, others will rejoice in the greater ease with which dialogue and common enterprises can now be undertaken.

NOTES

1. Alexis de Tocqueville, *Democracy in America* (New York: Alfred Knopf, 1966).
2. Robert N. Bellah, Richard Madsen, William M. Sullivan, Ann Swidler, and Steven M. Tipton, *Habits of the Heart: Individualism and Commitment in American Life* (Berkeley: University of California Press, 1985).
3. Max Weber, *The Protestant Ethic and the Spirit of Capitalism* (New York: Charles Scribner's Sons, 1958).
4. Robert Jackall, *Moral Mazes: The World of Corporate Managers* (New York: Oxford University Press, 1988), p. 7.
5. *Ibid.*, p. 201ff.; see also cf. Dillenberger and Welch, *Protestant Christianity*, p. 213.
6. For the other side of Calvin and Calvinism that continued to see the individual essentially and integrally linked to the larger community and sometimes, especially to the believing community, to the Church, see Andre Bleier, *The Social Humanism of Calvin* (Richmond: John Knox Press, 1964).
7. A. Whitney Griswold, "The American Cult of Success" (Yale University dissertation), 1934, published in part in the *American Journal of Sociology* (1934) and the *New England Quarterly*, cited in John G. Cawelti, *Apostles of the Self-Made Man* (Chicago: University of Chicago Press, 1965), pp. 32–59.
8. Cawelti, *Apostles*, p. 5.
9. Ibid. See also Jackall, *Moral Mazes*, on this contrast.
10. Ibid., p. 184; On seventeenth-century Puritanism, see Richard Baxter's much earlier statement: "If God shows you a way in which you may lawfully get more than in another way (without wrong to your soul, or to any other), if you refuse this and choose the less

gainful way, you cross one of the ends of your Calling, and you refuse to be God's steward" (as cited in Harkness, *Calvin*, pp. 184–185).

11. *Encyclopedia Americana*, Vol. 7. (Danbury, CT: Grolier, Inc., 1987, p. 713); see J. Wesley's "earn all you can, save all you can, give all you can"—John Wesley, "The Use of Money" in Waldo Beach and H. Richard Niebuhn, *Christian Ethics: Sources of the Living Tradition* (New York: The Ronald Press Company, 1955), pp. 372–379.

12. Cawelti, *Apostles*, pp. 169, 195.

13. Ibid., p. 197.

14. Dillenberger and Welch, *Protestant Christianity*, p. 215.

15. Ibid., pp. 221–222.

16. *A Theology for the Social Gospel* (New York: 1917), p. 5ff., as cited in Dillenberger and Welch, *Protestant Christianity*, p. 225.

17. Dillenberger and Welch, *Protestant Christianity*, p. 222.

18. Ibid., p. 227.

19. Ibid., p. 224.

20. *The Amsterdam Assembly Series*, "Man's Disorder and God's Design," 4 vols., Section III, "The Church and the Disorder of Society," as cited in Dillenberger and Welch, *Protestant Christianity*, p. 229.

21. John C. Bennett, "Protestantism and Corporations," in Oliver F. Williams and John W. Houck, eds., *The Common Good and U.S. Capitalism* (New York: University Press of America, 1988), pp. 83–106.

22. Paul F. Camenisch, "Recent Mainline Protestant Statements on Economic Justice." *The Annual, Society of Christian Ethics, 1987*, edited by D. M. Yeager (Washington DC: Georgetown University Press, 1987), pp. 55–77.

23. Michael Novak, *The Spirit of Democratic Capitalism* (New York: Simon and Schuster, 1982).

24. Andrew M. Greeley, *The American Catholic: A Social Portrait* (New York: Basic Books, 1977), pp. 50–68.

25. George Gallup, Jr., and Jim Castelli, *The American Catholic People: Their Beliefs, Practices, and Values* (Garden City, NY: Doubleday, 1987), pp. 3–6.

26. David Knowles, *Christian Monasticism* (New York: McGraw-Hill/World Universal Library, 1969), p. 74.

27. Eugene Kennedy, *The Now and Future Church: The Psychology of Being an American Catholic* (Garden City, NY: Doubleday, 1984), p. 4.

28. Jay P. Dolan, *The American Catholic Experience: A History from Colonial Times to the Present* (Garden City, NY: Doubleday, 1985), p. 221.

29. Will Herberg, *Protestant, Catholic, Jew* (Garden City, NY: Doubleday, 1960).

30. Dennis P. McCann, *New Experiment in Democracy: The Challenge for American Catholicism* (Kansas City: Sheed and Ward, 1987).

31. Dolan, pp. 330–333.

32. Ibid.

33. Dolan, p. 344.

34. McCann, pp. 21–22.

35. McCann, pp. 64–90.

36. National Conference of Catholic Bishops, *Justice for All: Pastoral Letter on Catholic Social Teaching and the U.S. Economy* (Washington, DC: United States Catholic Conference, 1986), p. 36.

37. National Conference of Catholic Bishops, p. 52.

38. National Conference of Catholic Bishops, p. 59.

39. Ibid.

40. Ibid.

41. National Conference of Catholic Bishops, pp. 174–179.
42. National Conference of Catholic Bishops, p. 174.
43. National Conference of Catholic Bishops, pp. 175–178.
44. Theodore Maynard, *The Story of American Catholicism*, (Garden City, NY: Doubleday, 1941).
45. Ibid, Volume 2, p. 72.
46. Ibid., p. 73.

REFERENCES

Bellah, Robert N., *et al.*, *Habits of the Heart: Individualism and Commitment in American Life*. Berkeley: University of California Press, 1985.

Bieler, Andre, *The Social Humanism of Calvin*. Translated by Paul T. Fuhrmann. Richmond, VA: John Knox Press, 1964.

Camenisch, Paul F., "Recent Mainline Protestant Statements on Economic Justice." *The Annual, Society of Christian Ethics, 1987*. Edited by D. M. Yeager. Washington, DC: Georgetown University Press, 1987: 55–77.

Carey, Patrick W., ed., *American Catholic Religious Thought: The Shaping of a Theological and Social Tradition*. New York: The Paulist Press, 1987

Cawelti, John G., *Apostles of the Self-Made Man*. Chicago: University of Chicago Press, 1965.

de Tocqueville, Alexis, *Democracy in America*. 2 vols. New York: Vintage Books, 1945.

Dillenberger, John, and Claude Welch, *Protestant Christianity: Interpreted through Its Development* (2nd ed.). New York: Macmillan, 1988.

Dolan, Jay P., *The American Catholic Experience: A History from Colonial Times to the Present*. Garden City, NY: Doubleday, 1985.

Gallup, George, Jr., and Castelli, Jim, *The American Catholic People: Their Beliefs, Practices, and Values*. Garden City, NY: Doubleday, 1987.

Greeley, Andrew M., *The American Catholic: A Social Portrait*. New York: Basic Books, 1977.

Jackall, Robert, *Moral Mazes: The World of Corporate Managers*. New York: Oxford University Press, 1988.

Kennedy, Eugene, *The Now and Future Church: The Psychology of Being an American Catholic*. Garden City, NY: Doubleday, 1984.

Knowles, David, *Christian Monasticism*. New York: McGraw-Hill/World Universal Library, 1969.

Maynard, Theodore, *The Story of American Catholicism*. 2 vols. Garden City, New York: Doubleday Image Books, 1960.

McCann, Dennis P., *New Experiment in Democracy: The Challenge for American Catholicism*. Kansas City: Sheed and Ward, 1987.

Novak, Michael, *The Spirit of Democratic Capitalism*. New York: Simon and Schuster, 1982.

Stackhouse, Max, *Public Theology and Political Economy: Christian Stewardship in Modern Society*. Grand Rapids: Wm. B. Eerdmans, 1987.

Weber, Max, *The Protestant Ethic and the Spirit of Capitalism*. New York: Charles Scribner's Sons, 1958.

Williams, Oliver F., and Houck, John W., eds., *The Common Good and U.S. Capitalism*. New York: University Press of America, 1987.

Wogaman, J. Philip, *Economics and Ethics: A Christian Inquiry*. Philadelphia: Fortress Press, 1986.

III

PERSPECTIVES FROM LAW, SOCIOLOGY, AND INDUSTRIAL RELATIONS

The water between religious and secular analyses can be transited rather handily by riding the boat of theory built by Max Weber, a man thoroughly at home in both ports. He called his craft the "Protestant Ethic."[1] In using the term, Weber did not simply mean that the United States was a Protestant society but rather that its religious ethic could be applied to any nation that determined to master the world through disciplined work and moral consensus. This, plus the church–state separation doctrine, gave to the United States a "signature" quite different from those found in other Protestant countries like England, Prussia, and Holland. The difference led some observers to speak of this country as the "first new nation" peopled by a hardy race who took the Puritan notion of personal *calling and extended it to a* collective *calling.[2] And the calling was expressed sequentially in such slogans as winning over the wilderness, winning the west, winning over the developing nations, winning the race to outer space.[3]*

Winning meant willingness to risk themselves and their resources against competitors, both physical and human. Because trees could not cry out when forests were ravaged, it was obvious that only humans hurt by ruthless winners would protest. And protest they did in the late nineteenth century when business competition turned ugly and managers turned arrogant. Because both protests are still heard, it is important to see how they might be better handled today. To these twin protests have been added a new challenge posed by a series of fundamental shocks to the traditional culture. All these issues will be explored in the following chapters, each of which merits a specific comment.

I.   THE LAW AND COMPETITION

In the secular temple of business, competition has been the high altar before which all eyes reverently bowed. That, at least, was the theory. In practice the entrepreneur was invariably driven by the prospect of great winnings to create monopolies. The robber barons tried to do it in the late nineteenth century—and failed; the corporate raiders are moving toward similar goals in the late twentieth century and probably will fail unless competition is made both real and ethical in the mixed economy, *a term popularized nearly 30 years ago by Columbia Economist J. M. Clark.*[4]

In the following part, Lynn Sharp Paine undertakes a difficult, yet necessary, task to assess market practices in the United States from legal perspectives and then to consider both practice and law from the vantage point of moral principles. Animating her work is the idea that competition may be seen as a positive good: Spelling bees in the elementary grades, football games at high school and college levels, and teacher awards for excellence bring out the best in children and adults. The same practices in market activities bring out the best in producers and distributors.

Unlike aggression that sees the rival as an enemy to be subdued, competition emphasizes achievement of goals open to all. Today's loser may be tomorrow's winner. To prevent competition from running amuck, Lynn Sharp Paine applies five moral principles that are explained and applied to court decisions. The five, used to encourage a form of positive *competition, are:*

1.   The principle of independent initiative
2.   The principle of constructive effort
3.   The principle of respect for the rules
4.   The principle of the level playing field
5.   The principle of respect for officiating parties

II.   SOCIOLOGY AND THE NEW INTEREST GROUPS

This philosophy of winning assumed that everyone would play the game. But suppose, asks Ivar Berg, that the new wave of immigrants wants to sit it out—or watch the game as disinterested and uninterested spectators. Suppose further that when these new Americans decide to try to win something, it is at games whose rules and goals are framed by a culture quite different from what may be called the "typically Yankee" one. Amerasians want their own games, not the traditional ones. Much the same can be said of the Native American population. Young blacks are simply dropping out. And women who do participate in business life want the rules changed.

In terms of its conclusion, Berg's analysis recalls those made by two early French visitors to these shores: Hector Crevecoeur (1735–1813) and Alexis de Tocqueville (1805–1859). The first wrote a minor classic that he called What is an American? The answer to his own question was ambiguous. Tocqueville wrote a major classic that he entitled Democracy in America. Tocqueville was very clear: Americans are a new breed of liberty-loving, equality-claiming individuals, people to be admired and watched. Both Frenchmen eventually got down essentially to this: Does America represent a revolutionary force of monumental proportions? Both answered in the affirmative. Berg smells another social revolution in the making; one totally different from the country's previous revolutions because it is being caused by people who either do not want to play the game or who want the rules changed.

Himself a distinguished sociologist, Berg is keenly aware of the difference between the lay sociology learned informally by adults who participate in American life and the professional sociology expounded by the scholars. The latter is marked often by excessive statistical analysis and a form of model building that has come to rival the economist's use of the technique.[5] He is also, of course, wise enough to recognize that the profession has much to offer when it concentrates on the interconnections currently appearing in American life among interest groups. Because it is likely that domestic tensions will be greatly impacted by the developments in the global economy, Berg's insights become even more important to business philosophers who grapple with the values of a changing culture.[6] His view, incidentally, differs sharply from one held by many economists and financiers who feel that political and cultural distinctions matter little in what is now a multinational corporate economy. One unidentified government economist was quoted as saying that the country's trade deficits with Japan and Hong Kong have about the same weight as deficits Kansas might run with Montana: "It doesn't matter if Hong Kong fixes its currency to the dollar; they're just operating like a part of the Federal Reserve System."[7] Berg's analysis shows rather convincingly that culture does matter and will matter even more when the country enters the year 2000.

III.   INDUSTRIAL RELATIONS

Cynics have said of historians that they are excellent at predicting the past. In his essay on labor management relations, James Kuhn uses history in highly constructive ways to illustrate his thesis that the traditional adversarial relationships between management and labor will serve neither them nor the public well in the coming years. To the sources Kuhn used to indict management for its excessive antipathy toward labor unions might be added the comment made in 1903 by David Parry, then head of the National Association of Manufacturers: "Labor leaders know *but one law and that . . . is the law of the Huns and the Vandals, the law of the savage. . . . It is . . . mob power knowing no master except its own will."[8] The harsh assessment was used to justify the imposition of harsh conditions, conditions revealed only in momentary flashes of respite that were caught in Thomas Anshutz's painting for the Philadelphia Centenniel Exposition of 1876. In this painting that he titled "The Ironworkers' Noontime," the artist positions a group of workers enjoying a moment of relaxation against a background of dreary factory walls and belching smoke—the hell to which they would return in a few more minutes.[9]*

At the other end of the spectrum were the leaders of labor. In 1876, a fourth-of-July picknicking labor group of some 5,000 people in the tiny coal-mining town of Priceburg, Pennsylvania, heard Terence Powderly, head of the Knights of Labor, warn that the Declaration of Independence must never be forgotten. Powderly, alternating between anguish and anger, told his rapt listeners:

> Written over a hundred years ago, on reading it now, in these closing days of the 19th century . . . how it comes about that the indictment drawn up against the English king applies with such startling force to the agencies we now find usurping the divine right of kings.[10]

When Kuhn criticizes employers for arrogating to themselves "managerial preroga-tives," he is echoing a message that union leaders have tried to convey to workers and to the American people for over a century; it incidentally might be asked why workers in the final large-scale success story in labor history should have called themselves "knights" and why their leader should have orated in Priceburg in ways reminiscent of the English barons at Runnymede in 1215. There is one clear answer: As the barons wrested from the King their Magna Carta, workers were demanding from the corporate archons their own charter of rights.

There may have been more, however, to this management–labor story than the "petty Parry" ideological outburst previously quoted. Several investigators have said that regression analysis of the linkage between labor organizations and produc-tivity showed that the "employers were essentially correct in their assessment of the barriers to profitability posed by organized labor during the pre-New Deal years."[11]

Nevertheless, because profits were running at a rather handsome level during the major industrialization period (1872–1925), it may be the fear of worker power even more than fear of financial losses that animated management during this period. This is, at least, strongly suggested by Kuhn.

The next question in management–labor relations prior to the New Deal becomes one of strategies. What did management do to frustrate the drive toward strong labor organization? With considerable foresight, management recognized that the institutional powers of the labor movement would allow greater worker militancy and thereby give workers greater opportunities to use the strike weapon successfully. And success in a unionized industry would have ripple effects that would work to the advantage of nonunionized workers in an otherwise unionized industry.[12] *To ward off the growth of labor organizations managers utilized this multipronged strategy:*

- *Support generous immigration policies to increase the labor pool. By so doing they hoped the law of supply and demand would work to their advantage. The strategy was easy to implement because agricultural societies of Europe were happy to export their surplus people to the labor-hungry shores of America.*[13] *(Note: The post-Civil War experiences turned out to be a very different from the early period when textile owners in New England mill towns welcomed poor Irish immigrants to Massachusetts. At that time, the Irish, participating quite substantially in the town's prosperity, moved into a middle-class status; however, the future pattern became clear: When economic prosperity began to decline in 1837, the mill owners began to exploit the newcomers.*[14])
- *Factory owners rapidly introduced machines to increase production and to free themselves from dependence on costly high-skilled workers. Semi-skilled machine operators could be brought in to replace skilled labor.*
- *Employers developed a salaried supervisory core at the midmanagement levels that would, it was thought, identify with the owners.*
- *Owners developed a specialized work force and rewarded it by incentives. Here again the managers' logic was straightforward: Using the carrot, their stick remained covered.*
- *Management helped to form company unions where the workers' representatives were clearly dependent on the goodwill of the owners.*
- *Certain "welfare benefits" (retirement pensions, stock options, housing subsidies, educational benefits, health services, and the like) were adopted to capture and hold worker loyalty to the firm.*

So far as the last item is concerned, Kuhn sees corporate social responsibilities with some misgiving; he, therefore, seeks a more imaginative form of conflict resolution by management and labor—and in this he is correct. Results from experimental studies suggest that a general policy of reciprocity—combined with the use of unilateral cooperative initiatives—tends to break deadlocks and is generally effective in getting an adversary to cooperate. In the past, management and unions have played a tit-for-tat strategy designed to slow down an overly aggressive adversary. Both parties are being nudged by Kuhn toward acceptance of a GRIT strategy (Graduated Reciprocation in Tension Relations) as the wiser way to halt aggressive actions by either management or labor.[15] Perhaps true grit is the answer!

To sum up: In each of the essays are observations of importance to business ethics—the ethical restraints a competitive economic needs, the value structures of the new Americans, as well as the competing value structures of the young and the old, and the right to decent wages and decent working conditions.

NOTES

1. Max Weber, *The Protestant Ethic and the Spirit of Capitalism* (New York: Scribner's, 1958). Tr. by Talcott Parsons.
2. Seymour Martin Lipset, *The First New Nation* (New York: Basic Books, 1963).
3. Roderick Nash, *Wilderness and the American Mind* (New Haven: Yale University Press, 1973).
4. J. M. Clark, *Competition as a Dynamic Process*, Washington: 1961. See also his article, "Toward a Concept of Workable Competition," *The American Economic Review*, Vol. 30 (1940), pp. 241–256.
5. Herbert J. Gans, "Sociology in America: The Discipline and the Public," *American Sociological Review*, Vol. 54 (February 1989), pp. 1–16.
6. Edward Tiryakian, "Sociology's Great Leap Forward: The Challenge of Internationalization," *International Sociology*, Vol. 1 (June 1986), pp. 155–171.
7. *Wall Street Journal*, April 3, 1989, p. 1.
8. Reinhard Bendix, *Work and Authority in Industry: Ideologies of Management in the Course of Industrialization* (Berkeley: University of California Press 1956), p. 266.
9. Thomas H. Pauly, "American Art and Labor: The Case of Anshutz's 'The Ironworkers' Noontime,'" *The American Quarterly*, Vol. 40 (September 1988), pp. 333–358.
10. Quoted from Leon Fink, "The New Labor History and the Powers of Historical Pessimism: Consensus, Dissensus, and the Case of the Knights of Labor," *Journal of American History*, Vol. 75 (June 1988), p. 115.
11. Larry J. Griffin, Michael E. Wallis, and Beth A. Rubin, "Capitalist Resistance to the Organization of Labor Before the New Deal: Why? How? Success?" *The American Sociological Review*, Vol. 51 (April 1986), pp. 151–167.
12. Beth Rubin, "Class Struggle American Style: Unions, Strikes and Wages," *American Sociological Review*, Vol. 51 (October 1986), pp. 618–631.
13. David Montgomery, *The Fall of the House of Labor: The Workplace, the State and American Labor Activism* (Cambridge: Harvard University Press, 1987).
14. Brian Mitchell, *The Paddy Camps: The Irish of Lowell, 1821–1861* (Urbana: University of Illinois Press, 1988).
15. Martin Patchen, "Strategies for Eliciting Cooperation From an Adversary," *Conflict Resolution*, Vol. 31 (March 1987), pp. 164–185.

4

Ideals of Competition and Today's Marketplace

Lynn Sharp Paine

In the race for wealth, honors, and preferments, [a man] may run as hard as he can, and strain every nerve and every muscle, in order to outstrip all his competitors. But if he should jostle, or throw down any of them, the indulgence of the spectators is entirely at an end. It is a violation of fair play, which they cannot admit of.[1]

The ethics of competition is a much neglected topic. In a highly aggressive marketplace, temptations to exceed the bounds of fair competition are great. Indeed, there is a temptation to relax, or even abandon, the very notions of fair play and ethical limits on competition and to adopt the position that "anything goes" in the struggle for competitive advantage. The object of this chapter is to describe an ideal of competition that I believe is reflected in traditional law governing business competition and in our common consciousness about fair competition in many competitive enterprises. Thoughts about the principles constituting this ideal are based on my own reflections on competitive activities and on my readings in the law of unfair competition.[2]

There are indications that this ideal, "positive competition," is under

---

Lynn Sharp Paine • Harvard Business School, Boston, Massachusetts 02173.

considerable pressure in today's business world. Discrepancies between the ideal, on one hand, and practices and attitudes found in the marketplace, on the other, are particularly noticeable in the area of competitor intelligence gathering. These discrepancies invite reassessments of the ideal and reaffirmations or revisions of the principles that guide relations among business rivals as competition becomes more vigorous and as the competing players become more culturally diverse. The competitive ideal here postulated can only be described in an impressionistic way and is related only loosely to specific judgments about acts and practices. That is to say, specific judgments are not logically entailed by the ideal. Nevertheless, the ideal is discernible in certain judgments of fairness and recognizable to anyone who has engaged in a competitive activity.

I. AN IDEAL OF BUSINESS COMPETITION

Much of business law and ethics focuses on the relationships between businesses and their various "constituencies": customers, employees, stockholders, suppliers, and the public. Many of the legal and ethical norms governing these relationships are designed to prevent businesses from inflicting certain types of harm on these groups through its profit-making activities. Although competitors are often overlooked in the enumeration of constituencies, the relationship between competing entities— the relative rights and duties as between competing individuals or competing firms—is an interesting and somewhat complex one because competitors are actually permitted to harm one another.[3] Insofar as the superiority of one firm's products, services, operations, conditions of employment, and so on permit it to succeed at the expense of another, it is allowed to do so. One firm cannot receive compensation for the business it loses because a competitor's product is superior to its own.

This privilege to harm the competition is an acknowledged part of all competitive activities. In games played for amusement and in many sports, the harm is trivial, short-lived, and consists mainly in disappointment. In business, however, the stakes are much higher, and even the very livelihood of many people may be at stake. This privilege to harm the competition in business is granted, not because business is a particularly entertaining game, but because of the larger social purposes served by economic competition. This is believed to be the best way to provide the goods and services desired by consumers at a price ensuring an efficient allocation of the society's resources. Thus we have competition among firms for market share, for knowledgeable and hard-working employees, as well as for capital. We have competition among individuals for jobs, recognition, and rewards. In fact, we have a body of law—antitrust law—designed to ensure that this particular sort of competitive harm actually occurs.

Of course, this competitive model is an abstraction from a reality that has many elements of cooperation. And the privilege to harm one's competitors is far from absolute. There are many forms of unfair competition: acts and practices that may allow one to succeed at the expense of another but that are forbidden or against which the competitor may take legal action. Although national policy is to promote competition, we want that competition to be bounded or limited in certain ways. As one judge remarked, "Our devotion to free-wheeling industrial competition must not force us into accepting the law of the jungle as the standard of morality expected in our commercial relations."[4]

Moreover, although the competitive model is highly suggestive, it is profoundly incomplete. One may conceive of business competition along the lines of the competition that occurs among warring nations, film directors, poker players, figure skaters, football teams, or artists. There are important differences among these types of competitive activities. Some are zero-sum competitions: One player's gain is another player's loss. Others permit win–win outcomes. Some are defined very strictly by rules; others leave a great deal of room for individual differences and creativity. Some are most successfully engaged in by paying close attention to a rival's actions and strategy; others, by paying very little attention to one's rivals. The object of some competitive activities is to create a superior performance or work of art. In some cases, success or failure is completely determined by rules; in others, the rules define the competitive process, but judges make qualitative assessments that determine who wins. Some activities— writing novels, for example—are not typically thought of as competitive by those who engage in them but may be regarded as such by critics, readers, and publishers. How we envision business competition in these various respects is closely related to how we approach business and what we regard as fair and unfair competition.[5]

Business more closely resembles the highly creative activities in which the rules of competition impose certain requirements and prohibitions, and even define certain procedures, but which basically depend on the creativity of the participants to define their character.[6] The rules perform a limit-setting function; they do not define success in the sense that the rules of tennis define success: Two sets out of three win a match. Business, like competitive figure skating, has judges who decide not merely whether the rules have been followed but who make more highly discretionary judgments of quality. Consumers perform this function in business competition, whereas the government, through the legal system, acts as rule maker and referee.

II. COMPETITIVE IDEALS AND THE LAW
OF UNFAIR COMPETITION

The government makes authoritative pronouncements about the limits within which business competition is to be pursued and devises procedures for their enforcement. Some of these limits govern how customers are to be treated; some govern the exploitation of national resources; others affect the firm's methods of raising capital. It is useful at this point to focus on a particular subset of these limits: those governing the ways competing businesses may treat one another and whose violation gives rise to claims by competitors who are harmed.

There are many legal rules and doctrines that affect the relationships among competitors without being about those relationships. For example, environmental or discrimination laws may affect the relative advantage one firm has over another because of its size, location, or work force. There is a particular area of law, however, explicitly governing the rights and duties as between and among competitors.[7] Sometimes called the law of unfair competition, it is actually a collection of doctrines from a variety of areas. The law of unfair competition covers the familiar terrain of antitrust law, as well as certain other legislated and common law doctrines that set boundaries on how competitors may deal with and treat one another. Although the law of unfair competition does not reveal every aspect of the competitive ideal I wish to sketch, it contains traces of the ideal's key principles.

Judicial attempts to offer a general specification or definition of "unfair competition" have not been particularly helpful. Most of the commonly cited standards or definitions of unfairness are little more than restatements of judicial intuitions. One illustration is the Massachusetts Appeals Court that concluded that "the objectionable conduct must attain a level of rascality that would raise an eyebrow of someone inured to the rough and tumble of the world of commerce."[8] Mr. Justice Pitney suggested that unfair acts are those that are "contrary to good conscience."[9]

Enumerating a list of specific unfair business practices is equally difficult given the scope of human ingenuity and rapidly changing technology.[10] One can, however, begin to isolate some of the guiding principles of competitive fairness that have driven the development of the law of unfair competition and piece together a distinctive ideal of fair competition that informs many of these decisions. This ideal of fair competition comprises several general principles or maxims that I will elaborate briefly. It must be stressed that these maxims are highly general: They should not be understood as rules laying down specific forms of unfair conduct. As one late nineteenth-century legal scholar noted, maxims are "merely guideposts pointing to the right road, but not the road itself."[11] Taken together, they define an ideal of the highest and best form of competition and the spirit in which it should be undertaken.

Although the ideal is reflected in the law, it is not particular to the law of business competition. The ideal provides a generalized picture that both guides and explains our more specific judgments about what is fair and unfair in many competitive activities. Because it reflects this underlying ideal, the law of unfair competition provides a convenient starting point for sketching out the principal elements of the ideal.

Much of the law of unfair competition reflects the ideal I will describe, but not all departures from it are legally actionable. By its very nature, many aspects of an ideal are outside the law. An ideal comprises a set of attitudes and aspirations as well as characteristic judgments about people and practices; an ideal is reflected in the sorts of persons it holds up for admiration or blame as well as in the actions it forbids. The law does not often require the satisfaction of our highest and best ideals, especially when they require a particular attitude or state of mind. It is notoriously difficult to ascertain in after-the-fact legal proceedings the finer points about the attitudes or motivations behind people's conduct. In most cases, the multiplicity of motives makes it even more difficult to single out one particular motive for condemnation or approval. Nevertheless, the law does, in some cases, base its judgments on the absence or presence of a certain motive or purpose.[12] The law of unfair competition reflects this judicial ambivalence about policing purposes and motives. More characteristically, the law forbids or penalizes certain acts.

Many departures from this ideal of competitive fairness are not even blameworthy—let alone legally actionable. Just as we do not blame people for failing to be saints, we do not blame participants in a competition for failing to be the best competitors they might be. An ideal, in part, consists of aspirations to be striven for. There may be certain minimum requirements whose fulfillment is necessary for the satisfaction of an ideal, and we may blame those who fail at that level. But meeting the basic requirements is rarely sufficient for fully attaining the ideal. As the difficulty of satisfying the requirements of full attainment increase, our tendency to blame or criticize those who fail diminishes.

III. PRINCIPLES OF POSITIVE COMPETITION

The ideal of competition sketched here comprises the following five principles:

1. The principle of independent initiative
2. The principle of constructive effort
3. The principle of respect for the rules
4. The principle of the level playing field
5. The principle of respect for officiating parties

Reasons for calling this an ideal of "positive" competition will emerge in the discussion that follows. There are several senses in which the word *positive* applies to the ideal. My focus here is on the first three principles because they are of greater relevance for assessing the marketplace practices I wish to discuss.

A. The Principle of Independent Initiative

The principle of independent initiative requires competing units to work individually in producing the artifacts or performances upon which they are to be judged and prevents them from exploiting or appropriating certain efforts of fellow competitors. The principle envisions competitors as distinct units—individuals, teams, firms—working separately in their endeavors to outperform one another. In cases involving units that are collectives, the principle envisions relatively stable attachments to the unit by its members. All competitors are free to exploit society's common knowledge and property within the limits laid down by the rules, but they are not free to take from one another certain types of internally generated knowledge and information. The particular nature of the competitive activity determines which sorts of appropriations are forbidden or inappropriate. The principle puts a premium on qualities such as originality, self-reliance, and effort, as well as on respect for the independence and privacy of competitors. It also has roots in notions of equal opportunity because it prevents competitors from utilizing at reduced cost certain advantages that their rivals may have earned at considerable expense.

The most commendable realizations of the principle of independent initiative occur when a competitor independently originates a new product, a new technique, or a new approach by applying individual skills and abilities to the common knowledge available to all competitors. The tap dancer who changes the idiom of tap by introducing the idea of dancing on musical instruments reflects this ideal to a greater extent than the dancer who perfects a step introduced by a competitor.[13] The dancer whose routine is a composite of steps borrowed from competitors is perhaps closer to the ideal than the dancer who copies someone else's entire dance. At a minimum, this ideal requires that one not present someone else's work or creation as one's own.[14]

At a practical level, the principle translates into defining one's projects and aspirations, as well as failures, more in terms of one's own abilities and interests than in terms of what the competition is doing. The principle favors purposes defined positively over those defined negatively in relation to the voids created by the purposes of others. It requires eschewing the reactive mode of thought and action for an active one. It translates into recognizing that much of what one's competitors know and do is literally "none of one's business." The principle of independent initiative is closely related to the idea of integrity in the sense that one's endeavors are linked at the core by a unity of purpose. At some point, focusing too much on the competition is unseemly and betrays a lack of originality and individual resourcefulness. At the extreme, when one competitor appropriates valuable confidential information from another, it becomes theft.

The law of unfair business competition recognizes the principle of independent initiative. A significant part of that law consists in enforcing certain prohibited appropriations and interferences with information, ideas, and people employed by a competitor. Some limits on competitor activities flow directly from property concepts: Conversion and theft of a competitor's property are forbidden. Others are closely related to contractual notions: Certain interferences with a competitor's contractual relations, for example, are actionable. These limitations may be seen from the perspective of their effects on competition or their origins in property and contract ideas. In either case, they support a competitive system characterized by independent initiative and noninterference among competitors. The legal system does not envision firms as free to upset beneficial relations between competitors and their employees or suppliers.

The principle of independent initiative is also reflected in the doctrine against "passing off." Indeed, at one time the entire law of unfair competition was thought, in some jurisdictions, to be encompassed in the doctrine against passing off.[15] Based on the principle that "no man has a right to sell his own goods as the goods of another,"[16] the doctrine also protects against certain product and package imitations by competitors. Like the law of trademarks and trade names, the doctrine prevents a firm from trading on the effort and good name of its rival and also protects against consumer confusion.

Protection and promotion of independent initiative is an explicit purpose of patent and copyright law, violations of which are a form of unfair competition. Both seek to allocate rights in certain types of intellectual goods in a way that recognizes and rewards innovation and effort. Without such a protective scheme, these goods would be easily appropriated and exploited by others. Trade secret law, often an issue in intelligence-gathering cases, has a hybrid purpose that may account for the confusion and inconsistency with which it seems to be infected. It protects certain commercial intangibles but only if they are appropriated in certain unacceptable ways. It has been said that trade secret law protects primarily against unethical actions.[17] In that respect, it reflects not so much the principle of independent initiative as the principle of respect for the rules.

There appear to be several rationales for the principle of independent initiative. A competitive system stressing independent initiative might be thought more likely to promote innovation than one based on liberal copying and close attention to the methods and approaches of competitors. When businesses define themselves and their objectives narrowly in terms of the competition, when their research efforts focus on investigating each other, the scope for innovation would appear to be much narrower, and its pace slower, than in a system where competing firms function more independently. At the logical extreme, such an inbred system would cease to innovate altogether. One can observe in certain academic fields a gradual narrowing of topics and approaches considered legitimate. Scholars define their problems in terms of those set for them in the literature. One cannot help but wonder whether less attention to the literature in the field and a more liberal attitude toward legitimacy might not lead more frequently to significant intellectual advances. Still, the question is one of degree: Advances do often result from building on the work of others. Independence is not to be sought to the degree that one ceases to be aware of the work of others.

Besides the possible relationships among independence, liberality of thought, and innovation, economics provides another rationale for upholding a system of independent initiative. According to economic thought, it is the profit motive that provides the link between innovation and recognizing limits on what competitors can borrow from one another. A system that allocates to the creator or discoverer of knowledge an exclusive right to exploit it for profit offers a powerful incentive for investment in new knowledge. Our system does not grant perpetual monopolies to discoverers or creators of knowledge because it also recognizes the value of knowledge as a building block for innovations by others. From an economic point of view, a central problem in the system of independent initiative is allocating legal rights to protect and exploit innovations in a way that promotes the greatest social good: To provide public access to new knowledge as quickly and as easily as is compatible with offering adequate incentives to investors in new knowledge.

A complicating factor in this calculus of social good is the likelihood that, without legally protectible rights to valuable information and without a legal process that works efficiently, businesses will develop their own methods for protecting valuable information from competitors. As compared with legal protection, self-protective measures may be more or less efficient from a social point of view. But one must be concerned about the net losses that result when, for example, businesses avoid the use of telephones to insure that valuable information will not be lost to competitors who may be listening by means of electronic surveillance.[18] Courts have often seen the rationale for limiting the right of one business to appropriate and exploit a competitor's efforts in terms of compensatory justice.

In one well-known case, *International News Service v. Associated Press,* the Supreme Court upheld an injunction prohibiting the International News Service from publishing news gathered, written up, and published by the Associated Press at the expense of its members.[19] Without compensating or even acknowledging the Associated Press as the source, International News had copied and sold to its own members news that it had gathered from bulletin boards and early editions of the newspapers of members of the Associated Press. In some cases, the news was published by International News exactly as written up by the Associated Press. The Court reasoned that International News should not be permitted to reap where it had not sown—to appropriate to itself the harvest of the effort and expense undertaken by the Associated Press in gathering the news. According to the Court, the underlying principle is similar to the equitable principle that "he who has fairly paid the price should have the beneficial use of the property."[20] The Court emphasized the competitive advantage enjoyed by International News that was able to profit from using the news without being burdened by the expense of gathering it.

A similar concern was expressed by the Court that held the taking of unauthorized aerial photographs of a competitor's unfinished plant to be the misappropriation of a trade secret. The Court reasoned that one may not avoid the labor and expense of independent research by appropriating a commercially valuable process from a competitor without his permission when he is taking reasonable precautions to maintain its secrecy.[21] The idea of unjust enrichment is central to the court's reasoning: A business should not be permitted to enrich itself by exploiting a competitor's effort.

All these rationales tend to support a competitive system that weighs heavily the principle of independent initiative in contrast to, for example, a system that gives wider approval to copying and imitation as the Japanese system purportedly does.[22] American culture, on the other hand, has, from its Protestant beginnings, given broad sanction to the values of individualism, self-reliance, hard work, and originality reflected in this competitive ideal.

To say that our ideal of competition recognizes the principle of independent initiative is not to spell out the exact contours of the principle—

either within the law or outside it. Although there are some generally accepted doctrines about legitimate and illegitimate appropriations from, and interference with, a competitor's business, there will always be judgments that are disputed because different weights are put on conflicting considerations. Particular judgments may involve other principles of the business system—principles that are not especially about competitive relations but that affect them. For example, the prohibition of bribery or breaches of fiduciary duty may also be an important consideration in determining whether a business may exploit intelligence about a competitor if the information was acquired by those means. Nevertheless, *respect for independent initiative is an important principle for explaining and guiding our rules and judgments about what is fair and unfair in business competition.*

B.   The Principle of Constructive Effort[23]

The principle of constructive effort is illustrated by our notion that the best competitors are those who succeed by their own positive efforts rather than by undermining their competitors. They see their rivals not as obstacles to be eliminated but as fellow seekers after a common prize.[24] Mr. Justice Brandeis expressed the idea captured by the principle of constructive effort in this way:

> Competition consists in trying to do things better than someone else; that is, making or selling a better article at a lesser cost, or otherwise giving better service. It is not a competition to resort to methods of the prize ring, and simply "knock the other man out." That is killing a competitor.[25]

This principle requires that competition be approached in a certain spirit—with a certain attitude toward rivals. This spirit is most fully exemplified by competitors who focus on their own strengths rather than seeking to identify and capitalize on their opponents' weaknesses. There is something distasteful, for example, in the competitor who makes a point of drawing attention to a rival's shortcomings—even if they are genuine and relevant. A positive campaign is preferable to a negative one in politics as in other competitive arenas. More distasteful is the competitor who emphasizes or exaggerates a rival's irrelevant qualities. These practices inevitably arouse suspicion. Do they reflect the absence of positive qualities the competitor might advance in his own behalf? Or perhaps they reflect a disrespectful or even destructive attitude that in other circumstances could lead to efforts to undermine the competition in more serious ways. At the very least, however, the principle requires a competitor to refrain from sabotaging a rival's operations, reputation, or relationships in order to create a competitive advantage.

The principle of constructive effort is at its core a principle concerning appropriate attitudes and motivation. As such, it is more difficult to enforce through law than principles governing required and prohibited actions. Nevertheless, the law of unfair competition recognizes the principle. The purely motivational aspect of the principle is seen in the body of law governing the improper use of business tactics that are normally quite legitimate.[26] The test of improper use lies in the purpose for which the tactics are employed. A classic illustration of the principle can be seen in the case of *Tuttle v. Buck* in which a banker was held liable for setting up a rival barber shop with the sole motive of driving a personal enemy out of business.[27] Normally, of course, setting up a competitive business is not legally actionable. In this case, however, the competitor's purpose was judged to be improper. Litigation, too, can be an unfair method of competition when it is used as a "deliberate weapon of business aggression rather than as an instrument of adjudicating honest disputes."[28] Other conventional business tactics whose misuse has been the basis of liability include selling below cost and refusals to deal.[29] Even if these practices are not actionable under antitrust principles because they do not harm general competition, they may be actionable under the common law of unfair competition because they harm a competitor.[30]

Cases like *Tuttle v. Buck* in which the motive of the rival is both singular and clearly demonstrable in a court of law are rare. More commonly, as noted earlier, the motives are mixed, and the potential defendant's economic self-interest is at least a partial explanation of the activities in question. In these cases, courts will look at the relative strength of the improper motivation, the degree of the rival's injury, and the extent to which there is public injury.[31]

The principle of constructive effort is also recognized in the doctrine against commercial disparagement, the making of false statements about the quality of a business's products or services with intent to cause financial harm to the business. Although not exclusively concerned with disparagement by a competitor, the doctrine, like the related doctrine against defaming the integrity of a business, may be the basis of an action by a competitor.

From society's point of view, the principle of constructive effort appears to make economic sense. Undermining the competition is likely to be an attractive strategy in just those cases where a rival is comparatively strong and successful—when it is most difficult to compete on the basis of one's own strengths. Permitting the less successful to sabotage the more successful would frequently result in a net loss to society. If the sabotage were successful, the goods and services most desired by the public could become less widely available or not available at all. There is also the opportunity cost involved in utilizing resources to destroy competitors rather than to improve one's own performance. The opportunity cost to society would be significant if negative rather than positive competition were to become widely practiced.

On the other hand, it might seem that certain departures from the principle of constructive effort could be socially valuable. It is sometimes argued, for example, that consumer welfare is promoted when competing firms engage in comparative advertising, a practice regarded by others as verging on the unethical. Such advertising, it is argued, helps consumers become better informed about product differences. Of course, comparative advertising is not legally actionable unless untrue. It is not such a serious departure from the principle of constructive effort as sabotage, but it does involve deliberate efforts to capitalize on a rival's weaknesses. Whatever criticism one might have of the practice relates to this underlying attitude that may affect the objectivity and the truthfulness of the comparisons made and that may reflect a willingness to engage in more serious departures from the principle. *In summary, the principle of constructive effort calls for competition directed toward self-improvement and conducted in a spirit of respect for one's rivals.* The economic rationales for the principle may be buttressed by the fundamental ethical principle of respect for others.

C.   The Principle of Respect for the Rules

Every competitive activity is governed to some extent by rules: some explicit, some understood, some that define the activity, some that regulate its performance; some that govern relations among competitors; some that govern relations among cooperators. A third principle of positive competition, one understood as governing all competitive activities, is that these rules shall be followed.[32] The most blatant form of unfair competition is attempting to gain a competitive advantage by violating the explicit rules of the activity. The card player who takes more cards than permitted, the tennis player who calls an opponent's ball "out" when it is not—both are like the business that continues to emit illegal amounts of pollution when its competitors are in legal compliance. All are seeking to gain an advantage over their rivals by attempting to avoid following or abiding by the consequences of violating the basic rules of their respective activities. In a competition, the participants are equally obliged to follow the basic rules of the activity, and gaining a competitive edge by failing to do so is a form of unfair competition.

Specifying all the rules of a competitive activity may be difficult, especially when it comes to the rules that are understood but not officially or authoritatively stated in a designated source. For purposes of understanding how the principle of respect for the rules informs our judgments about fair competition in business, however, we may take the rules as including those requirements and prohibitions laid down in law and in basic principles of business morality or ethics. By principles of business morality or ethics I mean respect for law, honesty, contracts, property, and fiduciary relationships. There are two ways in which departures from the principle of respect for the rules can give rise to a charge of unfair competition. First, as in the case of the polluter or the tax evader, violating the rules can create a competitive advantage for the violator. Second, the basic rules may be violated in dealings between competitors. Stealing from a competitor, bribing a rival's employees, and even perpetrating fraud on a competitor demonstrate violations of the principle of respect for the rules. As violations of basic principles of business ethics, these acts are unethical independently of whether they are also instances of unfair competition.

It is not surprising that firms are expected to adhere to the basic principles of business morality in their dealings with one another. Relaxation of the prohibitions on theft, bribery, and fraud between competitors would probably lead very quickly to weakening respect for those prohibitions in other contexts. Moreover, violations may represent departures from the principles of independent initiative and constructive effort, as well. It should be noted that despite the clear competitive effects of violating the principle of respect for the rules, the law does not uniformly permit firms to seek injunctions or recover the damages they incur when a rival gains a competitive advantage by violating the law. But like other victims of fraud, theft, and bribery, firms do have a cause of action against competitors who employ these techniques against them.

D. Remaining Principles: The Level Playing Field and Respect for Officiating Parties

Because the remaining principles are less directly relevant to the marketplace attitudes to be discussed, they will not be elaborated here. Suffice it to say that the *level-playing-field* principle is concerned with certain types of inequities among competitors and prevents them from using certain advantages—advantages of size, for example—in their competitive efforts. For instance, the practice of "buying in" (bidding below cost in competitive bidding contests in the defense industry) is a practice frowned upon in part because it favors the large contractor.

The level-playing-field principle is perhaps of greater importance as a guide to the rule makers than to the competitors in a competitive activity. The principle has its roots in ideas of equal opportunity. Though equality among competitors is rarely required, frequently adjustments are made or qualifications imposed to insure that disparities in abilities and resources are not too great to permit genuine competition—competition that tests the resources of all participants. Handicaps, age and weight limits, levels of difficulty, for example, serve this function. The principle also has roots in ideas of formal equality requiring that the rules of the activity be applied to all competitors alike. In competitive bidding, for instance, the principle finds expression in the requirement that all bidders receive the same information and that all be held to the same deadlines.

The principle of *respect for officiating parties* concerns the relationships between competitors and the referees and judges of a competitive activity. In the case of business, this principle prohibits efforts to influence or mislead consumers, government officials, and officials of self-regulatory agencies in certain ways. For example, firms may not mislead customers as to the nature of their products nor may they coerce them into buying. Attempts to bribe or in other ways exert excessive influence over legislators, judges, and other government officials who have power to affect competitive relations are also violations of fair play, according to this principle.

IV. MARKETPLACE PRACTICES AND THE COMPETITIVE IDEAL

A review of intelligence-gathering practices employed in today's marketplace raises questions about the vitality of the ideal of positive competition. To espouse an ideal, as noted earlier, is to hold a certain set of characteristic attitudes and beliefs about which aims and conduct are proper, neutral, questionable, or forbidden and which are worthy of blame, praise, or neglect. These attitudes and beliefs may be seen in tendencies to act and to judge people and their actions in ways characteristic of the ideal. The principles of positive competition describe clusters of attitudes and beliefs characteristic of the ideal. Given the loose relationship among the attitudes and beliefs associated with an ideal and given the variety of nuances of attitude and belief, acceptance or rejection of an ideal is usually a matter of degree. One espouses the ideal to a greater or a lesser degree: Wholesale acceptance or rejection is relatively rare.

The degree to which a particular practice departs from the ideal of positive competition may be assessed in relation to each principle of the ideal. The means used to acquire the information, the type of information involved, and the purpose to which it is put are all relevant to this assessment. Consider the practice of posing as a potential customer to gain access to information, the subject of recent litigation between Continental Data Systems and Exxon Corporation in Pennsylvania.[33] An Exxon marketing manager, whose branch office was failing to meet its sales quotas and who personally was failing to meet his own quotas, arranged to have a new hiree about to join Exxon pose as a potential customer for a competitor's software. The marketing manager himself attended the software demonstration as a friend and consultant of the supposed customer but without identifying himself or his employer. His object was to acquire information that would permit Exxon to develop a similar program to be sold in competition with the originator. As a result of the misrepresentation, the Exxon employees were given a detailed demonstration of the software, received in-depth answers to their questions, were given access to the competitor's sales manual, and made unauthorized copies of critical information in the manual. Using this information, Exxon was able to develop a competitive program. Apart from the misrepresentation involved—a violation of a basic principle of business morality—this case illustrates a classic instance of a firm's attempting to reap where it has not sown. Information was sought from the competitor for the explicit purpose of piggybacking on the competitor's research and development efforts to create a competitive product.

Consistency with the principles of independent initiative and respect for the rules is also at issue when a firm rummages through a competitor's trash in search of intelligence, a practice that has received attention in the press and has been litigated in at least one case.[34] The practice may be criticized if access to the trash involved bribery, theft of personal property, or trespass, but quite apart from possible violations of basic ethical principles, trash surveillance also raises questions from the perspective of the principle of independent initiative. The surprise and amusement we feel when learning about the practice and the fact that it is usually done covertly indicate that generally accepted boundaries of firm privacy are being crossed. The practice belies the attitudes of self-reliance, willingness to compete on the basis of publicly available information, and respect for the privacy of one's rivals involved in accepting the principle of independent initiative.

Intelligence-gathering practices revealed in the most recent defense procurement scandal reflect similar attitudes. These practices, however, depart even more seriously from the ideal of positive competition if the allegations of bribery involving government officials are true.[35] Because these practices arise in the context of formal bidding contests, they involve departures from at least four of the five principles of positive competition: independent initiative, respect for the rules, level playing field, and respect for officiating parties. Depending on the motives and effects of securing information about the bids of competitors by bribing government officials, the principle of constructive effort may be at stake in some cases as well.

Another increasingly common practice posing a challenge to the ideal of positive competition is that of hiring away a rival's key employees to acquire competitor intelligence. The pirating of employees with valuable competitor intelligence has been the subject of numerous recent lawsuits and threatened lawsuits. When Wendy's International, Inc., decided to change from Pepsi products to Coca-Cola products in its restaurants, Pepsi-Cola threatened to sue Coca-Cola for pirating executive employees to gain information about Pepsi's contract and programs with Wendy's and for tampering with contractual relationships.[36] The raiding of a competitor's key people was also at issue in litigation between Johns-Manville and Guardian Industries,[37] Avis and Hertz,[38] AT&T and MCI.[39]

A novel twist to this theme is illustrated in the dispute that arose when an advertising agency used its access to information about the key competitor of a potential client in its solicitation of the client. In a letter soliciting the business of Microsoft, the advertising agency explained how it knew the plans of Microsoft's main rival, Lotus Development Corporation:

> You see, the reason we know so much about Lotus is that some of our newest employees just spent the past year and a half working on the Lotus business at another agency. So they are intimately acquainted with Lotus' thoughts about Microsoft.[40]

The practice of hiring key employees from a competitor to obtain information about a rival or its trade secrets departs from the ideal of positive competition in several respects. It cuts against the principle of independent initiative insofar as it reflects greater reliance on the competition for new ideas, for the identification and development of human resources, and for the definition of one's own objectives. It also assumes a much greater mobility of employees among rival firms than that envisioned in the picture of discrete, independent firms with a relatively stable cadre of loyal employees.

Fundamental ethical principles are also at stake: The practice typically involves an inducement for the newly hired employee to breach fiduciary, and in some cases promissory, responsibilities to the old employer by using confidential information acquired in the former position. Misrepresentation may also be a factor. The potential employee may not be told to expect to deliver up specific information or may be told, incorrectly, that revealing certain information is not legally actionable. Potential earnings may be exaggerated. Sometimes, but not always, the practice conflicts with the principle of constructive effort. When the primary motivation or effect of the practice is to disable or destroy a competitor's business, it becomes a form of destructive competition. The destructive motive or effect may more often be seen when one firm raids another by systematically inducing many employees to leave the competing firm.

The law has attempted to protect firms whose key employees are hired away against the most egregious violations of the principles of positive competition. The doctrine against tortious interferences with contractual relations, noted earlier, makes it legally actionable to hire away employees when the primary motivation for doing so is to impair a competitive business or to obtain access to a rival's trade secrets.[41] This doctrine applies even if the employee is not bound by contract or if the contract is one terminable at will. Establishing the requisite forbidden motivation is usually difficult, however, because the motives behind most attempts to hire from competitors are mixed. Even if the hiring firm is interested in acquiring trade secrets or confidential information, it typically also desires the legitimate services of a capable and skilled individual. Rarely does a firm single-mindedly set out to disable a competitor's business by hiring away its employees.

Moreover, although the principles of positive competition might point toward restrictions on hiring from rivals, principles of individual liberty, which must take priority, cut the other way.[42] Limitations on individuals' freedom to change jobs or to accept employment on more favorable terms may not be imposed lightly. Consequently, when the hiring firm's motives are not clearly of the forbidden type, and the means employed to attract the employee are confined to persuasion and the offering of better terms, courts quite understandably are loathe to find an actionable wrong.[43] Judicial opinions consistently reflect a concern for the hiring firm's motives, the means of inducement, and the relative weight of the rival firm's interests as compared with those of the employee in question.[44] Thus, although legal doctrine on the hiring of employees from rival firms lends support to the ideal of positive competition, in practice the doctrine does little to enforce the ideal. Many firms whose conduct departs from the ideal of positive competition have little to fear from the legal system because only in the most egregious cases will there be sufficient evidence of improper motivation as well as the requisite balance between the individual's and the employer's interests.

V. MARKETPLACE ATTITUDES AND THE COMPETITIVE IDEAL

One measure of the extent to which the business community's prevailing ideal of fair competition departs from the ideal of positive competition lies in the prevalence of the competitive practices I have mentioned and the degree to which they are expected and approved. Neither is easy to determine. Most of the evidence about the prevalence of these intelligence-gathering practices and the scope and degree of approval given to them is impressionistic. Nevertheless, these impressions suggest that the ideal is under pressure.

A flavor for the attitudes of the individuals involved can be gleaned from reading court opinions and newspaper accounts. For example, the individual who gained access to a rival's software by posing as a customer is reported to have commented later: "This was something we had to do. . . . If you were in my position, you would have done the same thing if you were getting the hell kicked out of you in the marketplace."[45] The supervisor of an individual who clandestinely rummaged a competitor's trash testified that when he learned of the practice, he "handled it very lightly because I did not consider it a terrible thing. I considered it kind of a joke."[46] An individual who was personally engaged in trash surveillance reported his interpretation of his company's attitude: "The only good competitor is a dead competitor."[47]

The sheer number of individual cases reported in the press and the involvement of large and reputable companies also gives the impression that some of the practices and the competitive ideals they reflect are widely accepted. Survey data indicate broad approval among executives of the practice of hiring a rival's employees to gain access to competitively valuable information. An old 1973 survey showed a significant increase in the practice between 1959 and 1973, and broad approval of the practice among all age groups in 1973.[48] Fifty-one percent of the smaller companies surveyed and 37 percent of the larger ones said they expected such employees to contribute all they knew to the new job, including the rival's trade secrets.[49] Broad approval for the practice was also found in a 1976 survey.[50] About half the responding executives said they would try to hire a competitor's employee to learn about a rival's important scientific discovery that would substantially reduce their firm's profits for about a year. Seventy-three percent thought that the average executive would use such an approach to competitive intelligence gathering.

Approval of the practice appears to remain high among some marketing professionals. In a 1988 survey, *Advertising Age* asked its readers whether it was ethical to hire an account supervisor from a competitor in order to gain information about the competitor's client: The hypothetical question was based on the Rossin Greenberg solicitation of Microsoft using information acquired by hiring a rival ad agency's employees who had worked on the account of Lotus, the main Microsoft competitor. Seventy-three percent of the 157 professionals surveyed—advertisers, agency personnel, media people, consultants, and "others"—said the practice was ethical.[51] When the Center for Communication, Inc., posed the same hypothetical to students and professors of marketing, 59 percent of the 626 students surveyed said the practice was ethical, and 70 percent said they would do it.[52]

Other competitive practices in conflict with the ideal of positive competition were widely approved by survey respondents. Hiring a competitor's employees to gain clients was regarded as ethical by 57 percent of the students and 79 percent of the professionals.[53] Although only 21 percent of the students said it was ethical to use valuable competitive information acquired through inadvertent disclosure by a competitor's supplier, 63 percent said they would do it. Among professionals, 41 percent said that practice was ethical.[54] It is interesting to note that using trade secrets disclosed by mistake by someone with a duty to maintain their confidentiality would probably be legally actionable under trade secret law.[55]

At least a partial rejection of the ideal of positive competition can also be seen in the competitive attitudes expressed in a leading business policy textbook. The authors stress the importance of knowing a competitor's goals, assumptions, and capabilities in order to know with whom to pick a fight.[56] The text seems to suggest that the point of business competition is to do in one's rivals and that the "mind set" one should bring to business should be directed toward that end:

> The best battleground is the market segment or dimensions of strategy in which competitors are ill prepared, least enthusiastic, or most uncomfortable. . . . The ideal is to find a strategy that competitors are frozen from reacting to because of their present circumstances.

The text contains no mention of limits on the lengths to which one should go in obtaining competitor intelligence or the purposes to which it should be put. More important, perhaps, is the spirit conveyed by the advice offered, a spirit that departs from the principle of constructive effort.

VI. CONCLUSION

Discrepancies between the ideal of positive competition and the practices and attitudes found in the marketplace indicate a rejection of the ideal by significant numbers of market players. Whether this ideal should and can be sustained is cause for reflection. The answer has consequences for business education, managerial practice, and the development of the law of unfair competition. As noted earlier, an ideal comprises a host of attitudes and judgments. Some are transmitted formally through the legal systems. Others are transmitted informally through the socialization that occurs in families, schools, churches, and the workplace. If the ideal of positive competition is to survive, its principles must find expression in competitive activities undertaken at all levels. They must inform the law. They must be reinforced in business school education and rewarded in the workplace.

NOTES

1.   Adam Smith, *The Theory of Moral Sentiments*, Oxford University Press edition, 1976, p. 83.

2. Rudolf Callmann, *Unfair Competition, Trademarks & Monopolies*, §§1,2 (4th ed., 1981).

3. For example, the Business Roundtable omits competitors from its list of constituencies in its *Statement on Corporate Social Responsibility* (October 1981). Many company standards of conduct do the same: *General Dynamics Standards of Business Ethics and Conduct* (2nd ed.); *Johnson & Johnson, Our Credo; Wells Fargo Code of Corporate Responsibility and Ethics.* Hewlett-Packard, by contrast, devotes an entire section of its *Standards of Business Conduct* to "Obligations to Competitors." The section includes guidance on antitrust, gathering competitor information, comparative advertising, and commenting on a competitor.

4. Judge Goldberg in *E. I. duPont deNemours & Co. v. Christopher*, 431 F.2nd 1012, 1016 (5th Cir. 1970), *cert. denied*, 400 U.S. 1024 (1971).

5. Readers will be familiar with Albert Z. Carr's view that business is like poker, and his conclusion that business bluffing is therefore ethical. See "Is Business Bluffing Ethical?" *Harvard Business Review* (January–February 1968), p. 143.

6. In elaborating the nature of the rules of business competition, one would want to make use of John Rawls's distinction between summary rules and constitutive rules. See "Two Concepts of Rules," *Philosophical Review*, Vol. 64 (1955), pp. 3–32.

7. Here, I ignore the difficulties in determining who is a competitor, a question on which a great many court cases turn. The variety of roles played by market participants and uncertainties about the substitutability of products complicate the determination of who is competing with whom for what.

8. *Levings v. Forbes & Wallace, Inc.*, 8 Mass. App. 498 (1979), later app., 12 Mass. App. 990. For a comprehensive collection of the intuitive standards of unfairness judges have sought to apply, see J. Thomas McCarthy, *Trademarks and Unfair Competition*, §1:4 (1973).

9. *International News Service v. Associated Press*, 248 U.S. 215, 240 (1918).

10. This point has been noted by many courts. See, e.g., *People ex rel. Mosk v. Nat'l Research Co.*, 201 Cal App. 2d 765 (1962): "Unfair or fraudulent business practices may run the gamut of human ingenuity and chicanery."

11. Jeremiah Smith, "The Use of Maxims in Jurisprudence," *Harvard Law Review* Vol. 9 (1895), p. 13, at 26, quoted in Callmann, §2.28, n. 2, p. 105.

12. Discrimination law and criminal law are two cases in point.

13. This breakthrough in tap dancing was reported on National Public Radio in August 1988.

14. The author of a recent *Wall Street Journal* article took issue with a politician's presenting as her own a humorous turn of phrase she had heard from someone else.

15. Callmann, §2.02.

16. *Croft v. Day*, 7 Beav. 84, 88, 49 Eng. Rep. 994, 996 (Ch. 1843), quoted in "Competitive Torts," *Harvard Law Review*, Vol. 77 (1964), p. 888, at 908.

17. E.g., *Synercom Technology Inc. v. University Computing Co.*, 474 F. Supp. 37, 44 (N.D. Texas 1979).

18. Among the countermeasures firms can take against industrial espionage, the trade secret expert Roger Milgrim recommends avoiding the use of phones. See 12 *Business Organizations*, Milgrim on Trade Secrets, §5.05 (1988), p. 5–170.

19. *International News Service*, 248 U.S. 215, 237–238 (1918).

20. Ibid.

21. *DuPont v. Christopher*, at 1015.

22. See George Melloan, "An American Views Japan's Copycat Culture," *Asian Wall Street Journal* (July 15, 1988), p. 6. It is interesting to note the traditional emphasis on copying in the development of Japanese culture, as well as the reputed thoroughness with which the Japanese study their competitors. See comment of George H. Kuper, executive

director of the National Research Council's Manufacturing Studies Board, cited in "Making Deals That Won't Give Technology Away," *Business Week* (April 20, 1987), p. 63.

23. I owe this terminology to Callmann. In his discussion of the maxims of fair competition, Callmann emphasizes the fundamental principle of constructive competition and stresses the centrality of constructive effort. Callmann, §2.2.

24. In Callmann's words, business competition should not be seen as a struggle of one competitor against the other but of all with the others for a common prize. Callmann, §2.19.

25. Mr. Justice Brandeis, "Competition," *American Legal News*, Vol. 44 (Jan. 1913), quoted in Mason, *The Brandeis Way, A Case Study in the Working of Democracy* (Princeton: Princeton University Press, 1938).

26. See "Competitive Torts," *Harvard Law Review*, Vol. 77 (1964), p. 888, at 923–932.

27. 107 Minn. 145, 119 N.W. 946 (1909), cited in "Competitive Torts," Ibid., at 924.

28. Recommendations of the Department of Justice, *Final Report and Recommendations of the Temporary National Economic Committee*, S35 77th Cong. 1st sess., Exhibit No. 2794, p. 249, quoted in Callmann, §2.32, p. 108, n. 1. *See also T. N. Dickinson Co. v. LL Corp.*, 227 USPQ 145 (D. Conn. 1985) (filing of false petitions for cancellation in the Trademark Trial and Appeal Board violates state common law of unfair competition).

29. See cases cited in "Competitive Torts" at 924.

30. Antitrust law, it is commonly said, protects competition, not competitors. E.g., *Redwing Carriers, Inc. v. McKenzie Tank Lines Inc.*, 443 F. Supp. 639 (N.D. Fla. 1977), aff'd per curiam, 594 F.2d 114 (5th Cir. 1979). Thus, certain practices that are morally objectionable and that harm a competitor may not be actionable as antitrust violations but may be actionable under other principles of unfair competition.

31. "Competitive Torts" at 924.

32. Most competitive activities do not include among their primary rules the rule: "These rules shall be followed." That the rules are to be followed is, however, understood by those who participate.

33. *Continental Data Systems, Inc. v. Exxon Corporation*, 638 F. Supp. 432 (E.D.Pa. 1986).

34. *Tennant Co. v. Advance Machine Co.*, 355 N.W.2d 720 (Ct. App. Minn. 1984). See also Robert Johnson, "The Case of Marc Feith Shows Corporate Spies Aren't Just High-Tech," *Wall Street Journal* (January 9, 1987), p. 1; "Businesses Struggle to Keep Their Secrets," *U.S. News and World Report* (September 23, 1985), p. 59 (Mentor Corporation of Minneapolis reports trash surveillance).

35. Tim Carrington and Edward T. Pound, "Pushing Defense Firms to Compete, Pentagon Harms Buying System," *Wall Street Journal* (June 27, 1988), p. 1. "[W]ith information suddenly so crucial, what makes the new Pentagon scandals differ from past ones are the allegations of bribery."

36. "Pepsi to Sue Coke over Wendy's," *The Washington Post* (November 13, 1986), p. E1.

37. *Johns-Manville Corp. v. Guardian Industries Corp.*, 586 F. Supp. 1034, 1075 (E.D. Mich. 1983), aff'd, 770 F.2d 178 (Fed. Cir. 1985).

38. Tamar Lewin, "Putting a Lid on Corporate Secrets," *The New York Times* (April 1, 1984), sec. 3 (front page).

39. "Information Thieves Are Now Corporate Enemy No. 1," *Business Week* (May 5, 1986), pp. 120 and 122–23.

40. Quoted in Gary Putka, "Lotus Gets Order Barring Ad Agency from Telling Secrets," *Wall Street Journal* (December 14, 1987), p. 16. See also Cleveland Horton, "Ethics at Issue in Lotus Case," *Advertising Age* (December 21, 1987), p. 6.

41. Callmann, §9.03, pp. 31–32.

42. See generally, "Post-Employment Restraint Agreements: A Reassessment," *University of Chicago Law Review*, Vol. 52 (1985), p. 703.

43. Even the offering of better terms may be taken as evidence of improper motivation or inducing a breach of contractual relations. *See Texaco, Inc. v. Pennzoil Co.*, 729 S.W.2d 768, 803 (Ct. App. Tex. 1987) ("It is necessary that there be some act of interference or of persuading a party to breach, for example by offering better terms or other incentives, for tort liability to arise.") Callmann cites an 1819 case in which the plaintiff was ruined because the defendant enticed away his workers by entertaining them lavishly and offering them higher wages. *Gunter v. Astor*, 4 J B Moore, 12 (1819). Cited in Callmann, §9.03, p. 32.

44. Callmann makes this point at §9.13, p. 74.

45. *Continental Data Systems Inc. v. Exxon Corp.*, 638 F. Supp. at 437.

46. *Tennant Co. v. Advance Machine Co.*, 355 N.W.2d at 722.

47. Robert Johnson, "The Case of Marc Feith," *Wall Street Journal* (January 9, 1987) at 12.

48. Jerry L. Wall, "What the Competition Is Doing: Your Need to Know," *Harvard Business Review* (Nov.–Dec. 1974), pp. 22, 34, 164.

49. Ibid. at 38.

50. Steven N. Brenner and Earl A. Molander, "Is the Ethics of Business Changing?" *Harvard Business Review* (January–February 1977), p. 57. This survey, an update of a similar survey done in 1961 by Raymond C. Baumhart, showed a slight increase in the percentage of executives approving of the practice between 1961 and 1976.

51. The survey is described in "Industry Ethics Are Alive," *Advertising Age* (April 18, 1988), p. 88. However, the results noted here are those reported by the Center for Communications, a New York-based nonprofit group, from whom I received tabulations of the results.

52. Survey results received from the Center for Communication, New York, New York.

53. Ibid., Question no. 9.

54. Ibid., Question no. 5.

55. "Uniform Trade Secrets Act with 1985 Amendments," §1(2)(ii)(c), in *Uniform Laws Annotated*, Vol. 14 (1980 with 1988 Pocket Part).

56. C. Roland Christensen, Kenneth R. Andrews *et al.*, *Business Policy Text and Cases*, 6th ed. (Homewood, IL: Irwin, 1987), p. 239.

57. Ibid. at 243.

5

America's Neopluralism
The Proliferation of Interest Groups and Their Crippling Effect on Older Norms

Ivar Berg

I. INTRODUCTION

I was favored, as I prepared to address Walton's assignment for the symposium from which this volume derives, by the opportunity to read a brilliantly crafted paper he delivered at Penn State University in the Spring of 1986. In that paper (and more recently in *The Moral Manager*[1]), he examined the implications of three propositions relating to the "warrants," the writs so to say, affording legitimacy in the eyes of other Americans to the nation's top managers', their owners', and their directors' multifaceted ways and means. To paraphrase:

1. Managers although continuing to scan labor, resource, product, and capital markets, must learn to read the "total culture."[2] The logic is straightforward: Writs of all kinds are at least partly rooted in established cultural traditions but may well lose their legitimacies as some of an enabling culture's major enthymemes—the syllogisms with implicit premises by which we live—change. The shift in the eighteenth–century West "from status to contract," in the governance of most social relationships, I would add, is perhaps the most apposite example; a shift with which we lived many years before it was so labeled by Sir Henry Maine.

2. More specifically: Many of the well-established and long-treasured

Ivar Berg • School of Arts & Sciences, University of Pennsylvania, Philadelphia, Pennsylvania 19104–6383.

ideas among a culture's traditions tend, in Walton's words, to be dethroned when the culture itself changes, a proposition that applies particularly to ideas, in bygone days, that supported many of management's traditional "rights, privileges and immunities." My own example: Plantation owners lost critical elements of long-enduring controls over chattel property when their slaves were manumitted; the abolitionist movement triggering emancipation was a moral expression as well as the embodiment of a variety of political demiurges.

3. Challenges to the legitimacy of managers' ways and means will be linked with other challenges, challenges to institutions—to property rights most importantly, for example—that will inspire philosophers to develop a subspecialization in their field that could be called *business ethics*. As business ethics courses develop, they will, in turn, force shifts in the contents of future business leaders' educations and lead them thereafter toward "professionalized" behavior.

I intend, in these pages, to discuss some specific social changes that will likely impact upon the "total culture" in ways suggested by the first and second proposition and in the first half of Walton's third, business ethics, proposition. This is to say that I will not treat further the portion of his last proposition, regarding business school education; I have delivered myself of (somewhat overstated) critical thoughts on that subject in an esquisse entitled "Teaching Business Ethics: Leave it to Sisyphus."[3]

The title of that paper was meant to suggest what I here reaffirm: It is exceedingly difficult to teach business ethics as what would amount, in business education settings, to a subdiscipline of economics, not business ethics in a philosophy department. It is only a little bit arch to point out, in passing, that many of the younger folks recently indicted and convicted for "insider trading" earned decent grades in such courses at one or another of our leading graduate business schools. The logic of economics, with its perfectly extraordinary emphases on the interests of individuals, is the dominant one in business programs. But the ethical implications of individualism are only rarely recognized for what they are—and then weighed against other "isms" in moral–philosophical terms. Indeed, the moral suasions implicit in economics are generally denied in favor of scientistic claims to value neutrality. The simple related fact is that "the good" is defined, for most of us, by the outcomes of a calculus of economizing, not of moralizing, in a society that regards self-interest—greed, some might call it—as a basic and inevitable trait in man. Indeed the author of one of the other chapters in this volume takes that position as the point of departure for his sobering critique!

In pursuit of my intent, I will add my own elaborations (and a few subspecifications) to Walton's other propositions by looking at several cultural changes, the signs of whose development are already in evidence, under five rubrics: political changes; demographic changes; economic changes; changes in the "American Economic Republic"; and ideological changes. So great is the number of values in flux that one item in my bottom line will remind some readers of Arlo Guthrie's refrain, in his popular 1960s song, "You can get anything you want in Alice's Restaurant."

Walton argues that managers (and not a few others!) have long enjoyed an intellectual as well as moral "safety margin" inhering in the ease with which personal responsibility regarding a plethora of moral and ethical issues could be gainsaid by pointing fingers at impersonal forces over which managers claim they have virtually no control either collectively or indirectly.

Some of these forces, from droughts and floods like those that contributed to Great Recession of 1975, to OPEC's sudden and brief successes in acting like a classic cartel in 1973, are in fact largely beyond American managers control.[4] But such forces, like "market forces," are indeed often very much subject to control![5] Walton argues, however, that pressures are building that will bring us back to enlivened concerns about individual liberty, which he terms a societal value, and thus to efforts to fix individual legal and moral responsibilities for an increasing number of acts and actions. Patience with "scams," "Gates," inside traders, polluters, "Robin HUD's," and innumerable other quotidian scandals in high places, in Walton's judgment, is simply running out.

It is my thesis that a consensus about the sins that are so regularly reported may indeed occur, as Walton suggests. It is further my thesis, though, that this consensus will collect and organize itself only with very substantial difficulties. These difficulties, I submit, inhere in the disunifying, disjoining, and similarly "hyperpluralizing" forces in business leaders' larger cultural environment, in fractionating forces within the so-called business community itself, and, more fundamentally, in the virtually (and virulent) antisocial ethic of individualism as we have come to know it.

The rubrics under which I will enumerate the changes I see to be especially consequential to the discussion are not presented in any particular order.

II.   DEMOGRAPHY AND ITS DISCONTENTS[6]

We need not here rehearse in great detail the most basic of the so-called demographic facts of life in the United States beyond enumerating and commenting briefly on a few of them:

We have a staggeringly large number of single-person households, among the "aged" especially, but also among young persons in all segments of the population. The Reverend Jesse Jackson, earlier on, Senator Daniel P. Moynihan (in a recent revision of his controversial essay on the black family in the 1960s), and both parties' contenders for the presidency in 1988 helpfully reminded us of the perils to and significance of the family. But one does not readily palpate forces that will soon revive any of the central tendencies of an older "family-driven" society. Although it is not quite the case that "the nuclear family is in a meltdown," as some columnist recently suggested, the family is in trouble. Consider that the percentage of American households in which the people who live together are related— by marriage or otherwise—has declined by 20 percent, according to a Census Bureau report on September 19, 1988; where 90.3 percent of all households were made up of families in 1948, the figure 40 years later has dropped to 71.5 percent.

Consider further that over the past decade, though the proportion of new households formed by married couples began to rise by 1988, the marriage rate fell by about 30 percent, the divorce rate went up 50 percent—11 million families contain at least one divorced parent—and the average age at first marriage continues to rise, while the birth rate has remained low—about 66 per thousand woman 15 to 44 (or about half the rate of the late 1950s at the baby boom's peak). We cannot now tell whether the slight reversal in the later rate—about 1 percent from 1987 to 1988—is the beginning of a reversal in the trend.

Although "Leave it to Beaver" has a few successors, meantime, the American family of other days is hardly celebrated in a variety of TV "sitcoms" populated by singles, by the pitiful and dispiriting creatures in "Dynasty," "Dallas," "Roseanne," or "Falcon Crest," or in any of a splendid collection of what their own authors call feminist novels in which enduring marriages to husbands enjoy far less favor than obligatory affairs with younger men. Sunday newspapers' summaries of the coming week's soap operas' plots make Eugene O'Neill's, William Faulkner's, and Henrik Ibsen's dreary families look, in comparison, like studies in gentility and bliss—and their viewers number in the millions.

Second and assuming, as most do, the benefits of family training in a host of ethical and morally laden areas of youths' development, I see little to be optimistic about in data bearing, for example, on some once critical family functions. The Census Bureau reported on September 19, 1988 that two-parent (versus one-parent) households dropped from 40 percent of all households in 1970 to 20 percent in 1980, whereas nearly 3 million unmarried and generally childless couples lived together in 1988, up 63 percent in 8 years.

A recent survey, "sponsored by health education groups and the

Health and Human Services Department . . . involved 11,000 *8th and 10th graders* from a nationally representative sample of 217 public and private schools," in the meantime will send chills down some traditionalists' spines:

1. About one third of these 11,000 blithe young spirits reported "that they had had five or more [alcoholic] drinks in the two weeks preceding the survey."
2. Although 10 percent had smoked pot, "one in fifteen said they had used cocaine during that period."
3. "Forty-two percent of the girls and 25 percent of the boys surveyed said they 'seriously thought' about committing suicide," whereas 20 percent of the girls and 10 percent of the boys said they had actually attempted suicide.[7]

One ought not automatically blame all these sickening developments on parents, of course, but this and many comparable surveys do leave one wondering where, in respect of our childrens' avocations, we have gone wrong. When neither general laws, norms, nor constructive familial controls have thoroughgoing impacts on *14- to 16-year-olds* we have reason to doubt that they will have them in greater magnitudes later, and "later" is not very relevant in the case of the boom in unwed teenagers' pregnancies.

It is happily the case that pregnancies among unwed teenagers, across the board, do not necessarily spell long-term catastrophes for youthful mothers, as my colleagues at Penn, Frank Furstenberg and Philip Morgan, have demonstrated, but they are not regularly coupled with the founding of traditional families. At the same time, the ranks of aged persons do swell, as our medical colleagues expand their life spans and perforce the numbers of ailing and impaired elders who survive and endure; not a few of them are without nearly enough help and support from their mobile progeny. Indeed this is a two-sided problem: Nearly $19 billion changed hands between elders and children in 1985 as 7 million people aided nearly 10 million others. Among those 17,000 householders involved in these exchanges, 63 percent were parents helping adult children to the tune of 80 percent of the provider's income. Keep in mind, too, that where there are now 19 people 65 or older for every 100 adults in the working population, that ratio will gradually increase to 22 per 100 and, by 2037—40 years hence—it will be 37:100.[8]

Nor are all the interests of elders, themselves, altogether supportive of "community" values. Consider that with the cheerful blessings of millions of aged Americans, we have extended benefits to them even as they walk away from our youths in large numbers—especially from our youths' educational needs. In a 1983 Gallup Poll, "those older than 50 were opposed [to raising taxes for schools] by 62 to 28 percent."[9]

The foregoing allusions offer abundant hints, at least, of changes in values that once specified rather different intergenerational obligations. And "clinical" evidence comes regularly to academics, on one side, from the turmoil in undergraduates' lives that accompany the separations and divorces of their parents and, on the other, from the dazed shocks of parents whose progeny have resolved, upon leaving home, for example, to live out their lives as self-indentified Gays and Lesbians. As a college dean I was accused a few years ago (by a psychiatrist) "for allowing" his daughter to respond favorably to the sexual advances of her female student boss "in order to get ahead" on the hierarchical staff of one of Penn's undergraduate activities.

The last thoughts call to mind the perfectly gigantic discontinuities, *whether one applauds or deplores them*, that have occurred in social definitions of deviant behavior over the past 25 years. Long segments of chapters in sociology textbooks that once discussed homosexuality as a subset of "deviant behavior," for example, are now located, in keeping with very apparently widergoing value changes, in new, separate, and open-minded chapters on "human sexuality." The point here is not how the reader may feel about the substantive issues but that, in the words of a favorite 1960s philosopher, Bob Dylan, "The times they are a-changin'." The sexual preferences business is in several senses a metaphor for this chapter and thus one to which we will return.

Consider that although there are no numbers on the subject that most students would take to be dispositive, it is evident that growing numbers of Americans have made and are making their Gay and Lesbian preferences public and that there is an equally palpable increase in the number of entirely sanguine bystanders who view these persons' so called affectional preferences with equanimity. For some, these shifts in values are appalling; for others, they are signs of Americans' progressive liberation. Either way the disagreements between these observers are neither friendly nor consensus breeding. Republican Senator Orrin Hatch drew what quite apparently many agreed were among the critical lines between his party and the Democrats on September 1, 1988, for example, in a speech in which he announced that his Republican party's opponents in 1988 were the "party of homosexuals." His was a certifiable effort to shame Democrats and to exploit widely popular misgivings about those with latitudinary sexual preferences.

One is obliged to ask further how the intergenerational tensions these trends imply will be managed as the broadly shared societal ideologies of the 1940s and before yield to the extraordinary fragmentation of interests among multiple population subsets—principally by age, race, ethnicity, gender, and sexual identity. Consider that the proportion of minority to nonminority workers among the shrinking ranks of employed sponsors (and benefactors) of retirees will continue to grow rapidly. What sensibilities, what sympathies, one may ask, will leave the sons and daughters of the victims of bigotry (and themselves still suffering from discrimination on many fronts) more than grudgingly disposed toward hordes of retirees from the majority population in 2037?

Add the problem inherent in controlling tensions among male and female claimants to better—and better paid—jobs, to equitable remuneration, and even to fairness in the distribution of accommodations in the nation's millions of public restrooms, accommodations that now apparently favor males.[10] And, whereas some of us look with pride on the legal constraints we have conceived to reduce the free play of bigots, others are simply appalled by the progress of women and blacks resulting from what is pointedly called reverse discrimination by student aid seekers, medical school applicants, firemen in several cities, and scholarly social critics like Harvard's Nathan Glazer.[11]

The first of the bottom lines in this paper: The imbalance, in scientific terms, favoring theorems over axioms regarding the prospects for a growing force that will produce an equivalent increase in America's sense of personal responsibility is depressingly large. To put it another way, we are far, far more inclined to postulate self-correcting swings of pendulums than we are able to mobilize evidence supporting well-established axioms in the more traditional sciences that strong "forces also generate equal and opposite reactions" in the social realm.

Under these circumstances, most social scientists must confess that they would cast their votes with considerable pessimism regarding the prospects for America's returning to many of our older values. Population trends, it appears to me, are more likely to compound problems that were once linked to differences in *class* interests in America than to ease them, as relatively large economic classes increasingly give way to large numbers of "single interest" groups. Class conflicts, moreover, have been historically reduced by economic growth—the take from larger economic pies even if the percentage shares remain constant; we are now scrapping over moral, not essentially just economic issues. The real conundrum may be identified as involving conflicts among parties claiming combinations and permutations of two different sets or clusters of rights: traditional rights grounded in haves' and have nots' circumstances vis-à-vis property, on one side, and not-so-economic rights—justice, fairness, equal treatment, humane treatment, respect—on the other.

The potentially most serious intergroup problem hinted a moment ago: Baby Busters will be supporting the early half of the Baby Boom by 2018, while competing simultaneously with the latter half of this boom's population members for promotions in their job settings. Baby Busters will clearly suffer less than Baby Boomers did from "intracohort" competition, which is to invite attention to the good news. But, all things being equal, Baby Busters cannot avoid the bad news, the two aforementioned types of Baby Boom fallout viewed as "intercohort" disjunctions, nor can they avoid the conflicts they will sense between their interests, the interests of the earlier Baby Boomers own surviving *parents*, and the interests of older persons, otherwise.

III.   THE DISESTABLISHED POLITY

We turn now to the polity in preliminary efforts to assay the prospects inhereing in that subsystem of society for an emerging consensus that would move more Americans toward reassertions of a sense of personal responsibility for the commonweal, for framing their personal ends in terms of collective purposes, and for controlling their choices among means to their ends with eyes to community standards. I would first reassert that Americans are largely given to the view that market-driven outcomes are the best of outcomes, a view not contradicted to any significant degree by most voters in the last three presidential elections. Indeed, there are additional facts that may dismay the observer; many of the facts are less than reassuring.

Consider (1) the reforms in the financing of political campaigns, part of the "fall out" from the Watergate revelations; (2) the "democratization" of the two mainline parties; and (3) the shift to primary elections. These three developments have dwarfed the roles of the two principal parties as major *de facto* agents of social control. That development may well please the many critics of our traditional two parties, but such pleasure-taking hardly changes the consequential results of what may not be just a short-term eclipse of parties.

The results of castrated parties, when joined with the aforementioned splinterings among demographic groups, are such that we have changed America's traditional and long-vaunted pluralism—"Big Labor, Big Business, and Big Government,"—in John Kenneth Galbraith's phrase, in his discussions of "counterailing powers"—into something we might call "crippling pluralism": We now have a number of features in the United States that, though by no means identical, are depressingly (even frighteningly) similar to those that contributed to Germany's Weimar Republic's demise and that stalled France from the late 1930s until the advent, much later, of General/President DeGaulle's efforts to bring greater unity to the French people.

The consensus that finally did emerge in Germany—organized around Fascism—is more and more regarded by contemporary scholars as the "pathology of modernity," that is, as the result of growing popular dissatisfactions with the "liberated" spirits whose ways were associated by critics after World War I with social decadence. Even Christopher Isherwood, though himself a nonconformist on all fronts, noted that development in *I Am a Camera*, an early 1940s novel on which the hit musical "Cabaret" was later based. Once again, there is some distance between reducing intergroup tensions and producing consensus on broad issues. And in Nazi Germany, one will recall, the tensions among other groups gave way to the majority's deeply shared hostilities toward Communists and Jews. Among the spookiest of these parallels—the disaffected German veterans of WWI, with the same bullet-ridden pasts and parade-less homecomings, and the highly disaffected minority among American veterans of our misadventures in Vietnam.

The largest political unknown: the significance of the very large number of "no shows" among eligible voters in all recent elections; fewer than 28 percent of our eligible voters, for instance, sent Mr. Reagan to the White House in 1980. Political scientists have long argued over the pros and cons of heavy election turnouts in abstract terms to be sure, but no one really knows what is truly on the minds of the 40-odd percent among us who regularly sit out elections. The partisan splits among blacks and nonblacks and between males and females among those who have voted in the last three presidential elections are not, meantime, in the least suggestive of harmony.

As it happens, Mr. Bush's election victory was assured by the votes he won from white males alone. And it will take some time to gain a decent purchase on the effects of America's newest form of Jacksonian democracy; what we do know is that the Reverend Jesse Jackson persuaded 7 million voters, in 1988's primary elections, that we should be moving in directions very different from those staked out, for example, by Israel's American friends, and by critics of progressive taxation, welfare programs, and Affirmative Action programs. The oft-heard argument that "no shows" are basically contented with the way things are flies in the faces of the clear divisions that occur in every poll on abortion, gender questions, race issues, law and order concerns, the death penalty, gun controls, and tax reforms.

In these events one's sense of one's responsibility, of "where one stands," tends to be very essentially informed, in Sam Goldwyn's marvelous malapropism, "by where one sits": "male dominance," "affectional preference," "gun control," "judicial activism," the "Red Menace," are only a few among the wide array of chimera, shiboleths, and desiderata that block detached views of right and wrong on larger issues and act as defenses against suffering personal moral agonies over one or another issue among large numbers of Americans. Nor have our political leaders apparently divined ways of—or needs for—articulating visions of the heavenly city. The pitched battles between partisans concerning the nomination of District Judge Robert Bork to the Supreme Court suggested that much "settled law" is far from settled; indeed, large numbers of older norms are all in much worse disrepair than the term *unsettled* would capture.

The New York Times, meantime, reported, during the week of August 1, 1988, that major American real estate developers supported *each* of the sundry Republican *and* Democratic aspirants for their parties' 1988 nominations for the presidency; these developers' leaders were able to obtain $1,000 for every one of these candidates from friends. Journalists' interviews with donors revealed no personal despair over being political if not moral eunuchs.

We should recognize as well that congressmen increasingly reject the option to compete in what would be reelection campaigns because they have not been able to deliver, conscientiously, to all the "PACs" that supported them their first time around; the challenges in reforming a coalition of former supporters are formidable once office-holding beneficiaries have discovered that the wages of PAC support are "role conflicts." It was for long the case, well within the memories of many readers, that a Washington politico's loyalty (and well-brokered commitments) to one of the two principal parties was rewarded with dollar support there from that elicited loyalty to their parties. A brief reassertion of indignant Puritanism in the early 1970s, following Watergate, gave birth to a reformed—some would say *deformed*—political party system, after the Campaign Finance Reform Act, a system that is more often paralyzed than not on most matters of public concern and interest.

Indeed, one of the two liveliest topics—the other being furloughs for convicts—of debate between Messers Bush and Dukakis was over the Pledge of Allegiance's precise place in America's public schools' classrooms; oddly enough, a "long-settled" constitutional issue suddenly came to divide the candidates—and the people—right about in half. And then, 9 months later, came the flag-burning case, following which the president of the United States sought to undo the legal work of five of the Supreme Court's members by urging that we amend our Constitution, starting a battle that will very likely occupy antagonists well into the future.

Mention of the Pledge, penned by an avowed Socialist, serves to remind us that we are in constitutional terms not a democracy at all but a polity whose flag stands for the "United States of America and . . . the

Republic for which it stands."[12] Our federal system was designed, very thoughtfully, to be pluralistic, though the term is a more recent invention. When we add regional, intergenerational, and other divisions to the proliferation of single-interest groups and to the legally trifurcated federal apparatus, however, we find ourselves with diminished capacities for achieving agreements among ourselves on anything like "first principles." Generally such agreements require the help of a Senator Joseph McCarthy or other demagogue, a congressionally and popularly supported war, like World War II, or a Watergate. Note carefully, though, that our few moments of genuinely moral and ethical righteousness on most matters of principle have had very short half lives. It is a fact, I recall, that many GIs interviewed directly after combat exposures in Germany in World War II, allowed as how they thought Hitler's "final solution" regarding Jews was an appropriate one[13]; such splits are, of course, not new—but their proliferating qualities *are* new, a fact that adds to one's apprehensions about the prospects for sociopolitico moral consensuses.

I turn now to the more stereotypically familiar segments of the "total cultural environment" of the business community, that part of its environment that includes religion, the media, art, and education; "ideology" will be treated separately.

IV. AMERICA'S CULTURE: MELTING POT AND PRESSURE COOKER

The term *culture* among social scientists, as Walton helpfully reminded us in his Penn State paper, has generally been conceived to describe "the customs, traditions and values that together produce a distinctive way of life." He proceeded, as I indicated earlier, to identify our commitments to freedom and liberty and, with them, to personal responsibility, as forming the core of Americans' values, customs, and traditions. When we stray too far from these enthymemes, many believe, there are at least decent chances that there will be both reactive and "proactive" forces that will help, mercifully, to bring us back to our senses.

One of the most recent, useful, and historically well-informed, full-blown studies in support of what may be called a social pendulum theory is by Harvard's Samuel Huntington. He examined

> the persistent, radical gap between the promise of American ideals [on one side] and the performance of American politics [on the other] and shows how Americans, throughout their national history, have been united by the democratic creed of liberty, equality and hostility to authority. At the same time, he reveals how inevitably these ideals have been frustrated through the institutions and

hierarchies required to carry on the essential functions of governing a democratic society.

The pendulum swings, self correctingly between these poles in Huntington's reassuring volume.[14] Once again: I do not fully contest the cases regularly made for pendulumlike swings in our values; they have frequently been both elegantly and eloquently argued. It is valuable again, though, to elaborate on some of the realities—changes in realities, really—with which the next reequilibration or restorative processes' leaders must contend.

The first point is that America's culture was, essentially and for a long time, an amalgamation of different shadings of Western European and in some measure Eastern European cultures; these cultures, languages apart, had much, in common. And our capacities for integration were tested historically in ways that are very different from today's tests largely because earlier pilgrims to what S. M. Lipset called "The First New Nation" wanted in some diffuse sense to be Americans. Our capacities today for blending have apparently been reduced, as Penn's Political Scientist Karl von Vorhys puts it, more to those for tossing a salad than for tending a melting pot. Many of our black, Hispanic, Latino, Chicano and Amerasian compatriots have not, however much some dream of "a consummation devoutly to be whist," been bought wholesale into "mainstream" commitments.

It should quickly be added that majoritarians, by and large, have not generally been very open hearted in their definitions of how open an open society should be, as bitterly fought battles over school desegregation in the North show. The memories of ethnic Americans with United Auto Workers membership cards rocking and stoning schoolbuses headed for newly integrated schools are still fresh in the minds of the citizens of Pontiac, Michigan. That union's reputation, earlier, for liberal ways did not stop some of its members from illiberal actions that left grade schoolers screaming in fear.

Not many of us have ever heard members of our newer minorities or their leaders, meantime, speak as specifically or even in the same debating terms, as American Jews once did about the pros *and* cons of "assimilation" versus "acculturation." Some Americans argue that if indeed these "new" minorities conducted such debates observers might not so often be (or act) confused by black students, for example, who seek integration, but often live and eat separately, in dorms and dining rooms, on the nation's campuses. The fact may be that these issues are not joined by minority leaders because, in accord with their lights, the implied analogies with other social groups are falsely drawn.

Many Americans tend, however, to empathize with ethnic groups who agonize, a little bit at least, over the respective virtues of separatism and integration; they are less than sympathetic if choices are made in straightforward ways. Thus, in their first edition of *Beyond the Melting Pot*, Daniel Patrick Moynihan and Nathan Glazer looked happily forward to the day when black Americans would begin to act, so to say, like other ethnic groups. In the preface to their second edition, however, they decried blacks' "failures" to come along like the others in tones that bespoke these authors' great frustrations. The growing numbers of these new groups, separately and collectively, may also help explain these newer forms of something vaguely like segregated arrangements that are at once imposed upon and preferred, for example, by young blacks.

A significant dimension of all this: although some of my fellow immigrants in the 1930s and 1940s variously attended foreign language church services, read foreign language newspapers, listened to World War II news reports by shortwave "from home," attended Hebrew School, and did gymnastics at the German Turnverein, and paraded on Columbus Day, we did not study English "as a second language" in our native tongues, nor did we speak pridefully of "Norwegian English." Schools historically owned a mandate to "make Americans" out of their young charges as well as to teach them the "three R's"; the Pledge of Allegiance was an affirmation not of our militant patriotism vis-à-vis other nations but of our pride in our new nationality, and it was intended by its author to be so, as I have indicated in a footnote, in his appeal to the polyglot socialists he was advising.

It is at the very least a little bit difficult to believe that the admirable efforts, of late, to support ethnic and other forms of group pride can contribute significantly to a reciprocal exchange of interests, trade-offs, and value systems among these groups until the contending parties reach some enduring agreements about the limits on stridency, on one side, and on obstinately exclusionary tactics, on the other.

The modern version of the battle of the sexes, for example, is quite an intense one in many quarters; with few exceptions, the angriest antagonists talk at and past each other, of "feminist crazies," "male chauvinist pigs," and worse. The fact that the most important bones of contention are economic and political ones, at base, does not make politely calm debaters of the more determined of the two groups.

I will not presume to judge precisely how distant these numerous groups' value systems truly are, one from the other's. Behavioral indicators, though, are not exactly scarce. One recognizes them in the uses of an explosive proliferation of new venues for aggrieved parties in employment settings; in the highly combative posture of Mr. Reagan's administration toward "class action" discrimination suits; in the startling number of so-called racial incidents (in the North at Ann Arbor, Columbia, and Dartmouth College, most notoriously) on academic campuses and, as I have noted, in the life and death struggles waged by antagonists in the last several rounds of nominations to the U.S. Supreme Court.

The women's rights and Gay/Lesbian groups' efforts to gain rights, meantime, are reminiscent neither of the melting pot, nor of Emma Lazarus's wonderfully crafted celebration in prose of what, these days, is called diversity. Nor are today's ascerbic arguments indicative signs of a rebirth of the dialogue, say, between blacks and nonblacks within the NAACP's ranks of the early 1960s and before. I can recall autobiographically that several of my white colleagues and I left off as "pro bono" consultants to New York City's chapter of The Congress for Racial Equity when dear and grateful black friends in its leadership told us that we had become an embarrassment to them in their relations with their larger constituency, a circumstance we recognized; not all Americans understand such redefinitions of social realities, nor should it necessarily surprise us that they do not understand them.

Our churches are also increasingly riven by intramural conflicts over doctrine, over the limits on clergymen's behavior, over homosexuality, foreign policy, abortion, "prayers in school," and more. These of us who were cotenants with a Jesuit enclave in a Morningside Heights, New York, highrise in the early 1970s can recall the Berrigan brothers' difficulties with other Roman Catholics while hiding in our midst from the F.B.I.

Growing church attendance, long taken to be an indicator of religious commitment in the most general sense, appears now as much an indicator of growing ideological schisms among devout Americans who turn their churches into partisan bastions of their interests in redemption and the life to come in the hereafter. I will resist the temptation to comment on the politically and socially activist interests of video clerics. Or of other video religionists, complete with their own universities who, like the Reverend Fallwell, use commencement exercises in their institutions to vindicate one or another of the key perpetrators of "Contragate" while their heros awaited their trials.

Neither the pecadillos of some of these religionists nor their sometimes hate-filled perorations are very new, in either types or in numbers; what is new is that they are better covered by their lay colleagues in the media than were the screamings and ravings on the radio, say, of Father Coughlin in the 1930s. It is far easier for pro- and antireligious zealots and their quieter admirers to scorn each other with the help of the 6 o'clock news on the tube than it was before mass TV audiences could have help in the hardening of their categories from TV pundits. And hardly a single newscast covering local events fails to afford millions of viewers with detailed coverages of the interracial problems in their precincts.

The 1986 volume, *Economic Justice for All: Pastoral Letter on Catholic Social*

Teaching and the U.S. Economy, discussed with clarity elsewhere in this volume, marks another significant step towards the accommodation to America's secular ethic of older Catholic values, as embodied in Papal Encyclicals, regarding work and regarding occupational success, but it nevertheless offended some of such well-known Catholic laymen as William Simon, a member of Mr. Nixon's cabinet, for its "liberalism" and its cognate misgivings about capitalism. The term *liberal*, meantime, has succeeded to the places once occupied by pinkos, comsymps and fellow travelers.

The media's products, in turn, are harder to place on the continuum from pleaders for "one nation indivisible" to "dissensus mongerers." Consider how dramatically Bill Cosby's upper-middle-class playfulness with wife and kiddies contrasts with TV's images otherwise of black Americans, especially those on the evening news. Dolly Parton and fellow cast members keep us abreast of the novel ways in which women might assert their rights in the workplace "from 9:00 to 5:00." Dan Rather plowed contemptuously into a sitting vice president about "Contragate." President Reagan replied to TV interviewers' questions about "equal worth" with the scornful urge that it is "a cockamamie idea." Phillis Schlafly's admiration and NOW's contempt for antiabortion groups gain equal time. A *Wall Street Journal* veteran columnist is convicted of sharing "scoops" with inside traders among his friends, while a well-known stockbroker eats breakfast with *Business Week* printers and makes personally and organizationally profitable investments before the journal appears on newsstands to guide less fortunate readers.

Students on dozens of campuses, across all regions, spend countless weeks (among the 112 weeks leading to an undergraduate degree in the United States) building and tearing down shanties, protesting (or endorsing) the presences of government recruiters, and in registering their disagreements (or disagreements), in company with divided faculties, over whether students should be required to enroll in studies of "non-Western, nontraditional" persons and their cultures. Others scrap over whether or not scarce resources should be invested in the founding and nurturing of novel studies programs focused on one or another group of socially victimized population members. This partial list points to dissensus, not consensus, and, to the fact that resources—dollars and, in the views of antagonists, "power"—are limited, a fact that only serves to heighten the tensions between "them as have and them as don't."

Dissensus, social criticism, and philosophical debates have, of course, long owned special claims on America's campuses' agendas and on Veblen's "captains of erudition" who set them. Indeed, academicians have regained (and have even extended) their purchases, since Senator McCarthy managed to intimidate all too many of them, on the position that agree-ment and consensus is an enemy of all who hold, with Clark Kerr, that "people should be made safe for ideas," not that "ideas should be made safe for people." We ought accordingly and specifically *not* look confidently to colleges' and universities' populations as "point men" in generating a new deal in values widely shared; universities and colleges are the places that historically were and are still supposed, by most, to be settings in which "all truths are temporary." That battle cry rings hollow in the ears of many listeners inclined to hold only their own truths to be self-evident, and not a few of them can count on some support from campus intellectuals who live unhappily with colleagues who march to secular and iconoclastic drummers.

An only slightly less vaunted tradition—that higher education (espe-cially in the liberal arts and sciences) is only indirectly to be related to work and careers—has been gutted as "college-level" jobs continued to grow, after the early 1970s, but not at the same rates as those with which graduat-ing classes' numbers increased. The result: College grads were increasingly placed, by the mid-1960s, in what were high-school-level jobs only a decade earlier. Some of these looked with growing bitterness at the harvest of "underutilized" college grads—about 50 percent of the class of 1970—as did many high school grads who were pushed, by their fellow Baby Boomers with mortar boards, into lower level, lower paid jobs.[15]

Although the situation involving the massive underutilization of col-lege alums began to reverse itself in 1984, thanks in large part to the new "Baby Bust's" thin ranks (a development on the "supply side") that can be coupled with the rapid expansion of the service sector (on the demand side), the sense of broken faith in both high-school and college groups will likely survive among many Baby Boomers. College and high-school blacks might justifiably be especially disenchanted: Their schooling rates in-creased appreciably just before the decline in the growth rates of "good jobs" began—and were "rewarded" with *both* customarily lower earnings than whites *and* the displacements here noted.

Some observers will see better news in the academy's "credentialing" role now, for example, than I could discern in the late 1960s: Graduates' common "careerist" interests may offset the gender, racial, and ethnic divisions among them; time, conceivably, will tell us something. We can most certainly, though, apply some discount to the happiest news about the baby bust's prospects: The rapid increases in service sector jobs that will absorb many of them will not offer incomes like those paid to the manufacturing sector jobs that are growing at very much lower rates.

My own assessment is that the bitternesses among the afflicted groups will as likely be manifest in the form of restless personal disenchantment, voter apathy, and alienation in the workplace as in noisy intergenerational contests that might serve boomers' shared consciousness over their bleak prospects (and their number are in the millions). But the implied quiescence of those with unpromising prospects ought not be confused with a broad consensus on principles and values, as the palpable brooding among many young white males over Affirmative Action initiatives, for example, clearly indicates.

In each of the areas touched upon in the foregoing paragraphs there are moral questions—given inequities in the larger system—about education as means and education as an end unto itself; or individuals' and others' responsibilities for assuring the "equality of opportunities" and perforce (if more controversially) for assuring "equalities in outcomes" in Americans' lives; and about the responsibilities of decision makers in an almost endless number of school-related settings. One cannot be totally sanguine about democracy's vitality and well-being in a republic in which white males' votes are so often dispositive of critical public policies and the outcomes of presidential elections. "Economic growth"—read, significant growth—would undoubtedly help a great deal to reduce both noisy opposition and "quiet desperation," but the forecasts we see in print and picture undermine all hopes that busy hands will perforce be happy hands.

There is little room, moreover for give-and-take where any and all causes are framed in dramatically moralistic terms—and where winners are lauded and losers blamed for their respective circumstances. Where there are both conflicts among the interests of particular individuals, as such, as well as among those of different groups of individuals, there are fewer prospects for the emergence of relatively clear, clean "moral" or "ethical" guidelines that capture little moralities under larger moral umbrellas. Single, unemployed black mothers whose children attend school with "beepers," coded for calls from drug dealers making their rounds, face moral dilemmas over income needs and the urge to straighten out their errant children that may, for all the rest of us know, cause them agonies of conscience that other, better situated Americans can make soluble in lunchtime martinis.

It is not possible at this writing, on a more conventional cultural front, to predict the outcome of Senator Helms's urges, as I write, to deny federal support for artists who portray a crucifix in urine baths or "homoerotic sadism" in their productions, but it is clear that the senator and his antagonists are not aiming at comprehensive detentes over artistic questions. Neither does one observe that the majority of the nosier combatants engaging each other agonize nearly as much as they rant at each other in the matter of abortion. It would take something out of me, I must say, to show "grace under pressure" when mine enemy's arguments are articulated by a capable and well-armed bomber.

Although most of the conflicts listed in this section on culture do not exactly all involve "life and death struggles," as Cassandras might want to believe, neither can they simply be papered over by Pollyannas who wish devoutly for untroubled consummations of even implicit, that is, normative, agreements among the many, and a few good principles for all.

Mention of the matter of morals and ethics calls two other possible long-term changes in our culture to mind: The emergence of blithe-spirited and highly relativistic views toward a variety of personal matters, not the least of them pertaining to sexual preferences, as I have noted, and the growth in the ownership shares of America's capital by investors from historically very different cultures. Together, these changes point to reaffirmations of a relativistic rhetoric that has always been part of Americans' philosophy, "except moreso," even as moralistic critics finger their puritanical rosary beads. Let us consider the matter of relativism first by returning to the valuable metaphoric role that evolving sexual preferences have afforded me in this discussion.

We are living in a time that may soon prove to have been, overall, a critical test of Freud's theorem, enunciated in his last book (*Civilization and Its Discontents*), that the modern capitalist chapters in the story of the world's industrial development went hand in hand with ideas about individual responsibility. Then again it may not be so.

In *Discontents*, Freud argued—as Herbert Marcuse reminded us—that preachments about hard work "by the sweat of your brow" would not have brought us as far as they did if they had not been accompanied by the *de facto* repressive character of managers of workers' impulses, especially of their sexual impulses,[16] whose tired employees could be punished for "soldiering," "goldbricking," "withdrawing efficiency," or other workplace signs of fatigue or malaise.

Although the term, itself, is not heard as frequently in the late 1980s as it was 20 years ago, the highly relativistic notion of "situational ethics" still describes the view of millions that virtually "anything one would like to do is 'o.k.' if it doesn't hurt another person," with special though not exclusive reference to sexual activities. I use the word relativistic in the philosophical sense—in graphic popular usage the philosophical position is captured in the urge: "different strokes for different folks," the strokes to be judged essentially by a given culture's (or in the present case by a subculture's) parochial standards. Thus many individual Gays and Lesbians deplore stereotypes of themselves inspired by the AIDS epidemic.

But, what if a culture's standards regarding individuals' responsibilities, overall, are in flux? And what if, as is not uncommonly the case, some persons' responsibilities are waived for them by virtue of their membership in one or another interest group? Critics of group-based rights, like rights claimed by victims of discrimination, deplore statistical tests of progress in a given employment setting. An individual's progress, they insist, should be gauged against a person's experiences with an employer and his or her merit, not against the progress of a group claiming that they are deserving of treatments that compensate members for past immoralities.

On one side, the residues and derivations of the notion of situational ethics have contributed significantly to the generosity of a growing number of Americans toward those infected with AIDS antibodies or by the AIDS virus itself, for example. To the unhappy surprise of most moral majoritarians, even President Reagan elected, during the summer of 1988, to endorse one of three proposals urging that HIV/AIDS victims not be discriminated against.

On another side, the notion of situational ethics has contributed, in the minds of an essentially uncounted but undoubtedly very large number of Americans, to the HIV/AIDS epidemic, given the situationists' indulgent views about what "consenting adults" may do with, to, or for each other. For the most logical of these critics, two facts relate to what they take to be the governing question, to wit: Why do the indulgent Americans conceive that the matter of "harm to others" will be sensitively (never mind accurately) measured by those who knowingly embark on one or another potentially dangerous course of action? The subspecification: The correlation, in San Francisco, between alcoholism and HIV/AIDS infections, is demonstrably both positive and robust; the attractive theorems are that alcohol is part of the hardcore culture of "Gay bars" and that alcohol is a "disinhibitor." How reasonable about "safe sex," how thoughtful about his own infection (if he has been tested), and how honest can or will a "disinhibited" Gay or bisexual person be in a sexual encounter with partners?

It may also come to pass that the matters of HIV/AIDS infections and individual responsibility may be regarded by the tolerant among us as all too available grist for pessimists' mills or, worse, that Gays' and Lesbians' fearful critics offer only cynically exceptional instances of the correlates of cultural changes in this realm in that their arguments are based on "outlier" cases. To such critics, I would offer the reminder that many cultural changes in the United States involve precisely the shifts in sensibilities about what behavior was (and what behavior no longer is) "deviant" that have made for greater accommodations to new life-styles. But rights to unfettered pursuits of new life-styles are not won without opposition.

The most trenchant discussion of the cultural changes we have endured or experienced since the 1960s is by Daniel Bell[17] who identifies "the idea of modernity" (as the aforementioned students of the Weimar Republic do) as lying at the core of America's increasingly soluble cutlure; Dr. Bell goes on to argue that there are irreconcilable contradictions between the

> axial principles of the economy [efficiency], the polity [equality] and the culture [self-realization or self-gratification and values that emphasize unrestrained appetite]. The contradictions [he sees] in contemporary capitalism derive from the unraveling of the threads which once held the culture and the economy together, and from the influence of the hedonism which has become the prevailing value in our society.[18]

Bell's analyses of the family, religious developments, modern art, and other key aspects of a culture he characterizes as "a psychedelic circus" are not at all easily gainsaid. His conclusion: Capitalism requires a series of commitments—the delay of one's gratifications, for example, among the most important of them—that are totally denied by "modernity." Their indulgent views, for example, add differently to a modernist couple's children's values than those that once emphasized self-denial, frugality, and the rest. Midge Decter has written widely about what many regarded as the abdication of parental responsibilities and the radicalism, relativism, and nihilism of liberals' children in the late 1960s and early 1970s.

The residual cultural effect of the other development—the growth in foreigners' stakes in the American Economic Republic—are both a little less palpable and less colorful than the effects of our natives' emendations of older ways of living as worshippers, parents, men, women, and children. The basic facts of ownership, however, have been clearly stated in a thoughtful book by Martin and Susan Tolchin.[19]

The Tolchins' book had its origins in one of the authors' conversation with U.S. Senator Jim R. Sasser of Tennessee following a successful reelection campaign. In that campaign, Sen. Sasser was opposed by a certain Robin Beard whose campaign enjoyed substantial financial support from American managers in Nissan USA, a wholly owned subsidiary of a Japanese "multinational" with a truck manufactory in Tennessee. Although Sasser was neutral, Beard had opposed federal legislation that would have obliged car manufacturers to build a portion of every car sold in the United States with parts manufactured in the United States; Senator Sasser's critics at the Nissan works in Smyrna, Tennessee, were angry with his neutral stance on the proposed legislation.

The Tolchins' book, amply documented and thoughtfully written, reviews an extraordinary range of political, social, economic and, yes, cultural incursions by our new foreign-based stake- and stockholders, ranging from their highly successful resistance to antipollution reforms to quests for U.S. taxpayers' subsidies and abatements, with stops off for zoning easements, low cost loans, congressional grants, and acquisitions of defense-related manufactories of "semiconductors," and more. These incursions each involve value-laden issues.

Of particular interest in this context is the virtually total lack of sympathy for (and, often, significant evasions of) labor laws and affirmative action "regs" by most foreign owners, whatever their American managers may think about such things. A good part of the problem: individual states, hungry for jobs, vie with each other to bring foreign investors to their precincts. As MIT's business dean, Lester Thurow, pointed out in a review in *The New York Times* on February 24: "Selling America is bad enough but, when we subsidize the purchase price, [through tax breaks, for example] it is sheer madness." The impacts of foreign owners' values on our culture, backed by bucks, are not exactly predictable, but some of them can be divined.

Americans, Daniel Bell's demonic hedonics, have long financed the difference between what they produce and consume through what amount to IOUs, that is, passive investments by foreigners. The reduction in the dollar's value, designed to increase our exports, has made those IOUs less valuable to foreign lenders even as they have made American property— both realty and reproducible capital (industrial companies, buildings, and financial institutions) increasingly attractive buys. To maintain our consumption levels, as the ascetic Protestant Ethic of other days gives further and further way to our cravings for gadgets and gizmos big and small, we will need to borrow $200 billion per annum. These billions, Thurow reckons, will come in the form of foreign dollar holders' expanded active investments: "To put $200 billion in context," Thurow writes,

> In 1985 the value of all the reproducible capital in the U.S. was $10,900 billion. At the current rate of sale, all of these assets will have been sold in a little over 50 years. . . . America is in no danger of being completely sold tomorrow, but if current trends continue long enough, Americans will have sold off their capitalistic heritage. They will have become workers for the rest of the world, while the rest of the world will have become owners of America.[20]

The last clause in Thurow's summary is a *stunning* one. Given the significance of ownership, among the most basic of America's values, to the American creed, it is hard to imagine that most of us will not gradually be *unraveled* should the "selling off" be quickened.

The British lead the pack, but Canadian, Kuwaiti, Japanese, Dutch, West German, French, Swedish, and Australian investors (and their governments) collectively hold at least 10 percent and perhaps as much as 20 percent of our national debt and well over 16 percent of our bank assets. Foreign investments accounted directly for 2,536,553 jobs in the United States in 1983, up 8.3 percent from 1981, in such all-American companies as Hardee's (fast food to you gourmets), Doubleday, Viking Press, Smith and

Wesson (which arms both our policemen and not a few of those they check after), Grand Union, Carnation, half of National Steel, and, of all things, the Watergate complex. A French firm may, since the Tolchins' book appeared in 1988, be America's largest TV manufacturer at this writing, in the fall of 1989, while our top chemical and auto tire companies and more than half of our cement industries are already essentially in foreign hands. And, by withdrawing all interest in $2.9 billion in "T Bills" in 1987, these foreign investors forced a price reduction and an increase in yield by then-Treasury Secretary Baker; the Japanese promptly bought nearly half of the $9.3 billion 30-year bonds on public sale. As Ibsen urged: "Think of that." Will giant creditors *totally* abstain from using their leverage to influence the patterns of public expenditures for improving what Bell calls "the public household"? Or, more mundanely, on controls of automatic weapons, especially since (a minority of) such guns can no longer be imported.

The purpose here is not to weigh the economics of all this; foreign investments involve arguably both bad and good news. Rather, my concern is with the reversal of our "Cocacolonization" of the world, in the early decades after World War II, to the recolonization of America, from Rockefeller Center (Celanese's building), "Baby Doc" Duvalier's $1.65 million condo on the fifty-fourth floor of New York's Trump Tower and, but for an observant CIA agent, the sale of the Central Bank of California's banks in Fresno, Tahoe, and Burlingame, California, to Moscow Narodny Bank. Most Americans look with hope to Comrade Gorbachev's experiments with *perestroika*, but they are not joined by the Central Bank of California's cheers about the successful elements of "restructuring" of the U.S.S.R.'s economy that would materialize at the expense of the California bank's owners.

The recolonization of America has some significant cultural undertones. Assuming that our new patrons do not suddenly "pull the plug" on us for good, as they did not, in the short haul, do in the "T-Bill" case, and that we are well beyond the point at which one asks simply whether or not there will be impacts on American ways—the Tolchins demonstrate many workplace effects—the question now is how deeply these impacts go. Kuwati investors, for example, will not likely insist on having Miss America candidates wear veils at the annual Atlantic City pageant; indeed, that event's managers may themselves get away from cheesecake. But neither they nor the Japanese have taken at all kindly to American women's claims to "comparable worth," either at the plant level or in the largest sense of that term, though the language they use on this subject has not been as offensive to this cause's champions as Mr. Reagan's judgment that comparable pay is a "cockamamie" idea.

It is not likely, meantime, that we will require "cultural impact statements," as we do "environmental impact statements," for foreign business (and government) ventures, as when Japanese investors bought yet another large moviemaker in September, 1989. But we may very well wonder, as foreign investments increase, how much foreigners' holdings will add to the pressures in our pressure cooker society. The majority of nineteenth–and twentieth-century immigrants, we must remember, were poor people who moved into tenements, gratefully took what jobs were available and, for several generations, allowed American urban political machines to speak in their names; not many of them could buy million dollar houses in southern California, build multimillion dollar plants in Smyrna, Tennessee, or literally shape American consumers tastes, or augment their basic corporate activities by the formation of PACs, as our newcomers have, or mount media campaigns against policies they abhor, as in the case of tax proposals in California.

None of this is to suggest that the American business community will suddenly become a single interest group united with other American's against wealthy and demanding immigrants, foreign investors among them, a matter to which we turn in the next section.

V. CORPORATE LEADERSHIP: MANAGERIAL REVOLUTION OR DEVOLUTION?

It will soon be 56 years since A. A. Berle and Gardner C. Means published their ominous warnings about the implications of the separation of stock holding stakeholders from their hired "professional" managers and 46 years since Robert A. Brady delivered himself of an updated warning in *Business as a System of Power*. Neither study's forebodings about *a* single truly exploitative managerial elite would fully materialize: Powerful they may well be in small groups, but business leaders have not become a "class" with a coherent ideology and intramurally harmonious interests.

Indeed, the ranks of managers are quite well populated, thank you, with Adam Smith's individualists who, far more often than not, serve themselves individually far better than they serve a true community of fellow industrial magnates, captains of industry, or corporals of business bureaucracies. The testimony of some "inside traders," against others facing trials, in pursuit of favored treatment for themselves, are only among the more notorious instances of the lack of communitarian values among our business leaders; the familiar aphorism about the sad fate of honor among miscreants has earned considerable credibility from the actions of some of the alums of our finest law schools and most lauded MBA programs. Perhaps the rest of us should be happy, given the difficulties prosecuters face, that communitarian impulses are less widely distributed among some of these persons than they are even among piranhas that they otherwise resemble.

We note the fragmentation of our management "community," many of us, with only a little pleasure though, because a collection of powerful management-run interest groups is evidently not (and not automatically) the absolute opposite of a single more powerful interest group. "White Knights" may be preferred by a targeted company's chieftains to "sharks," but a few observers are perhaps justifiably worried about the public's interest, in a merger-mad world, in the growing concentration of ownership and management of manufacturing wealth in fewer and fewer hands: When titans have at each other, the losers' falls are perforce a good deal more ground shaking than when small businesses, as bankers colorfully put it, "go belly up."

Owners and managers are also divided on matters of protectionism and free trade, depending on their interests as exporters and importers. Generally, moreover, managers tend to be far more enthusiastic about the regulation of their competitors than they are about regulations that limit their own firms' freedoms of actions. Managers have also been known to engage their own stockholders, in the courts and in annual meetings, over their salaries and "perks," their performance, their policies, their response to would-be acquirers–raiders, their treatment of corporate personnel, their operations in South Africa, their sales of milk substitutes to postnatal Third World mothers, and so on and on. And the growing volume of intercorporate litigation calls Rousseau's savages more readily to mind than it does his "social contracts."

The conflicting interests, among business leaders thus add to all the others in the United States that we are reviewing. Although this is a fairly happy circumstance in a *de facto* if not a *de jure* democracy, it may leave one concerned about the resolution of moral–ethical issues, the best sides of which, as Walton allows, need wide support, and the worst sides of which need to be contested. Neither corporate businessmen—and women—nor stockholders have truly fulfilled Adam Smith's strongly worded apprehensions in *The Wealth of Nations* about their disposition to conspire endlessly at the public's expense behind their "corporate veils," nor have doctrinaire Marxists' forebodings about the ultimate successes of only a few large entities materialized.

But the evidence does not suggest that we can count on business leaders either guarding against or cleaning the nest foulers in their circles who bilk customers, pollute shorelines and inland waters with industrial wastes and oil spills, shut down plants without or with only trivial notice, pay bribes to ex-Pentagoners with friends still in high places, produce unsafe cars or airplanes despite whistleblowers' warnings, carcinogenic cigarettes, diluted fruit juice, sex orgies on video cassettes, or who draw upon the Department of Housing and Urban Development's funds as an income source after they leave the public's service to become "consultants."

VI.   IDEOLOGICAL TRENCHES AND FRONTIERS

There are of course, a number of principles on which most large corporate stakeholders and executives have long agreed "in principle": (1) Market forces should be given wide berths, especially by agents of central government; (2) economist Gary Becker's urge that "the combined assumptions of maximizing behavior, market equilibrium, and stable preferences, used relentlessly and unflinchingly, form the heart of the economic approach" is an urge that resonates well in executive suites even if, in a number of details, these suites' occupants will seek subsidies or rig prices and otherwise avoid the chill winds of the market place; (3) business leaders seem frequently to say "a thing worth doing at all is worth doing until marginal costs exceed marginal revenues"; however troublesome such a view of "worth" is, I confess have never met a business leader who has plotted these curves outside of a classroom; and (4) as Sir Edwin Chadwick put it, "When the sentimentalist and moralist fails, he will have as a last resource to call in the aid of the economist." So go the refrains in the neoorthodox anthem. Beyond them, the belief is widely held in business circles that life is ordered in ways that lend themselves to careful measurements and thus to quantitative analyses that yield objective results.

For all the disingenuous claims to objectivity, we may insist, there is a moral imperative immanent in the underlying model: The collective interests of a society's members, "the good of all" with only a few exceptions, are best served in a system in which free men and women doggedly pursue their legal interests in accord with their individual preferences; all men are, in fine, islands unto themselves in a society in which prices can be put on anything, as any life insurance salesman knows, and in which the marketplace becomes the arbiter of values in what we nevertheless pledge that we devoutly conceive to be "one nation, under God." There is only trivial evidence that those who live by these contradictions suffer, even a little bit, from the disconfitures that psychologists suppose are the correlates of "cognitive dissonance."

Business owners' (and usually their managers') more-than-nominal commitments to aphorisms (and the narrow definitions of personal business's responsibility they clearly imply) should only be mocked by business's critics, however, if these critics are also prepared to blow corporations and their captains, as we know them in legal and conceptual terms, clean out of the water; mockery is one thing; active pursuits of fundamental reforms of structures are quite another thing. It is the case, and it should be recognized in this context as a point of departure, that corporations formally earned several basic legal rights of American persons in 1819 in Chief Justice Marshall's opinion for the Court in the Dartmouth College case.

In that case all the stockholders of a corporation were made as into one person, with specific rights to enter into binding contracts and with its owners' liabilities for the corporation's doings significantly limited, among other attributes of natural persons.

So limited have these liabilities been that persons-cum-corporations were, for a long, long time, seen to be victims of an illegal conspiracy perpetrated by its individual employees if their workers *acted* collectively under the aegis of a labor union, membership in which was otherwise legal. It is neither an accident nor an entirely miserable preoccupation with their own welfare, in these events, that business leaders impute power to impersonal forces beyond their control, a defense Walton suspects will be increasingly less effective as popular misapprehensions about business leaders' conduct continue to grow.

But the defense these leaders can and will mount against the popular legions Walton hopes will be mobilized against derelictions by business folks follows from the logics built into the formidable protections with which business leaders and their owners enjoy. These protections have been regularly accorded them through acts of incorporation by the several states and by constitutional safeguards. The advantages that corporations derive from legal doctrine are of no small moment to our economic system; to deny their owners "limited liability" while making *persona ficta* of them, for example, is to deny one of the very appeals of the corporate form to investors who would not otherwise risk their fortunes, large or small, in these ingenious products of social technology.

On one side, one thus has a valuable economic form rooted, long before the Dartmouth College case, in natural law.[21] Corporations are serviceable entities and, as they have evolved in the United States, they have been extraordinarily important component parts of our progress as an "economic republic." One's admiration for them, though, should not blind us to the fact that these valuable social inventions are, by law, the *very opposite* of agencies that can be called to moral account.

Put another way, one has a basic institution in our capitalist system whose essential raison d'être is predicated upon the relocation of responsibilities from "natural" to corporate persons. Those who seek more responsibility from men and women of business might well ask themselves how we can best deal with what is a conundrum wrapped in dialectics;

how, logically, can we simultaneously stress the great value of the business community's owning limited liabilities and truncated personal responsibilities while urging that its rank (if not its filers) be personally responsible for what they undertake in the names of their corporations? We have, according to a cherished legal adage, no right, as such, to ask a corporation to act morally, for "there is no right without a remedy." Even in the case of antitrust law, criminal provisions applicable to corporate principals have been, until recently, rarely applied. (While I have not reviewed the data, a colleague, W. Bruce Bassett, reports that there have recently been hundreds of convictions of executives for violations of legal prohibitions against "vertical integration.")

Some, recognizing that our 50 states charter corporations in accord with 50 different configurations of rules and regulations, have urged that corporations be federally chartered. Among the arguments favoring such a reform: There could prospectively be full-fledged formal debates in Congress about just how limited the liabilities—read responsibilities—of a corporation, its owners, and its managers should be, with prospects that a specific list of sins would be beyond redemption. It is my clear recollection that this proposal, the child of antiestablishmentarian passions in the late 1960s, was a victim of infanticide; the Ralph Naders who were the progenitors of the idea returned, after the interment, to chasing after living delinquents, most prominently at General Motors in those days, "one on one."

Stockholders, protected by the doctrine of limited liability, were soon joined in the ranks of those who were assured that though their sins would be discovered, they would be neither punished nor even very seriously maligned by any but Nader's Raiders' press releases or by muckraking "investigative reporters." The protective mechanism involved is a costly one for consumers given that the sky-high costs of malpractice insurance for corporations' executives and directors are passed on to the rest of us in the prices we pay for goods and services. Malpractice insurance in common with some other private insurance plans, meantime, is America's answer to the problem of socializing risk such that there is barely a hint of an antiindividualistic premise while "perpetrators" are insulated from those who might dream of pursuing them.

Walton does not address the conundrum as such, but he does correctly point out and forcefully against the case I have outlined, that the courts are increasingly holding even unknowing and unwitting corporate chiefs (and corporate board members) responsible for the actions of their employees. These cases derive from the conviction by a court of a certain Mr. Dotterweich whose employees in his Buffalo plant adulterated and misbranded pharmaceutical products in 1943. It is also true that 29 executives from the then 29 largest heavy electrical equipment manufacturers who engaged in bid rigging from 1935 to 1959 were jailed for 30 days, and that others have been indicted as vertical integrators, in accord with the rarely applied section of the Sherman Anti-Trust Act noted a moment ago.

But the boom in sales of insurance policies, on one side, and the rush of indicted executives to join up as witnesses against their confreres, for the prosecution, in return for trivial sentences, on the other, cannot exactly inspire hope that personal responsibility will be elevated to dizzying legal–philosophical heights.

These misgivings call to mind an enduring asymmetry in our sense of owners' and managers' responsibilities and those of workaday Americans.[22] Thus, unemployed American workers, especially the least skilled and educated among them, are quite generally held responsible, personally, for their trying circumstances when the economy is moving sideways; our prejudices against them are marked clearly by the declining numbers of laid-off or redundant workers who are eligible for unemployment insurance. But, on the upside, their employment is also held against these would-be workers because most of us have been urged by economists to believe that the threat of inflation grows in proportion to increases in employment whenever these increases are coupled with declinations in unemployment. I have never been able to satisfy myself that one can forever persuade the millions to which we here allude that they are legitimately damned whatever they do. One realistically responsible reaction to their two possible fates, in these events, is to yield to the schizophrenia such conflicting treatments might understandably induce: If I lose my job, it is essentially my fault; if I regain it, under otherwise good circumstances, I contribute blameworthily to inflation.

Speaking of such two valued logics, consider the views of conservatives that the workplace must essentially be managed bureaucratically but that the larger social system's logic should stress liberty, freedom, and free private enterprise; planning, thoroughgoing divisions of labor, and detailed orderings of tasks and authority should, however, occur in factory, mill, lab, and office, not in Washington. In a waggish moment, Marx summed it up in his preface to *Das Kapital*: "It never ceases to amaze me," he wrote, "that the simple, strongest criticism that the factory owner can make against Communism is that it would make a factory out of all society." Many liberals, I hasten to add, simply turn this position on its head: Let us democratize the workplace, expand workers' participation in decisionmaking, and otherwise reform the workplace. At the same time, let us explore the prospects for a "new industrial policy," new "social contracts," "incomes policies," detailed regulatory arrangements, and some significant elements of macroeconomic planning.

What is interesting about these two camps' demiurges is that one group of ideologues cannot realistically attack the other's inconsistencies without confessing to its own. I do not see too many signs of a "centerist" position between the two contradictory ones. Employee Stock Ownerships Plans (ESOPs), involving a kind of centerist reform, have pretty generally turned into new mechanisms of capital formation in pursuit of leveraged buyouts, not industrial democracy, whereas "work reform" programs appear and disappear with booms and busts in the economy. And the main debate between Democrats and Republicans continues to be over the role of central government in the economy. In these debates, the question of responsibility is addressed not at all—in favor of bizarre tax laws and juggled interest rates that, with the help of technical momenclature, become the "fiscal" and "monetary policies" that will afford *persona ficta* with incentives to do well if not, necessarily, to do good.

VII.   CONCLUSION

We have found ways in America of extolling the virtues of individualism in ways that couple the concept with individual responsibility. On the contrary, we uncouple them in dedicated, systematic, and highly imaginative ways. Schisms among proliferating and militant single-interest groups assure that would-be recouplers face formidable odds.

If and when the sensibilities of the majority are offended by excesses, we litigate, we do not moralize; and, in the process, our perpetrators often plead *nolo contendre*, as my son pleaded when he was small and was questioned about a suspicious development: "I didn't do it, Daddy, and I won't do it again." And we actively help prospective corporate miscreants to be happy and not worry, as the song has it, by allowing their companies' accountants to deduct their fines from corporate taxes as "costs of doing business."

Readers can surely add additional case instances of the types reviewed in these pages, but the conclusion that we are not, at the moment, heading either very quickly or forcefully toward major revisions in the writs and warrants that govern the American Economic Republic's principal economic actors, appears to be a reasonable one. The number of investigations, indictments, congressional and court proceedings involving leading White House figures from Mr. Reagan's residence in the capitol might trigger some groundswells that will wash over a miscreant here and there, but the rallies mounted in their support are equally determined to urge that we look the other way.

A pragmatic view of all this would leave one persuaded that the price we pay for a lack of consensus on key principles of behavior may not be an excessive one, in the views of a majority of Americans. The old pluralism, "Big Labor, Big Government, and Big Business," was not, after all, without its own well-informed critics, particularly from the flanks on the far Left and Right. Perhaps it is enough, as Daniel Bell notes in passing, that we urge moral virtues on all without being too bent on puritanical enforcement programs, absent consensually argued-upon norms. Bell points to the practical wisdom, in the meantime, of La Rochefaucauld's dictum that "hypocrisy is the homage that vice owes to virtue"; hypocrites do help us by pointing out the evil ones among us and, as Bell sees it, we at least *salute* the norm.

Whatever we can sensibly expect of our leaders in all our other precincts, meantime, will have to be informed in large measure by the examples set at the highest levels of governance, private and public. Revelations about misbehavior and essentially subversive beliefs in *those* circles can only reinforce the misgivings we can nurse about the prospects for progress on the moral frontier.

NOTES

1. Cambridge, MA: Ballinger Publishing Co., 1988. I should state at the outset that these pages benefit greatly from conversations with Jack P. Gibbs, at Vanderbilt University, during 1983–1984.
2. Whereas Walton refers to "the Market," I note that *four* distinctive but interrelated markets need to be scanned to emphasize that market scanning, itself, will have to become *far* more sophisticated than it was in bygone days. A few markets actually do require a sense of the changing cultures in which they operate: Labor markets in an age of affirmative action are not what they were in many respects; Ralph Nader's name in the products arena, moreover, is about as well known as any business leader's. And the *Kulturdebat* over mergers and acquisitions, in the capital markets, very evidently is getting noisier. For an elaboration, see Arne Kalleberg and Ivar Berg, *Work and Industry: Structures, Markets and Processes* (New York: Plenum Press, 1978).
3. This paper appears in Murray Murphey and Ivar Berg, eds., *Value Theory in 20th Century America: Essays in Honor of Elizabeth Flower* (Philadelphia: Temple University Press, 1988). The late A. A. Berle offered a primitive version of Walton's thesis in *The American Economic Republic* (New York: Harcourt, Brace and World, 1963), in which he argued that America might well be saved from the worst excesses of capitalism by the evolution of what he called a "transcendental margin," that is, normative constraints understood by and applied by conscience-stricken business leaders to the decisions they must make.
4. See O. Eckstein, *The Great Recession with a Postscript on Stagflation* (Amsterdam: The North-Holland Publishing Company, 1978), and a discussion thereof in Arne Kalleberg and Ivar Berg, *Work and Values: Structures, Markets, and Processes* (New York: Plenum Press, 1987), Chapter VI. For a discussion of America's contributions to the apparently not so inevitable emergence of OPEC, see Jack Anderson, *The Great Fiasco* (New York:

Times Books, 1983), and Anthony Sampson, *The Seven Sisters: The Great Oil Companies and the World They Shaped* (New York: Viking Press, 1975).
5. For examples, see Walter Adams, ed., *The Structure of American Industry*, 6th ed. (New York: Macmillan, 1982), and F. M. Scherer, *Industrial Market Structure and Performance* (Chicago: Rand McNally, 1980).
6. The phrase borrows from Daniel Bell's "Work and its Discontents" first published in *The End of Ideology: On the Exhaustion of Political Ideas in the Fifties* (New York: Collier Books, pp. 227–274).
7. "Responses 'Dismaying' in Poll of Teen Agers," *The New York Times*, August 10, 1988, p. A13.
8. "People Aiding People to Tune of $19 billion a Year, "*The New York Times*, October 27, 1988, p. A22.
9. See Samuel H. Preston, "Children and the Elderly in the U.S.," *Scientific American*, December 1984, 251, No. 6, pp. 44–49.
10. Harvey Molotch, "The Rest Room and Equal Opportunity," *Sociological Forum*, Volume 3, Number 1, Winter 1988, pp. 33–47.
11. Nathan Glazer, *Affirmative Discrimination: Ethnic Inequality and Public Policy* (New York: Basic Books, 1975). See especially, Glazer's Chapter 6, "Morality, Politics, and the Future of Affirmative Action," in which the author summarizes many Americans' abhorrence of recent legislative and judicial efforts to effect both more equal opportunities and, especially, more equal outcomes in the economic race.
12. It is an irony that Mr. Bush, an avowed critic of the state as an agent of intervention, is the Pledge's champion: It was written by Edward Bellamy's brother, in an effort to win support for the state among Socialists.
13. The fact was reported in series of massive studies of the American Soldier by Samuel Stouffer and a corps of social scientists soon after World War II.
14. Samuel P. Huntington, *American Politics: The Promise of Disharmony* (Cambridge, MA: Harvard University Press, 1981). Citation from dust jacket. Italics added.
15. I. Berg, *Education and Jobs: The Great Training Robbery* (New York: Praeger, 1970).
16. H. Marcuse, *Eros and Civilization* (Boston: Beacon Press, 1955).
17. *The Cultural Contradictions of Capitalism* (New York: Basic Books, 1978).
18. Ibid, pp. ii and iii.
19. *Buying Into America: How Foreign Money is Changing the Face of Our Nation* (New York: Times Books, 1988).
20. *The New York Times*, February 24, 1988, p. C9; italics added.
21. See Otto Gierke, *Natural Law and the Theory of Society, 1500–1800* (Boston: Beacon Press, 1957 edition), pp. 162–198, and passim. I note, en passant, that the Dartmouth College decision was handed down by the Supreme Court in 1819. Slaves—*property*—were emancipated in 1863; for 44 years *things* were accordingly made *persons* while many black *persons* remained things.
22. As these pages were undergoing revision, the Johns Manville Corporation settled claims from workers and clients suffering from one or another version of asbestiosis by converting 60 percent of its assets into a trust benefitting claimants. The company's assessment of the "social accounting" process involved here will have to await future progress reports. Meanwhile, the company will be operating nearly two-thirds of the time for its own victims.

6

Unions in the Nineties
Implications for Business Ethics

James W. Kuhn

The significance of, and difficulties involved in, managerial abandonment of an anachronistic adversarial ideology can best be understood through a capsule history of corporations and unions over the last century. During that period, the nation made only slow ethical advances in its treatment of workers.[1] Primary responsibility for this slowness rests with business managers, though most labor leaders and unionists have comfortably adapted an adversarial stance. Both groups are going to have to change attitudes and behaviors if advances are to be made and the past is very relevant to present needs.

I. UNIONS AND CONSPIRACIES

In the latter half of the nineteenth century, American businessmen sought to combine property, capital, and managerial control in such a way that they would win legal approval and legislative encouragement in order to fully reap the rewards of efficiency and of size. First in railroads, then in retail trade, and quickly thereafter in the processing of basic raw materials, large organizations promised large financial returns and better services than the economy had ever before known. They tried pools and then trusts, but the courts ruled that these devices were combinations in restraint of

James W. Kuhn • Graduate School of Business, Columbia University, New York, New York 10027.

trade, inappropriate, and illegal. However, courts could not continue to deny relief to the large business organization: The efficiencies of scale it permitted, given the emerging and prevailing technology, made the argument compelling—despite historic theory and traditional principle. With impressive legal legerdemain, the Supreme Court was able to discover in the newly approved Fourteenth Amendment, the rationale it needed to squeeze the huge bulk of the new, looming business corporations behind the mask of the Constitutional term *person*.[2] Magically, an artifact became a constitutionally protected species.

By 1901, when J. P. Morgan and his associates created the then-gigantic United Steel Corporation, it would have appeared to an outsider that every large combination was now possible, but not to the public or, particularly, to judges. Unions continued to be seen as combinations, pure and simple, and thus dangerous as well as illegal, if not in their existence, at least in any serious activity they might undertake. Because judges could find no property behind unions, as they easily discerned in the case of corporations, they found no good Lockean reason to declare them persons.[3] More than a third of a century later, when the Supreme Court had to decide whether Congress could constitutionally encourage labor unions, it still found no substantial reason for ruling in their favor; the best justification the majority could provide was that of expediency. Unions were declared legal simply because of "the necessities of the situation."[4]

II.   UNIONS AS THREATS TO TRADITIONAL AMERICAN INDIVIDUALISM

Not only did business managers succeed in winning an advantage over unions in the legal definition of their personhood, but they also skillfully redefined the meaning of traditional American individualism. That individualism, displayed most widely among the nation's small, independent farmers was not well suited to the needs of large business firms. Through the latter half of the nineteenth century business managers found themselves directing hundreds, then thousands, and sometimes hundreds of thousands of employees in vast, cooperative efforts. individualistic employees, withdrawing from the group and pursuing their own interests, directing themselves and seeking to achieve their personal goals, were not apt to make up a productive, useful work force.

Early corporate leaders attacked individualism as out of date and harmful in an industrial society. However, individualism and the values it identifies were so deeply embedded in the American ethos that the attackers quickly discovered the dangers of rejecting it. Managerial reinterpretation served the needs of the large corporation very well, and all the better if unions had to contend with the originally defined notion of individualism. Many workers, and a large segment of the public appeared, to accept the redefinition but applied it only to the business firm, not to other institutions. The term continued in use, but with a bifocal meaning that gave it a peculiar twist indeed.

A few of the early business leaders, such as John D. Rockefeller, Sr., bluntly rejected individualism; it was obviously wasteful and incompatible with the operation of the new business organizations, he declared:

> [The combination movement] had to come, though all we saw at that moment was the need to save ourselves from wasteful conditions. . . . The day of combination is here to stay. Individualism has gone—never to return.[5]

Chauncey M. Depew, in an 1897 address at the unveiling of a statue in honor of Vanderbilt University's benefactor, Cornelius Vanderbilt, disagreed with Rockefeller. He asserted that "the American Commonwealth is built upon the individual," of whom Commodore Vanderbilt was a conspicuous example.[6]

Andrew Carnegie also declared that his own success exemplified the promise of, and the opportunities for, individualism. He reveled in his own "intense individualism," mixing with it a thoroughgoing paternalistic concern for his workers and poorer neighbors. Even as he preached and wrote about his individualism, the giant company he had helped create, Carnegie Steel, in 1901 became the core of United States Steel. Depew's and Carnegie's praise of individualism accorded well with the traditional American ethos, but their own business activities flagrantly contradicted it.

The *American Bankers' Magazine* suggested that the decline of the old individualism and the rise of business corporations would help, not hurt ordinary Americans. In 1902 it offered the opinion that:

> The general character of the charges against modern business methods is that they injure the individual in his opportunities to acquire wealth. . . . It is probable that the new business order may reduce the number of great prizes, but that it will increase the opportunity for a large number to arrive at a competence. . . . It is too soon to assert that in the long run, after the combination system has been fully developed and perfected in all its details, it will bring about a greater equality in the distribution of wealth than could be hoped for under the competitive system, but there are many signs that lead to this conclusion. It is highly probable from existing indications that the intense individuality that characterized the average citizen of the United States during the first century of the republic is gradually softening.[7]

To attack individualism, as Rockefeller did, or to point to the benefits available in giving it up, as the editorialist of the *American Banker's Magazine* did, was not convincing to many Americans. De Tocqueville had first recognized the fierce independence of the American character and called it *individualism*.[8] He recognized it as a powerful and appealing social ideal, arising from the condition of social equality common throughout the nation. Both praise for, and defense of, individualism were woven tightly into almost every strand of American thought. Ralph Waldo Emerson, a characteristic spokesperson for his time, provided an individualistic philosophy; President Andrew Jackson offered a political expression for it; and the Historian Frederick Jackson Turner constructed a theory of American history around the notion of individuals moving from crowded society to a new beginning on the frontier.[9] As late as the 1930s, in the midst of the worst depression the economy had experienced, Herbert Hoover extolled individualism in extravagant terms:

> While I can make no claim for having introduced the term "rugged individualism," I should be proud to have invented it. It has been used by American leaders for over a half a century in eulogy of those God-fearing men and women of honesty whose stamina and character and fearless assertion of rights led them to make their own way of life.[10]

The realities—advancing technology, urban living, and the spread and growth of the large corporation—made traditional individualism more difficult to achieve and created even greater economic and social interdependence. As Rockefeller realized, they indeed made the older concept and practice of individualism anachronistic. Individualism, as de Tocqueville perceived it and as managers feared it, was a detachment of the individual from the group—the cutting off of persons from each other. Such separation was not desirable in the large corporation. The ties of interdependence could not be undone without destroying economic progress and the American level of productivity. By the middle of the twentieth century, the editors of *Fortune* could celebrate the solution that modern professional business managers had effected—a reconciliation of traditional individualism with the needs of the interdependent corporation:

> The concept that appears to be emerging, as the answer of the modern individual to this challenge, is the concept of the *team*. It is an old concept but it is being put to new uses. As a member of a team an individual can find full opportunity for self-expression and still retain a dynamic relationship to other individuals . . . the concept of the team has the power to challenge the individual to seek his self-expression, not along purely egotistic channels. . . . A community—big or little—is created, and through it the individual finds a higher expression of himself.[11]

Employees, and even middle-level managers, often confused the old individualism with the new. Workers who inventively bargained with supervisors for special benefits for themselves and the members of their work groups might realize a self-expression at the place of work that helped themselves, but their side agreements created precedents that caused trouble for top officers as well as industrial relations managers. A subordinate manager who refused, when ordered by his superiors, to sell dangerous, below-standard oil-well casing for use under conditions of high pressure might lose his job.[12] A bank manager who protested his superior's illegal transfers of funds to avoid paying taxes was fired.[13] Such employer expressions of individualism are not often appreciated by managers in many firms. Managers usually expect employees to follow the late Sam Rayburn's injunction to incoming members the House of Representatives: "To get along, *go* along."

In short, corporate individualism, to use an oxymoron, is the freedom to participate in the corporate community. Where originally individualism was freedom *from* society, it now becomes freedom *within* society. Self-reliance has been transformed into other-directed sensitivity; independence has been changed into team play; autonomy has become initiative within organizational bounds. John W. Ward has pointed out that there are two different systems of values going under the same name that verge toward opposites—one toward the isolated person, the other toward society. For a century, at least—since the rise of the large business corporation—Americans have held both views to be valid, judging unions by the former and the corporation by the latter.[14]

One should note, however, that the traditional understanding of individualism rested upon a moral foundation that the new does not. That foundation was rooted in the Puritan tradition that gave religious sanction to both individualism and work as a "calling." Prudence, sobriety, propriety, and dignity in work easily attached themselves to the worker imbued with the old values of individualism. Whether they accompany the new individualism is a question to consider carefully. Do those who sit at or close to the apex of many layered hierarchies have a careful regard for the values generally held by those beneath them? Only with such respect, and affirmation, of those values will managers win the necessary cooperation that makes productive, effective, and efficient coordination of their corporate enterprises possible. Yet so commonly accepted is the nontraditional, other-directed individualism in business organization that union leaders themselves sometimes ignore the relevance of, and need for, the older form in the union. The result is to hold unions to a dysfunctional and destructive standard, not applied to business.

Both courts and public have persisted in their views of unions as combinations of people who should be free to express the rights and values of traditional individualism. A popular view, certainly held at least by many conservatives, libertarians, and free-market advocates as well as by others in the electorate, is that unions are vast and sprawling organizations, governed by "bosses" intent upon forcing members to support disliked political actions, to join unneeded, dangerous strikes, and to work only when and where union rules dictate. Unions, almost by definition, form, and purpose, in pressing their members and employees to a conforming behavior, threaten to extinguish the value that original individualism extolled.

The result is curious: One kind of corporate organization called the business firm is perceived as a promoter and protector of individualism, whereas the other corporate organization, called the labor union, is seen as a threat to individualism. The first therefore deserves support, whereas the second needs to be regulated and constrained. Unionists thus find themselves in a double bind: They are found guilty of squashing individualism within their unions, and also as third parties, are guilty of interfering with the expression of business employees' individualism within the firm. In fact, the two corporate bodies often treat their members much alike, neither being able to tolerate a high degree of traditional individualism. Nevertheless, the public focus of attention on unions' threats to individualism has diminished their organizing appeal to workers who have "brought" the corporate definition of individualism. Few business managers show much concern about the misperception involved and we may presume that most accept the bifocal view of individualism in business firms and in unions as both natural and right. If true, one may ask such questions as these:

1.   Have managers too often—and too casually—established a neo-feudal society at the place of work?
2.   Have organization managers developed legitimacy that is viable only because of special and temporary economic conditions when competition favored American business?
3.   Are there other and more effective ways managers might structure their organizations so they can serve their various constituencies more in accord with traditional American social and economic ethos?

III.   PROBLEMS OF ORGANIZING UNIONS

This excursion into the past helps us to understand our future, but it must also address another moral issue: If individuals are to be treated as ends in their own right, not as means for managerial ends, must they not have a right to form associations that protect their other rights? Workers must morally have the right to organize, and for more than 50 years they have enjoyed the legal right to form unions, though it is hedged about with many judicially prescribed constraints and limited by a suspicious public. Consequently union organizers have never had an easy task. In addition, industrial problems have compounded the difficulty of pulling together and maintaining unions. Given the high level of ordinary labor turnover,[15] the closing of old and the opening of new plants, and the rise and fall of firms as well as industries, unions have had to organize continually, even to maintain membership, let alone increase it. As a consequence, organizing ran ahead of labor force growth only in the two decades after the passage of the Wagner Act in 1935. Even during the period of this rapid growth, some unions gained far more than others, for there exists a variety of unions that pursue quite different purposes.[16]

On the one hand, unionists of the Knights of Labor (a vast, but poorly organized union in the early 1870s) hoped to reform the economy and improve the working conditions that oppressive employers then offered. Members of the International Workers of the World (IWW), on the other hand, sought to overthrow the capitalistic business system and replace it with one that would serve workers better. The union never attracted many members, but their aims and tactics gave them a notorious reputation. In the big cities, predatory, corrupt, and racketeering unions developed and flourished in the building trades, in the Teamsters, among some dockworkers, and, before the 1930s, even in parts of the needle trades. Corruption has continued to the present time—all too common in construction, the trucking industry, and in some of the other service industries, particularly at the local level. Unfortunately, the labor federations have seldom possessed either the will or the authority to combat such besmirching activities; they have continued as an all too prominent strain in unionism, reducing public acceptance of, and confidence in, organized labor.

All along, from the early 1800s, organized workers practiced another form of unionism, which during the early twentieth century, was to become dominant. Labeled *business unionism*, it developed first among craft workers whose skills and usual ownership of tools provided them a strategic position from which to negotiate. Those joining the American Federation of Labor (AFL) were the most stable and enduring. Samuel Gompers led them in their acceptance of the capitalistic market system as well as the dominating role that managers, as representatives of stockholders, held in directing the affairs of business. Before the turn of the century, Gompers asserted that "we are living under the wage system, and so long as that lasts, it is our purpose to achieve a continually larger share for labor, for the wealth producers."[17] Business unionists directed their efforts toward winning employer recognition of collectively negotiated terms defining wages, hours, and conditions of work through which they gained a measure of control of the job or rights attached to it. They sought to take wages out of competition, as much as possible, requiring employers rather to compete among themselves on the basis of technological innovation, process, product, marketing, and design. In return for the relative stability gained, business unionists used strikes and other forms of economic pressure only as a tactical weapon, not as part of a strategy to undermine the economic system.

Employers dealt with business unions when they could not otherwise avoid them, but the rising cadre of professional managers in the large corporate firms, particularly after World War I, resisted both them and their attempts to bargain collectively. Managers championed "The Open Shop" and "The American Plan," both antiunion programs designed to forestall union organizing, and if workers did form unions, the organizations would be essentially powerless, dependent upon employers' largess.[18] In 1920 Gompers, seeking to quiet managerial fears that unions were seeking to replace managers, wrote:

> Collective bargaining in industry does not imply that wage earners shall assume control of industry, or responsibility for financial management. It proposes that employees shall have the right to organize and deal with the employer through selected representatives as to wages and working conditions.[19]

His words brought no reassurance to managers. The more progressive among them sought to avoid unions by proactively and unilaterally introducing paternalistic personnel policies designed to improve and regularize their workers' welfare.

The unremitting hostility unionists faced and the marginal position they had won for themselves over a century of struggle had gradually persuaded them to mold their organizations, ironically, into defensive, distorted smaller mirror images of business management: hierarchical, authoritarian, property minded (about work rules), adversarial, and eventually bureaucratic. The weaker party borrowed the surface form and some of the substance of the stronger; some unionists adopted formal business values and traits such as undemocratic organizational procedures and managerial goals of maximizing returns; some even sought personal enrichment as a right of union office. When unionists were locked into battle with management, they were wary of introducing more democracy than their opponents. John L. Lewis put the common view succinctly: "Democracy means labor union inefficiency."[20]

Authoritarian unions proved fertile sources of corruption and racketeering in industries where *employers* already were temped to collude in price fixing, market-sharing schemes, and restraining the market. Even when not engaged in corrupt practices, unions acted as monopolists, ready and willing, whenever able, to exploit a market to improve their own wages at the expense of the unorganized. Studies have shown that union wages and benefits enjoy a significant margin over nonunion wages and probably at the expense of some unemployment for those not in unions. One should note, however, that managerial hostility to unionism, persisting in a virulent form unto today, discouraged union pursuit of more benign goals and stunted or restrained more productive and economically responsible union programs.

For over half a century managers unwittingly acted as Frankensteins, helping to transform the labor movement into a kind of hamstrung, limited-capacity monster. Its potential shortcomings and limitations were not always appreciated in the 1920s and even during the next two decades, despite the dramatic rise of unions throughout the 1940s and into the 1950s, most union leaders manifested the stumbling gait, inarticulate speech, and ineffective (but sometimes scary) behavior that Boris Karloff so well portrayed on the silver screen. If this characterization is too strong, at least one may say that the labor movement, developed since the turn of the century in response to business managers' unremitting antagonism, has all too often produced leaders with a trained incapacity to perceive, let alone make, the most of new and different opportunities for themselves or their members. George Meany, long-time president of the unified AFL–CIO, was a sorry and typical example. Labor leaders were satisfied with their limited agenda; they accepted a defensive role, preferring to be reactors rather than aggressors or initiators. John L. Lewis of the United Mine Workers and Walter Reuther of the United Automobile Workers were the rare exceptions.

The only period of great organizing success union leaders have enjoyed arose out of managers' failure to keep faith with their employees. During the Great Depression, managers abandoned many of the reasonable labor policies of the 1920s, when they had begun to show some sensible consideration for employees' needs and rights. They severely cut wages, laid off workers in large numbers, and reduced or eliminated many paternalistic welfare and fringe benefits. Angry employees and a disillusioned public pressed for federal legislation that would remove the legal restrictions upon union activities. Successful in that effort, unionists and their supporters then sought to win from the federal government new, positive encouragement of organization and protection of bargaining rights.

With the passage of the Norris–LaGuardia and Wagner acts, workers began to organize so rapidly that the old unions had difficulty in adapting their structures, procedures, and programs to the needs and desires of the new members. In a series of tumultuous organizing drives, workers created new unions and expanded old ones, so that within a decade member-ship had almost quadrupled. In another decade union members accounted for more than a third of the labor force. The form of collective bargaining that prevailed was that advocated by Gompers, which, as noted, was greatly influenced, if not shaped, by management's belligerence. Those who administered the new laws and the judges who interpreted them, still influenced by the public's skepticism, trimmed both unions and collective bargaining to fit the prevailing limiting notions about the proper sphere of unions and an appropriate ambit for collective bargaining.

Industrial relations practioners, labor leaders, and the public were so caught up in the dramatic surge of unions and spread of collective bargain-ing that few considered how well formed either was to meet future de-mands and the needs of a continually changing industrial society. They still concentrated upon fitting unionism to the hostile managerial climate that had lasted for decades. Few considered how stunting it might be to a flexible, creative, and imaginative use of the labor force in a truly competi-tive world economy. Only with time did Americans come to realize how narrowly defined was the union role. The law proclaimed that unions and management might voluntary bargain over anything they chose, but its interpretation and application in practice focused both parties' attention on those few items over which they *legally had* to bargain—wages, hours, and conditions of work as traditionally defined.[21]

Corporate management remained satisfied with the restrictive legaliz-ation of the scope of bargaining. Because the law required most business managers in large corporate firms to recognize unions and bargain in good faith, they wanted to set definite limits on any union challenge. They meant to defend their managerial positions. Most managers fiercely op-posed the Wagner Act legalizing unions, but having lost that battle, contin-ued to resist organizing efforts, insisting that collective bargaining had to be kept within bounds, lest it encroach upon the necessary powers of management. They even invented the term *management rights*, contending that they were protecting vital *prerogatives*, a term that implied the obsolete claims—and long-rejected values—of imperious kings from the seven-teenth century. Certainly it was a most peculiar term to find currency in a democratic society.

By the end of World War II, managers in the nation's large manufactur-ing firms, as well as those in transportation, communications, utilities, and mining, had obeyed the law by recognizing unions and engaging in collective bargaining. For the most part, they resisted any broadening of the scope of bargaining, though in thousands of agreements, scholars found examples of unions participating in a wide array of formerly manag-erial activities.[22] Although most agreements covered only the traditional, conventional items of union concern, the detailed specifics, however, sometime covered hundreds of pages that were, or written like, complicated legal documents. The lawyers and industrial relations professionals, who increasingly took over negotiations, argued for as narrow an interpretation of the terms as they could secure. Bargaining under this legalistic approach naturally remained adversarial.

Clearly managers continued to view unions as outsiders, "third parties" who had no role in the directing of company affairs. As representatives of the stockholders who owned the company, managers insisted they were the only legitimate source of authority, direction, decision making, policy, and control. Union leaders were to be kept at a distance, and employees, particularly those who were union members, were to follow managers' rational instructions, supervisors' correct rules, and in general, managements' sole definition of efficiency. If they disagreed with management, they could grieve, but first they were to obey. *Collective bargaining thus, became frozen—crystallized—into a form that may have fit the conditions of the depression years but became less and less germane to the needs of either employees or management.*

Through the halcyon post-World War II production years, when American manufacturing firms appeared to have reached a mature stage of capitalism, unions and management established a stable adversarial system of negotiations and bargaining. Yet the public was most impressed with, and at times most alarmed about, the resulting strikes, picketing, and boycotts. The power of unions appeared to many to be overweening, though the terms won through collective bargaining were usually only quantitatively, not qualitatively, different from the benefits provided voluntarily by management in the 1920s. The ambit of collective bargaining and the interests of unions continued in its narrow range—perhaps well suited for the peculiar economic conditions of the 1930s, acceptable during the uniquely noncompetitive years, 1947–1972—but all too inflexible, constricted, and confined to prove adaptable to a dynamic, rapidly changing world and domestic economy.

Differences between union and nonunion wages increased from the 10 percent to 15 percent range in 1950s to 15 to 20 percent in the early 1980s, to as much as 30 percent if fringes are included.[23] Throughout the 1970s, and into the early 1980s, managers in two highly unionized industries—steel and automobiles—agreed to provide unions ever-larger, unprecedented wage margins, even when foreign producers were eroding the American firms' markets, when plant closures were epidemic, and when millions of manufacturing employees were losing jobs. Neither party could find a more imaginative strategy than that of the end game.[24]

To summarize: The lofty view managers held of their role in production, and the high status the chief managers of large firms claimed for themselves, did not encourage wider worker interests or develop broader union concerns than those of wages and protective work rules. Managers made clear to union negotiators that they were quite satisfied to provide ever higher wages and more complicated and detailed work rules, as long as all other business affairs were excluded from negotiations. Managers insisted that such matters as investment policy, plant closings, financial arrangements, technological development, research and development, marketing, inventory policy, shipping schedules, and the other multitudinous activities of a company were to be handled by managers alone, with no input needed or wanted from unions or employees.

Given such a managerial approach to industrial relations, it is hardly surprising that unionists concentrated upon those few items about which managers were willing to bargain and ignored other basic matters. Furthermore, business managers found themselves in the decades after World War II in positions of power and respect that history had thrust upon them but that they considered a consequence of their exceptional merit. It enabled them to indulge their preference for containing unions and limiting collective bargaining. Circumstances had so favored them that no constituency, certainly not unions, could exert more than weak and intermittent influence upon them.

Managers, therefore, enjoyed a freewheeling style of operations, well described by John Kenneth Galbraith in 1967.[25] Managers in DuPont or General Motors, to choose two representative companies, were answerable to almost no one;[26] they directed the activities of hundreds of thousands of employees through a decentralized system of command and control, relying upon central service staffs (which Galbraith awkwardly termed *the technostructure*) to oversee personnel practices, define budgets, and set overall policy.[27] At the time, such firms and such style of managing appeared to be a final accomplishment of an industrial economy; in fact, they turned out to be a transient organizational form, able to flourish only under the very special circumstances of the time.

IV.   THE PUBLIC CHARACTERISTICS OF THE AUTONOMOUS CORPORATION

The business corporation of the 1950s and its managers could be easily identified by four characteristics: (1) the pursuit of economic growth, with stability, (2) a bureaucratic, hierarchical organizational structure, (3) an embracing sense of social responsibility, and (4) an authoritarian relationship with employees, involving both an adversarial stance toward unions and often a paternalistic attitude toward employees. In developing these characteristics, managers worked to make collective bargaining a limited process with which they and employees have to contend today. A comment on each is appropriate.

A.   Stable Economic Growth

Few managers had any doubt that a primary purpose of their firms was pursuit of economic growth, carried out in a controlled and stable way. Although managers sought constantly to enlarge production, expand sales, and increase revenues, they also realized the benefits of stabilized markets. This meant control of all developments and activities that surrounded and affected production and sales. Galbraith had noted the imperatives of the massive technologically driven demand for capital and the long lead times required to transform big capital investment into productive operations. Because uncertainties over costs and demand endangered the stability of the firm (and the position of managers), they had to be controlled if detailed, long-run planning was to be carried out successfully. The control and planning function that managers assumed was both daunting and audacious. Eventually it became presumptuous. The social, political, and economic setting is so changeable that even very powerful organizations cannot become reliable instruments of control, of either their internal or external activities.[28] At the time, however, it enhanced managers' illusion of complete control—particularly over their employees.

In the automobile industry, a few large domestic firms constituted an oligopoly; in steel, the huge United States Steel company was of such a dominating size that smaller companies operated in its protective shadow; other firms in communications, transportation, and financial industries benefitted from a government-regulated, monopolistic status. One example was the old American Telephone & Telegraph Company. Given such protected status, managers were able, to a remarkable degree, to plan and control the environment of their firms. Not surprisingly, managers whose whole professionals careers were played out in such organizations came to accept economic growth (the production of more and more through larger and larger firms) as an unquestioned, unquestionable organizational purpose. If growth could be assured only through the stability brought by the continued, even permanent existence of their corporations,[29] overall planning, centralized control, and managed demand, then the necessities of the situation defined their rights and legitimated the ways they exercised their power.

B.   Bureaucratic Hierarchies

To handle the burgeoning work of planning and the ever more complex problems of control, managers of large industrial corporations created arrays of staff offices to offer specialized advice, propose policy, collect data, and monitor performance in all divisions and all parts of the firm. They followed the hierarchical structure that early corporate managers in the mid- and late-nineteenth-century corporations had first used, probably borrowing from the command organization of the armies in the Civil War.[30]

The size and extent of business firms' bureaucratic hierarchies were remarkable. By 1975 a fifth of all industrial employees in the United States worked in firms with at least *six levels* of managers.[31] As late as 1987, General Motors, one of the largest business corporations, still maintained as many as 14 management levels. Its organizational form contrasted strikingly with that of a chief world competitor, Toyota Motor Company, which managed with only five levels of managers.[32] Firms built up their professional and technical staffs at a particularly rapid rate throughout the 1950s and 1960s. The various levels of their hierarchies swelled enormously. The manufacturing nonproduction labor force increased far more rapidly than did employment in general. In the years between 1950 and 1970 firms in the durable goods industry, where most of the large corporate firms were found, hired managerial, professional, and technical employees in such numbers that their share of the industry labor force increased from about 17 to more than 28 percent. Though employment in the industry accounted for less than 4 percent of total private employment, the hiring in these occupations was so large that it accounted for 13 percent of the net employment gains for the *entire economy* over the period.[33]

The result was an ever-longer reach between top and bottom managers, large-scale bureaucracies (far bigger than those in comparable European and Japanese firms) that rivaled only those of the Department of Defense and the U.S. Post Office whose bureaucracies are infamous for their sluggishness and inefficiencies. But the same adjectives were seldom applied to corporate bureaucracies. Of course, such large bureaucracies allowed much room for slack; they also encouraged another invidious corporate development, namely the pushing of responsibility for performance downward and of rewards upward. The overall result was a dangerous split between performance and recognition of achievement, and thus a pathological "game playing" among managers to the detriment of the firm.[34]

C. Social Responsibility

To win public acceptance of the power they wielded, managers developed a third corporate characteristic, a credo of social responsibility. Business leaders recognized that the control they exercised and the planning they deemed essential had to encompass more than the immediate interests of their own firms. The prestigious Committee for Economic Development (CED) noted that because business corporations often included millions of employees, stockholders, customers, and community neighbors in all sections of the country and in all classes of society, this made them "a microcosm of the entire society."[35] The chief executive of Exxon, in 1978, concisely expressed a widely held view of the corporation's social responsibility in these words:

> Corporations are part of the life of the communities in which they do business. Their operations affect not only the economic and physical well-being of such communities, but the social and cultural environment as well. Consequently, corporations carry responsibility well beyond conducting their primary business.[36]

The managers of General Electric introduced, in the early post-World War II period, the concept of corporate *stakeholder*—all those affected by the policies and programs of the firm. Managers were responsible to all of them and thus had to assume a wide social responsibility, far beyond that owed to stockholders alone. Implicit in the notion was the possibility that managers might responsibly subordinate stockholder claims to those of other stakeholders. By the 1980s, many managers, threatened by hostile takeovers and corporate raids, explicitly declared the desirability of that subordination. The members of the Business Roundtable wrote in 1981:

> Balancing the shareholder's expectations of maximum return against other priorities is one of the fundamental problems confronting corporate management. The shareholder must receive a good return but the legitimate concerns of other constituencies also must have the appropriate attention.[37]

When taken to task by Paul MacEvoy, a prominent economist, for such a stand,[38] Andrew C. Sigler, chairman of Champion International Corporation and then-president of the Business Roudtable, responded that too few shareholders were long-term, personally involved individual investors; large numbers of them were institutions—"unidentified short-term buyers most interested in maximum near-term gain." According to Sigler, managers had to balance such interests with those of other stakeholders; the simple theory that only shareholders count in managers' responsibility was a discredited notion to be found only in old economic dissertations.[39] In 1987, Hicks B. Waldron, chairman of Avon Products Inc., boldly proclaimed his belief that managers not only *might* but *have* a positive duty to subordinate the maximizing value for stockholder.

> We have 40,000 employees and 1.3 million representatives around the world. We have a number of suppliers, institutions, customers, communities. None of them have the democratic freedom as shareholders do to buy or sell their shares. They have much deeper and much more important stakes in our company than our shareholders.[40]

Sigler, agreeing with Waldron, put the matter into a rhetorical question, with his own answer: "what right does someone who owns the stock for an hour have to decide a company's fate? That's the law, and it's wrong.[41]

Managers had taken a dangerous path in applying the logic of their industrial relations policy to that of their shareholders. They insisted that *they, and they alone*, were capable of choosing among the various competing demands put forth by the many stakeholders. The managers of General Electric had long made clear *their* claim of autonomy in the company motto repeated again and again in advertisements and company literature all through the post-World-War-II decades: "Do Right Voluntarily in the Balanced Best Interest of All." In 1971 the Committee for Economic Development described the full meaning of social responsibility.

> The modern professional manager also regards himself, not as an owner disposing of personal property as he sees fit, but as a *trustee balancing the interests of many diverse participants and constituents in the enterprise,* whose interests sometimes conflict with those of others. The chief executive of a large corporation has the problem of reconciling the demands of employees for more wages and improved benefits plans, customers for lower prices and greater values, vendors for higher prices, government for more taxes, stockholders for higher dividends and great capital appreciation—all within a framework that will be constructive and acceptable to society.
>
> This interest-balancing involves much the same kind of political leadership and skill as is required in top government posts. The chief executive of a major corporation must exercise statesmanship in developing with the rest of the management group the objectives, strategies, and policies of the corporate enterprise. In implementing these, he must also obtain the "consent of the governed" or at least enough cooperation to make the policies work. And in the long run the principal constituencies will pass judgment on the quality of leadership he is providing to the corporate enterprise.[42]

This remarkable description of social responsibility placed corporate managers in a very special position, particularly in a nation that values democratic procedures. And a decade later, the members of the Business Roundtable described their role very much as the CED had earlier:

> Carefully weighing the impacts of decisions and balancing different constituent interests—in the context of both near-term and long-term effects—must be an integral part of the corporation's decision-making and management process. Resolving the differences involves compromises and trade-offs. It is important

that all sides be heard but impossible to assure that all will be satisfied because competing claims may be mutually exclusive. . . . Balancing the shareholder's expectations of maximum return against other priorities is one of the fundamental problems confronting corporate management . . . some leading managers have come to believe . . . that by giving enlightened consideration to balancing the legitimate claims of all its constituents, a corporation will best serve the interest of its shareholders.[43]

In both the earlier and more recent statements, the managers made clear they were not to be *accountable* to any of their various constituents, not even stockholders. On their own, in their wisdom, and from their positions of high status, they would set social priorities, choosing which interests to favor and which to slight. They alone would decide, in light of the general welfare, what, if any, resources might be devoted to community activities, social needs, or constituency demands.[44]

The statements of the CED and Business Roundtable were typical descriptions of corporate social responsibility as it had come to be accepted by the managers of most large business corporations since the late 1950s. By 1958 three-quarters of 700 companies queried had formulated statements of managerial responsibilities.[45] Business managers may have felt that they publicly had to advertise their responsibility because, in fact, they were *not* responsible. More accurately they were not easily accountable to anyone or any constituency for many of their decisions and actions, except through the market. They could close a factory, mine, or mill and move an operation to Tennessee, Texas, or Taiwan without securing permission from any group but their own colleagues and officers.[46] They might tear out the economic roots of a well-established community and build a new city in the open countryside without having to account to anyone directly or immediately. Within the market's often wide limits, they were responsible only as they choose to define responsibility.[47]

Even those who otherwise endorsed managerial direction and the business system had doubts about such a sense of responsibility. Philip Sporn of American Electric Power and Reed O. Hunt of Crown Zellerbach dissented from the CED statement. It was entirely too ambitious, they argued; managers' responsibilities should be limited to discharging their business responsibilities as business managers.[48] University of Chicago economist Milton Friedman had denounced such formulation years earlier and called the enlarged definition of corporate social responsibilities a "fundamentally subversive doctrine." He asked how business managers could determine the best balance among the contending interests and how they would justify the balance selected. In a democratic society, elected officials and their civil servants set the taxes and allocate public revenues for the general welfare, but they are accountable to the electorate. Should self-selected managers of private firms act in a similar way, pricing their products or services to raise revenue for distributing among the interests they rate highest? If they arrogate a public function to themselves, managers will be sooner or later "chosen by the public techniques of election and appointment."[49]

Other economists also expressed alarm. Yale professor Paul MacAvoy argued that the Business Roundtable statement "implies that the large corporation is a political entity subject to the votes of interest groups, rather than an economic organization subject to the market test for efficient use of resources."[50] Peter Drucker warned that the social responsibility enunciated by managers in the last few decades was incompatible with the realities of America society. Comparing those who espoused the doctrine to the enlightened despots of eighteenth-century Europe, Drucker wrote:

> [Management] gloried in its good intentions. And American managements busily engaged in removing what they considered as the last obstacle to their enlightened rule, an independent and powerful board of directors.[51]

The managers' definition of their own—and their firms'—social responsibility obviously allowed managers great leeway. Great power can lead to great corruption. From the perspectives of the late 1980s, however, the social responsibility of the large business firms over the preceding quarter century had been quite remarkable. In the automobile industry, for example, the major producers raised their workers wages steadily through the 1970s, as already noted, they assured a steady and profitable market for thousands of parts suppliers, particularly in the mid-West, who in turn were able to provide steady jobs and good pay to thousands of blue-collar, industrial workers. As a result, many small communities, as well as larger manufacturing towns throughout the country, flourished and supported what most Americans took to be the good, middle-class life. Plant closings were rare; there was no "Rust Belt"; and the stable prosperity of middle America commended itself to most people. In retrospect it was a time when corporate social responsibility appeared to be working reasonably well.

As might be expected, however well off the various constituencies were, they were seldom satisfied with their benefits. Unionists, along with others, complained that managers should have been far more generous and wiser in their enlightened choices; economists described managers' sharing of earnings among constituencies as merely shared gains of quasi-rents or oligopolistic gains won in protected markets. But more important than criticism was a new reality: a global, more intensely and more widely felt competition that forced managers to realize that they could no longer protect their various constituencies as they had over the decades following World War II.

V. AUTHORITARIAN MANAGEMENT

Few American employers or corporate managers have believed that there should be any balance in bargaining power between them and their employees—or their other constituencies. They generally have assumed that the proper relationship of employer and employee was the one defined in English common law—that of master and servant. Most managers perceive no reason why they should not possess the right to uncontested, unilateral authority within their organizations. Managerial attitudes toward employees have changed in their style of expression over the years, but their substance is remarkably similar. Consider the bluntly worded declaration made in 1851 by the editor of the *New York Journal of Commerce*:

> Who but the miserable, craven-hearted man, would permit himself to be subjected to such [union] rules, extending even to the number of apprentices he may employ and the manner in which they shall be bound to him, to the kind of work which shall be performed in his own office at particular hours of the day, and to the sex of the persons employed, however, separated into different apartments of buildings? For ourselves, we never employed a female as a compositor, and have no great opinion of apprentices, but sooner than be restricted on these points, or any other, by a self-constitued tribunal outside of the office, we would go back to the employment of our boyhood, and dig potatoes, pull flax, and do everything else that a plain, honest farmer may properly do on his own territory. It is marvelous to us how any employer, having the soul of a man within him, can submit to such degradation.[52]

George F. Baer, president of the Reading Company, during the 1902 anthracite mine strike declared: "The rights and interests of the laboring man will be protected and cared for . . . by the Christian men to whom God in his infinite wisdom has given the control of the property interests of the country."[53] The rhetoric has changed, but the antiunion attitudes have not. J. P. Stevens fought unions from the 1950 into the 1970s; managers of Texas Instruments and Litton Industries have engaged in similar fights. If managers have learned to express themselves more moderately than Baer and to act less openly hostile to unions than Texas Instruments and Litton, it is a good guess that most were still firmly opposed to unions. Royal Meeker, commissioner of the U.S. Bureau of Labor Statistics, reported on the President's First Industrial Congress in 1920 in these words:

> The employer group in the conference must be taken as representing the majority of employers the country over. The speeches made by these representative employers were often difficult to understand, but their attitude of mind was never for a moment in doubt. They had been driven by hard experience [during World War I] to abandon individual bargaining, but they vigorously maintained their right to *dictate* the terms of the collective bargaining.[54]

That attitude seems quaintly out of date. But is it? Though about a sixth of the labor force employed by private firms works under the terms and provisions of collective bargained agreements today (down from nearly a third a generation ago), most American managers find even that much unionism a standing threat to managerial authority. In the late 1970s the National Association of Manufacturers created the Council on Union-Free Environment, with 450 member companies joining together to discourage unionization and collective bargaining. The announced purpose of the council was to benefit themselves and their employees.[55] Corporate antiunion programs are widespread and used by the largest business firms. The AFL–CIO reported in 1983 that 401 consulting firms had conducted antiunion programs in the preceding 3 years. An additional 126 firms had conducted seminars on union avoidance.[56]

Of course, not all the managers of large business corporations have been antiunion, but the perception has been widespread among them until very recently that unions are a necessary evil rather than useful contributors to the firm or society. Managers have usually assumed that Yale Professor William Graham Sumner was right in saying that "industry may be republican; it can never be democratic."[57] Some managers, though, have recognized the nature of the power they defend. Robert E. Wood, president of Sears, Roebuck, noted:

> We stress the advantages of the free enterprise system, we complain about the totalitarian state, but in our individual organizations we have created more or less a totalitarian system in industry, particularly in large industry.[58]

A Unilever factory manager, writing for the company magazine in 1974 described his reactions in these words:

> It is my submission that the worker in the large industrial enterprise is accorded the status of a child . . . when he walks into the factory he is given a number; "punches the clock"; is closely supervised; and is assumed to be capable of accepting no more than a bare minimum of responsibility. If he then reacts to this in either an apathetic or aggressive manager, management reacts by tarting up the physical environment or putting another quid in the wage packet, and is comfortably confirmed in its stereotype of the average worker as solely motivated by irrational and childish impulses. If, in desperation, the worker then latches on to the "militant" who appears to offer hope of escape from this morass, he is branded a sheep.[59]

The two indictments are too sweeping; only a minority punch time clocks, and managerial styles are more sophisticated and benign. Some scholars have identified a variety of styles—autocratic, democratic, and laissez-faire management,[60] and others have specified elitist or participatory styles.[61] Nevertheless, whatever adjective, the power is often authoritarian and widely exercised in the hierarchical business corporation.[62] By

1975, one of every five industrial workers in the United States and Europe was employed by a large, hierarchically structured, company. A far greater proportion is employed in lesser, but still multilevel, hierarchies.

Few scholars have explored the reasons why managers have adopted an authoritarian hierarchical employment policy. Competitive market theory does not predict such a management policy; nor do practical market operations require it. Why then is it so common? Alternative ways of coordinating production and distribution are possible. Small companies, with little or no hierarchical structure, could have coordinated their activities through trade associations, interest groups, loose combines, or even cartels, negotiating among themselves the details of their membership and relationships. In fact, business managers had experimented with such arrangements in many industries through the nineteenth century, but a popular dislike of cartels, trusts, and monopolies made these arrangements politically suspect and legally unenforceable or unlawful. Alternatively, managers might have coordinated their activities through the competitive market of small units, guiding their production and marketing decisions according to price information supplied through market exchange. In such a case, most firms probably would not have grown to the sizes of the large corporation today, but cumbersome hierarchies might have been avoided or greatly flattened, and managerial power might have been defined more easily and exercised in different ways.[63]

On the basis of the bureaucracy's prevalence, and with little or no other evidence, economists conclude that the hierarchical, authoritarian corporate form must have been more a more efficient way to coordinate production and distribution than either federations or market coordination. Assuming that business managers are always profit maximizers, the record suggests that corporations were particularly efficient in capital- and energy-intensive, high-volume, standardized production, mass-marketing industries. But managers' choice of the large corporation is not necessarily proof that it was made primarily to secure efficiency; however once made, the organizing choice proved efficient enough to sustain itself.

Nevertheless, a caveat is in order. Hierarchy, and the bureaucracy it creates, can all too easily pose barriers to both rational decisions and efficient operations. Managers in such notable industries as automobiles, steel, and air transportation have not always acted to gain and maintain the most efficient production; they are often quite willing to settle for enough efficiency to produce satisfactory profits. Apparently other values than those of efficiency influence managers' perceptions, and other goals than those of maximum profits motivate their actions.

Furthermore, if hierarchical, authoritarian corporate businesses were sufficiently efficient to have maintained themselves in the past, that is hardly proof that those characteristics will serve them well in the future. Corporate managers employ workers whose skills, schooling, and specialties are very different from the workers of even a generation ago. They are knowledgeable to a degree unimaginable to their predecessors; they are better able than ever before, and more apt than in earlier times, to insist upon the right to participate in decisions that affect their work and lives; in addition, employees' skills, training, and education have prepared them increasingly to work on their own with minimal or no supervision. The critical question, therefore, is whether this contemporary work force will be used in so constructive a manner where enlightened individuals can still play a part. The signals are mixed.

VI. UNIONS IN THE NINETIES

Research results from Harvard's Elton Mayo were published through the 1930s and 1940s. He and his associates reported, in the famous Hawthorne studies that workers spontaneously formed groups and enjoyed a social life at the place of work; here they must be seen as social creatures who achieved complete freedom only in submerging themselves in the group, what managers popularly call team individualism.[64] Workers naturally rely upon social routine to deal with the daily on-the-job problems rather than on logical thinking and systematic analyses. If unproductive and uncooperative, workers probably suffered from anomie and low morale. Managers controlled the industrial environment within which employees worked. If they behaved as if they were bewildered, lost, isolated, and discontented, then managers were not managing properly. They had in all likelihood stripped away the reassuring customs and traditions that made work meaningful for employees. It was management's responsibility to make the workplace both human and humane.[65]

Mayo suggested that managers were more than mere employers. They were neither managing workers nor work—they were administering a social system. Their goal was not to gain a bit more efficiency or a bit less waste, but social stability. As rational directors of an industrial civilization, managers carried the burden of interpreting the emotional conditions of workers, molding their feelings and mastering the facts of human–social life at work.[66] Managers had to learn the art of "human relations" to eliminate workers' misunderstandings and to provide useful facts to those in the shop, all in the promotion of teamwork necessary to the achievement of managerial goals.

Mayo's contribution to managerial ideology lay in its emphasis upon managers as an elite—trained, rational, and possessed of a kind of industrial *noblesse oblige*. He saw no need for unions, government regulation, or outside pressures to guide managers in the fulfillment of their social responsibilities. He assumed that managerial goals were—and out to be— the basis for social and industrial cooperation. The effective working of the social order thus depends upon the full and unquestioned authority of managers.

Since the 1950s, American managers have not developed their managerial ideology beyond that based on the Mayo's human relations, though as we report later, some managers realize that it needs to go far beyond it. Most have been unwilling to contemplate sharing authority with employees—or any other constituency. Cooperation has almost always been defined as employees joining managers in pursuit of managerial goals, never a joint exploration of joint goals. By definition, managers are assumed to be superiors and all other inferiors; only managers are the source of ideas, suggestions, or production know-how. The result is that many business leaders still defend managerial prerogatives without embarrassment.[67] Managers have been intent upon maintaining their "right to manage," as if the basis of that right was obvious and necessary. Those who negotiate with unions have almost universally demanded and secured a "management rights" provision in the labor agreement. It has become a symbol of managers' reach for authority but at the same time an indicator of their fears. They know full well that managerial rights extend just as far— and no further than—the cooperation, respect, and willingness of workers who choose to recognize them, no matter what the labor agreement declares.

In a free society no person has special claim over another unless, by superior economic position, the claim can so squeeze the inferior positioned person that free choice is in fact not allowed. Managers claimed hierarchical, authoritarian autonomy. Such a right-to-manage ultimately rested upon the power of economic coercion. It is a power that fits American traditions and ethos no better than does prerogative. Economic coercion has always generated resentment and fear. Neither is a good base on which to build loyalty and cooperation at the place of work. When labor scholars and researchers suggested ways to win more employee loyalty, managers ignored them. Almost always, scholars included recommendations that workers be provided opportunities for them to exert influence on the decisions of importance to them.[68]

In the quarter century after World War II, managers of large corporations conducted business affairs without having to account to any of many of their constituencies, except for those employees who had gained certified union representation. With this one exception, they neither had to listen to, nor to communicate with, their various constituencies, most of whom were still unorganized. Out of a self-defined sense of social responsibility, however, they often did listen carefully, seeking through opinion surveys to discover the desires and preferences of individuals who could be presumed to be members of informal constituencies. Many of the large firms communicated regularly, and at length, to the public at large through newspaper, television and radio advertisements, company brochures, magazines, and pamphlets. Much of the listening and communicating, though, was more a public relations exercise than a truly responsive encounter with constituencies. Many Americans were persuaded that the means used were all too self-serving, and "PR" (*public relations*) came to be an invidious term.

While corporate managers increasingly demonstrated their awareness of the social impact their firms had upon community life and the effects they produced for different interests, they continued to insist that they alone could make operative decisions. Few considered the possibility that they might formally recognize and use unions and their members—or any constituency—as sources of information or as aides and assistants in dealing with the complex problems confronting them. They presumed that it was their right—even their duty—alone to fashion *their* firms to serve community needs and constituency preference; they saw nothing odd about the exercise of such autonomy in a democratic society.

The technology of the period and the sheltered markets for which they produced coincidentally worked together for more than two decades to insulate managers from the formal demands and organized pressures of shareholders, unorganized employees, consumers, suppliers, and all the other variety of constituencies, whose number and variety increased rapidly after the mid-1960s. An environment increasingly inhospitable to both managerial presumption and unchecked corporate progress was changing dramatically. As the 1980s approached, managers were discovering that the assumptions of, and the expectations generated by, the 1950s corporation were not sufficient to support their claims to either social autonomy or organizational authority. A note on some of the major forces that suggest the necessity for change includes the following.

VII. WINDS OF CHANGE

Only ever-increasing rates of production and a rising standard of living in the two decades after World War II had allowed managers to maintain their claims to autonomy. As industrial productivity declined through the 1970s and many industrial workers' standard of living also fell (or at least remained steady), managers found themselves confronting more challenges than any time since the Great Depression. By the 1980s, it was apparent that the economy and the society had changed markedly over the previous generation. Some of those changes require specification and comment.

A. Globalization and Domestic Deregulation

As the European and Japanese economies began to recover from the World War II, they proved to be formidable competitors, producing goods of higher quality and lower price than American manufacturers were able to deliver. Even by the late 1960s the rate of increase in American labor productivity began to fall behind that of Japan and West Germany. Few managers paid much attention so that as the 1980s approached, they were shocked by what had happened. For example, Xerox engineers visiting Japan in 1979 discovered that their competitors' production costs were half of theirs, and the defect rate in parts was better by a factor of 30![69] In addition, a number of other developing economies, particularly those on the Pacific Rim—South Korea, Taiwan, Singapore, and Malaysia—began to serve the America market. Imports began widely to supplant American manufacturing providing, as noted, lower priced and higher quality goods. By 1987 imports (in constant dollars) were more than double those of 1971 increasing from less than 9 percent of GNP to nearly 15 percent. At the same time, there appeared a new and widely supported movement to deregulate industries that had long enjoyed government protection against rampant competition. Under both Republican and Democratic administrations, Congress weakened or eliminated long-established forms of industry-by-industry regulation, particularly those in transportation, communications, and finance. The rise of foreign competitors, accompanied by domestic deregulation, increased effective competition enormously, affecting almost every sector of the economy.[70] Managers used to the special, protected markets after World War II confronted an economy of unprecedented harshness, challenging them as none of their predecessors had been. Although two-thirds of managers in large business firms still believe they are as—or more—powerful than ever, over than three-quarters admit that their job is now much harder. Twenty-five percent find globalization of business the cause, 23 percent blame increased competition, and nearly a third see shareholder pressure, merger and takeover pressures or technological change as the source of their difficulties.[71]

B. Industrial Shifts

Over the past half century, the most prominent and preimminent American business firms have been found in durable manufacturing, the same sector that unions had organized dramatically in the two decades after passage of the Wagner Act. In 1987, however, absolute employment was less than it had been in 1967, and only a bit higher than it was in 1953, a generation earlier. The share of nonagricultural employees working in durable manufacturing shows a marked declined over the same period— from 20 percent in 1953 to 18 percent in 1967, to 11 percent in 1987. Employment growth took place elsewhere. More significantly than the shifts in durable goods employment was the decline in real manufacturing output in the 1970s and 1980s. Taking into account the considerable increase in parts and supplies imports for domestic assembly, real manufacturing output (both durable and nondurable) has probably declined over the past decade by large and unprecedented amount.[72] The wasting away of manufacturing output is a startling indicator of the increasing stress under which large American firms now operate.

C.   Decentralization of Production

The managers of large, centrally managed, hierarchical business firms may believe they are as powerful as ever, but the rising tide of competition and technological changes suggest that increasingly they and their approach to production are becoming obsolete. Certainly they have not proven to be significant creators of jobs. Small companies are growing faster and showing themselves quicker and more flexible in adapting to the rapid pace of technological change. Between 1975 and 1984 firms with under 500 employees increased their work force by more than a third, whereas firms with over 500 employees increased theirs by a bit more than an eighth.[73] As *The Economist* pointed out:

> Across the country as a whole, the number of people employed by the largest 500 companies (ranked according to market capitalisation) fell by 1.5 million between the end of 1981 and the end of 1986. The average size of companies has been inching down since 1977. Within manufacturing itself, small businesses are taking over from large ones. Manufacturing companies with fewer than 250 employees now account for around 45 percent of the manufacturing workforce; in 1975 they accounted for only 42 percent. In the economy as a whole, firms with fewer than 20 employees account for 25 percent of all jobs. Between 1981–1986 companies with 20 employees created 88% of the net new jobs in America.[74]

George Gilder argues that modern computer technology is making possible ever more decentralized production, with less and less need for large, hierarchical organizations to manage and control. He is quite sure the possibility will be realized in the information industries and is it likely to spread to other, older technologies as well.[75] Brian H. Rowe, senior vice president of General Electric Aircraft Engines argues that manufacturing firms had better adopt a small-is-better philosophy of expansion. In all of his companies new facilities are small satellite plants: "We believe that if you limit a plant to 600 to 1,500 people, the management is closer to workers."[76]

D. Mergers, Hostile Takeover, and Managerial Risk Taking

Hedged about by competition as never before, discovering size and many-layered hierarchies unresponsive to change, managers have discovered their performance questioned, not only by customers and the public, but by those whose support—or tolerance—has always been critical— their stockholders. Through most of their history, corporate managers have usually been able to treat stockholders as rentiers, legitimate claimants to decent return, but with no serious role in the running of the operations. However, the recent rise of huge pension and mutual funds have concentrated enormous ownership power in the hands of professionals, both able and increasingly willing to use it.

By 1986, institutional investors collectively controlled 35 percent or more of all publicly traded shares.[77] Their share has increased for two reasons: first, because pension funds have grown enormously since 1970, and second, because individual stockholders appear to be putting more and more of their investments into mutual and pension funds rather than holding shares in their own accounts. Pension funds owned assets of publicly traded stock amounting to $1.5 trillion in 1986, up from $548 billion in 1970, and the amount was rising fast toward at least $2.0 trillion. In 1965, pension funds held only 6 percent of all corporate equity, but by the late 1980s they owned about a quarter of it. By the year 2000 that share should rise to 50 percent.[78] Mutual funds were increasing their share of corporate assets as well: By the end of 1986, roughly half of the 47 million U.S. households owning stock held it through mutual funds, whose accounts numbered over 42 million.[79]

Institutional investors have, unsurprisingly, begun to exert no little influence upon corporate business policy; and if their exertions bring little response, the profession investors have gone further, encouraging mergers, takeovers, divestitures, and restructuring, often at the expense of managers and despite managerial attempts to fend them off. Corporate managers have been surprised—and dismayed—by the boldness with which institutional investors have challenged management policies.[80] Many managers or large business corporations have reacted with anger at the loss of their former autonomy.[81]

The appearance of a powerful and legitimate constituency—organized shareholders through institutional investors—poses a fundamental challenge to managers.[82] Defenders of the business system have always grounded the authority of managers on responsibility to the corporate owners. Institutional investors claim a more direct and immediate right to speak and act for the owners than do managers and thus can preempt the chief support of managers' authority. If the interests of managers diverge from those of the institutional investors, acting for the owners, by the logic that managers themselves have long used—indeed, insisted upon—it is managers, not the owners, who must give way. Managers are not apt to push institutional investors aside, for law and tradition are clearly on the side of owners; therefore, the kind of managerial autonomy that characterized the 1950s, "classic" corporation is not apt to be recovered. As these stockholders pressed managers for improved performance, managers began to recognize that the autonomy they had long claimed was isolating them from potential allies and supporters. Managers may begin to realize that their interests and those of their employees, unionized or not, may be more complementary than conflicting. At least, middle managers have reason to think so, for they have been losing "safe and assured career" jobs as well as have ordinary production workers.[83]

If managers hope to find allies in their employees, or even if they expect workers to respond positively and productively to competitive pressures and stockholder demands for improved performance, they are apt to be disappointed. For too long managers have disdained their employees, manipulated them rather than won their loyalty, and sought to control them rather than encourage them to contribute their own and unique talents to a joint effort.

E. Dependent, Discontented Employees

More than 9 out of 10 members of the work force are employees— working for another person or a corporation. A high proportion of them find such dependence less than satisfactory. Well it might, for it contradicts fundamentals of the American mythos. It binds workers to groups rather than allowing independent work, requiring them to merge their efforts with those of others in joint activities. The Harris polls found that a majority of those interviewed in recent years agreed that business did not allow "people to use their full creative abilities."[84] A survey conducted by the Public Agenda Foundation of New York in 1983 showed that many workers distinguished between *agreeable* jobs and jobs that *motivate* them. They would work harder, they said, if there were potential for advancement, a chance to develop abilities, and a challenging job. Most workers reported, however, that employers had little knowledge of how to motivate workers, and less than a quarter of those surveyed said they were performing on the job to full capacity. Sixty-one percent identified "pay tied to performance" as a feature they wanted most in their work.[85] They hankered after forms of remuneration and restructured jobs that might offer, at least, the illusion, and perhaps some of the substance, of traditional American self-employment, independence, self-reliant individualism. As long as managers of large corporate bureaucracies do not, or cannot, fulfill such hope for their employees, they can expect widespread worker discontent. The traditions are kept alive in workers by the frontier myths with which Americans grow up. The discontent may well find generalized public expression, blending with consumer dissatisfactions and other disappointments that will bring about unexpected and unintended consequences.

If employees do not find satisfaction at work, there are few alternative opportunities in which to find it. Whereas 40 years ago 1 out of every 5 persons in the labor force was self-employed, since the early 1970s, fewer than 1 out of 10 has been able to claim that independence.[86] Those who find self-employment may be exemplars of the nation's mythic rugged individualism, but they pay an increasingly high price for it. The shares of national income accruing to them appear to have declined markedly over the past 40 years. At least proprietors, who are among the self-employed, have lost economically. Their shares of national income, both nonagricultural and agricultural have dropped even faster than their share of the work force. Where in 1948 they received nearly one-fifth of national income, in 1986 their share was just a bit more than one-twelfth. If self-employment or setting up a small business is still an option for a few Americans, they are pinched and relatively unrewarding opportunities. Probably they are chosen more out of desperation than in pursuit of independence or as a declaration of self-reliance.

Employees' dissatisfaction with their condition at work may lie at the heart of the economy's lagging economic performance. Andrew C. Sigler, chairman of Champion International Inc., warns that managers are going to have learn more sophisticated ways of increasing productivity than the traditional solution of cutting costs alone, which he pointed out can be all too easily by "stupid arbitrary judgments." "Competitive companies must understand how to motivate people to be productive and that is hard as hell."[87] More important than new robots, more computerized machines, or automated plants, industry needs systems that get management and labor on the same side.

Ford Motor Company has pulled ahead of General Motors in recent years, primarily because it has included its workers and their union in every step of its changed operations. The new, unprecedented cooperation on joint, not just managerial goals, has probably been more important than the massive capital investments Ford has made. Companies that have delegated authority down the line report excellent results. At two of Champion International's smoothest-running plants, workers—called members—belong to teams that do their own hiring and firing. This is a remarkable—startling—innovation for a major manufacturing firm. TRW has also experimented with pushing production responsibility down, rather than maintaining it at the top. Small groups of employees at a few plants now possess responsibility for maintaining their equipment and interacting with customers. The increase in productivity and quality has been tremendous, according to local managers. However, such experimentation is still rare in industry.[88]

With the educational level of the U.S. work force continually rising, it is surprising that managers have held on to old modes of supervision and worker control. One out of every four workers is now a college graduate, compared with one out of five just 10 years ago. An additional 20 percent have had some college training, up from 16 percent a decade ago.[89] Moreover, the fastest growing employment is in high technology. Between 1978 and 1987, whereas manufacturing employment fell by almost 7 percent, hi-tech employment increased by almost a third.[90]

F.   The Changing Demography of the Labor Force

Demography and education have joined together to supply a cadre of constituency leaders for the discontented and dissatisfied. One of the responses to the revivified economy after World War II and the unexpected prosperity it brought to many young families was the Baby Boom. Between 1945 and 1960 the birth rate was over a third greater than it had been the decade of the Great Depression. It produced the immense Generation, 70 million persons born between 1946 and 1964, large enough to create and sustain a "youth culture," a new social phenomenon. That generation questioned and disturbed the major institutions through which it flowed—suburban family, church or temple, elementary and high schools and then the universities, culminating in the student riots and rebellions that swept across the country in 1968. The sheer number of youths was larger than the nation had ever beheld. As they aged and moved through their stages of life, there was a crowding of every entry port from hospital maternity wards to positions as bank tellers and jobs on auto assembly lines. The members of the Immense Generation have had to compete fiercely among themselves for preference. As the young people have graduated from colleges and graduate professionals schools, always seeking to gain a leg up on their competitors and enhance their chance of winning the good life, they have honed their instincts for opportunity. Competition has encouraged those with ability and imagination to try new and innovative services.

Some were able to discover "needs" that the public had not previously recognized; they proceeded entrepreneurially, creating new markets as earlier business leaders had done.

The successful and innovative among the Immense Generation were better equipped to lead than any of their predecessors. It was the most schooled generation in American history. The educational effort revealed new and untraditional notions about the world to millions of Americans. They were generally inculcated with a more rational and skeptical view of the nation's institutions and a more critical approach to values than were people with little or no schooling. They probably understand better how government operates and are less mystified by business operations than their parents were. Lipset and Schneider found that, indeed, the level of schooling adversely affects people's *confidence* in institutions. They conclude:

> The less well educated and the less sophisticated are more likely to express a "naive faith" that the people running our major institutions know what they are doing. Those at higher educational levels are less likely to say they have "a great deal of confidence" in the people running things. This relationship did now show up at first because the better educated also show higher personal satisfaction and greater trust in others. These factors increase confidence in institutions and therefore counteract the negative effect of education. . . . When all three variables are taken into consideration simultaneously, each has a distinct impact: education (negative), and personal satisfaction and trust (both positive).[91]

The more schooled Americans may still use the rhetoric of patriotism, glory, myth, and ideology to describe their nation and economy, but they are not apt to mistake soothing assurances for remedies to their perceived injuries and expressed discontents. They know how to raise their voices in protest; when they appeal through broadcasts and broadsheets for public support, they can sometimes mobilize millions. From among the ranks of the well-schooled Immense Generation there are sufficient numbers of young professionals of all kinds to provide an ample supply of leaders for all the various corporate constituencies. If they have not had unions available as institutions within which to display their talents, they have been all too successful in influencing government, at all levels, seeking and winning protection for employees. Instead of developing employee protection through flexible, decentralized collective bargaining, they have helped pass legislation against discrimination on the basis of race, sex, and age, assure safe working conditions, protect pension benefits, and even to encourage and support whistle blowers. If American business firms are to improve their productivity and competitiveness so that can cope with the changes that have challenged them in recent years and prepare themselves for the continuing challenge of an industrializing world economy, they will have to modify their style even more than they have yet contemplated.

The titles of two articles in issues of *Business Week* illustrate how far corporate managers are from understanding the needs, demands, and aspirations of their most valuable resource: the members of their own organizations. "GM bets an arm and a leg on a people-free plant"[92] and "GM's new 'Teams' Aren't Hitting any Homers."[93] A technological fix for the problems of production is a weak reed upon which to support the economy. Managers might consider some investments in dignity and consideration of the worth of human beings. Why not refer to their fellow members in their organizations as associates, colleagues, members, or partners? They might well consider using such terms rather than those that carry the denigrating status of the past, "hand," "worker," or "employee." The change might be only semantic, but if it signified a change of ideology, it could carry the day. It would open the possibility of joining with unionists, seeking increased production and productivity through cooperation rather than the traditional adversarial combat.[94]

VIII.   THE FUTURE OF UNIONS AND COLLECTIVE BARGAINING

This review of managerial ideology—as well as practice—and union response over more than a century does not suggest much promise that the major parties in American industrial relations will be able to meet their present challenges. There is little indication that present-day managers generally recognize how dysfunctional their adversarial policies have become or how alienating is their managerial ideology to employees and to other constituencies. There are few signs that union leaders and members will find it easy to trust managers and help create a more flexible, open, less legalistic collective bargaining system. John T. Dunlop, a long-time scholar and experienced participant in the national industrial relations system finds that the parties have made no fundamental changes over the last decade, despite a few experiments here and there in economically stressed industries.[95] Younger students of labor are more optimistic, finding in the changes occurring in some firms indications that a fundamental change is beginning to take place.[96] It may well be younger managers—a new generation of them—will comprehend how obsolete traditional American managerial ideology has become.

Some of the recent changes in large business corporations may be more than temporary responses to economic pressure; certainly a few managers recognize that not only were past industrial relations practices defective but that the ideology out of which they grew was inappropriate in a modern, democratic, high-technology world of work. Elmer W. Johnson, sometime executive vice president of the General Motors Corporation, for example, has identified the problem that America managers

> have long preferred to ignore. By hindsight, it now appears that management and labor struck successive shorterm bargains over the years to the detriment of the company's long-term competitiveness. That is, in the name of efficiency, management bargained for the perpetuation of authoritarian structures in exchange for ever-increasing economic benefits. But authoritarian structures tend over time to produce oppressive managers and an alienated work force, with grave implications as to productivity and quality of the product. . . . Well before 1987, both parties had come to realize that they must break away from old patterns, think in much longer time horizons, and pay far more attention to dignitarian values. . . . Yet, it was not simply that the old ethos was right for one time, only to be rendered obsolete by changes in competitive conditions. It was morally flawed from the beginning.[97]

We agree with Elmer Johnson but wish that other and more managers were as forthright as he. If his colleagues and associates in corporate management admit that flaw, there is a chance that they may win the trust of their employees and, with union leaders, develop a new form of collective bargaining that will serve them, employees, and the public far better than the present form has served. A more participatory, "dignitarian," responsive industrial relations system will not eliminate conflict and disputes, but we believe it will contribute to enhanced productivity and productive efficiency, even as it also encourages the creative abilities and imaginative contributions of employees. In short, it will offer the nation morally sounder relationships at the place of work. Like all questions raised in the face of historic change, the role of human, even more than socioeconomic, imperatives will determine our future. Business ethics has much to offer and much to give as corporate managers and union leaders seek to answer important ethical questions:

> As human beings, should employees expect and receive different treatment, rights, and responsibilities from those as citizens?
> What of life's purposes can be fulfilled at the place of work?
> In an economy where competition presses ever harder, can more humane role for employees allow greater contribution than in earlier times?
> If business organizations offer an enlarged role for employees, what role can and should the union play? Will it not have to change its organization and the expression of its members' concerns and interests?
> Is the American public prepared for redefinitions of managing and working, as well as job rights and job responsibilities that better fit traditional American notions of democracy, participation and egalitarianism?

NOTES

1. Though American employees have made significant gains over the last century, including markedly higher real wages, shorter hours, and fringe benefits, including safer, more

enjoyable places of work, in general, they have not won several rights that surely are basic to ethical treatment. The most important of these is the right to due process at the workplace. Skilled, technical, and professional employees often can not find alternate jobs through a competitive labor market, if they believe themselves mistreated in a particular job; many other employees find alternatives more scarce and thus are denied even a kind of procedural due process through the market. Outside of unionized firms, few organizations offer due process procedures of appeal that include third-party arbitrators or "neutrals." Without such a final appellant level in the process, due process will be suspect, both to employees and to the public at large. A second right few employees have gained is that of "blowing the whistle" on illegal, questionable activities by others in the organization, particularly managers. Typically managers penalize whistle blowers, unable to recognize the help they may offer in maintaining quality standards, protecting consumers and thus the firm's reputation, and assisting managers in making sure those within the organization take seriously the various codes of ethics that many firms promulgate. A third right, closely related to the first two, is the right of free speech, something that American employees might particularly expect. A fourth right to which managerial attention has not been paid in recent decades, particularly among the rapidly growing retail trade and services sectors, is that of a more, rather than less, egalitarian wage structure. Occupational barriers in education and the health industries have promoted wider wage differentials than were usually found in modern manufacturing industries.

Recent surveys of employees and top executive perceptions of work satisfactions suggest that managers are out of touch with those they work in their firms and have not carefully considered how rights, such as the four mentioned, might be offered to enhance worker satisfaction. A 1987–1988 survey by Louis Harris and Associates, Inc. indicated that whereas 46 percent of office workers were very satisfied with their jobs, and 41 percent were somewhat satisfied, 75 percent of top executives believed their workers were very satisfied, and 19 percent believed that they were somewhat satisfied. See Louis Harris and Associates, Inc., *The Office Environment Index, 1988 Summary Report* (Grand Rapids, MI: Steelcase, Stow & Davis, 1988), p. 4.

2.   County of Santa Clara v. Southern Pacific Railroad Company, 118 U.S. 394 (1886).

3.   See Commonwealth v. Pullis (1806), reported in Commons and Gilmore, *A Documentary History of American Industrial Society*, pp. 59–236; Commonwealth v. Hunt, 4 Metcalf, 111 (Mass. 1842), Plant v. Woods, 176 Mass. 492 (1900), Pickett v. Walsh, 192 Mass. 572 (1906), and American Steel Foundries v. Tri-City Central Trades Council, 257 U.S. 181 (1921).

4.   NLRB v. Jones & Laughlin Corp., 301 U.S. 1 (1937).

5.   Quoted in Allan Nevins, *Study in Power: John D. Rockefeller, Industrialist and Philanthropist* (New York: Charles Scribner's Sons) 1953, vol. I, p. 402.

6.   Sigmund Diamond, *The Reputation of the American Businessman* (Cambridge: Harvard University Press, 1955), p. 53.

7.   Alfred L. Thimm, *Business Iedologies in the Reform-Progressive Era, 1880–1914* (Tuscaloosa: The University of Alabama Press, 1976), p. 166–167.

8.   John William Ward, "The Ideal of Individualism and the Reality of Organization," *The Business Establishment*, Earl F. Cheit, ed. (New York: John Wiley & Sons, 1964), p. 43. The ideas of this section are based on Ward's arguments.

9.   See Henry Nash Smith, *Virgin Land: The American West as Symbol and Myth* (Cambridge: Harvard University Press, 1950).

10. Herbert Hoover, *The Challenge to Liberty* (New York: Charles Scribner's Sons, 1934), pp. 54–55.

11. John William Ward, "The Ideal of Individualism and the Reality of Organization," *The Business Establishment*, Earl F. Cheit, editor (New York: John Wiley & Sons, 1964), pp. 39–40.

12. Geary v. U.S Steel Corporation, 319 A.2d 174, Supreme Court of Pennsylvania, 1974. For other such cases, see David W. Ewing, *"Do it my way or You're Fired!"*: Employee Rights and the Changing Role of Management Prerogatives (New York: John Wiley & Sons, 1983).

13. See the case of David Edwards, Citicorp, Roy Rowan, "The Maverick Who Yelled Foul at Citibank," *Fortune*, January 10, 1983.

14. John William Ward, *The Business Establishment*, p. 73.

15. The Bureau of Labor Statistics no longer publishes turnover figures, but over the years that it did, for manufacturing production workers, turnover typically involved from 4 to 5 percent of the measured labor force each month. Although the core of any work force may be quite stable and some employees may be hold jobs for years, a sizable portion of them come and go all the time.

16. Robert F. Hoxie, *Trade Unionism in the United States* (New York: D. Appleton & Co., 1917).

17. Quoted in the "Report of the Industrial Commission on the Relations and Conditions of Capital and Labor," *Hearings*, April 19, 1899, 7 (Washington, DC: Government Printing Office), p. 645.

18. Charles M. Schwab, chair, Bethlehem Steel, in a speech to a Chamber of Commerce group, 1918, declared: "I believe that labor should organize in individual plants or amongst themselves for the better negotiation of labor and the protection of their own rights; but the organization and control of labor in individual plants and manufactories, to my mind, ought to be made representative of the people in those plants, who know the conditions; that they ought not to be controlled by somebody from Kamchatka who knows nothing about what their conditions are." "Capital and Labor," *Annuals of the American Academy of Political and Social Science*, January 1919, p. 158.

19. Samuel Gompers, *Labor and The Employer* (New York: E. P. Dutton & Company, 1920), p. 102.

20. Charles C. Heckscher, *The New Unionism: Employee Involvement in the Changing Corporation* (New York: Basic Books, 1988), p. 28.

21. The Norris–LaGuardia Act, 1932, passively encouraged union organizing, only by relieving unions of the previously imposed judicial restraints. The Wagner Act, 1936, actively encouraged union organizing and protected collective bargaining. In 1947 Congress passed the Taft-Hartley Act, which imposed some restrictions upon unions and limits on collective bargaining. The Landrum–Griffin Act, 1959, increased both the number of restrictions and limits and sought to regulate some of the internal affairs of unions.

22. Neil W. Chamberlain, *The Union Challenge To Management Control* (New York: Harper, 1948).

23. Thomas A. Kochan, "Adaptability of the U.S. Industrial Relations System," *Science*, April 15, 1988, p. 280.

24. Kathryn Rudie Harrigan and Michael E. Porter, "Endgame strategies for declining industries," *Harvard Business Review* (July/August 1983), pp. 111–120.

25. (Boston: Houghton Mifflin Company, 1967). This volume had been preceded by two other influential studies of the modern corporation and its considerable but not necessarily benign contributions to society. The first was *American Capitalism: The Concept of Countervailing Power* (Boston: Houghton Mifflin Company, 1952), and the second was *The Affluent Society* (London: Hamish Hamilton, 1958).

26. Adolf A. Berle and Gardiner C. Means, *The Modern Corporation and Private Property*, rev. ed. (New York: Harcourt Brace & World, 1968), first examined the new industrial

corporation that had emerged after the turn of the century. They emphasized the separation of ownership and control, with managers effectively exercising power.

27. See Peter Drucker, "The Coming of the New Organization," *Harvard Business Review* (January/February 1988), p. 53.

28. S. Frederick Starr, president of Oberlin College, has noted that even so centralized, powerful, and all controlling an organization as that of the Soviet government has not been able to control its external and internal environments. He writes that "the regime had become petrified and oligarchic, thereby repressing the very forces that might have stimulated economic renewal . . . while the official economy lagged, an entrepreneurial 'second economy' burgeoned. . . . Economic stagnation . . . occurred because the system failed to adjust to the emerging values of the populace, especially its best educated and technically most competent elements." "Soviet Union: A Civil Society," *Foreign Policy*, No. 70 (Spring 1988), pp. 26–27. It is ironic that the large American business corporation should suffer some of the same troubles that the centralized state planning system of the Soviets has encountered. As the reader will see in the following analysis, the sources of those troubles are remarkably similar; both capitalism and Socialism are subject to them. Or more accurately, one can characterize the large, Galbraithian business corporation as the closest Americans have come to a socialistic system.

29. See the description of the modern corporation given by the Committee for Economic Development (CED): "One of the most important changes is that the corporation is regarded and operated as a *permanent institution* in society. . . . [The] aim is to further the continuous institutional development of the corporation in a very long time frame. . . . As a permanent institution, the large corporation is developing long-term goals such as survival, growth, and increasing respect and acceptance by the public." CED, *Social Responsibilities of Business Corporations*, June 1971, pp. 21–22. In the light of the continual change in a capitalistic economy, with even large firms appearing and disappearing, this statement is more an expression of hubris than fact. In the 70 years between 1917 and 1987, 78 percent of the firms on a list of the 100 largest in the earlier year did not survive to appear on the list during the latter year. See *Forbes*, July 13, 1987, pp. 49ff.

30. Peter Drucker, "The Coming of the New Organization," *Harvard Business Review* (January/February 1988), p. 45. Richard A. Gabriel notes that the military, during World War II, borrowed the same hierarchical, bureaucratic model back from the large corporations. It had become the recognized standard of what "a large organization should be," if one wanted to gain both efficiency and control. See Richard A. Gabriel, "What the Army Learned From Business," *The New York Times*, April 15, 1979. The Roman Catholic church may also have been a indirect model for the newly emerging business corporation. A large proportion of the industrial work force were probably Catholic, and many were immigrant. Both their new arrival in the country and their acceptance of the church's organization may well have conditioned them to the authoritarian, hierarchical form of their employing corporations. The workers acceptance of a similar form in their unions, as well as in the business firm, may thus have been facilitated.

31. Alfred D. Chandler, Jr., and Herman Daem, *Managerial Hierarchies* (Cambridge: Harvard University Press, 1980), p. 1.

32. William J. Hampton and James R. Norman, "General Motors: What Went Wrong?" *Business Week*, March 16, 1987.

33. See *Employment and Training Report of the President*, 1982 (Washington, DC: Government Printing Office, 1982), Table C-2, p. 241. "Administrative and managerial personnel" made up over 10 percent of all nonagricultural employment in the United States in 1980, compared to 4.4 percent in Japan, 3 percent in West Germany, and 2.4 percent in

Sweden. See Mark J. Green and John F. Berry, "Taming the Corpocracy: The Forces Behind White-Collar Layoffs," *The New York Times*, F3, October 13, 1985.

34. Robert Jackall, *Moral Mazes: The World of Corporate Managers* (New York: Oxford University Press, 1988), and Michael Maccoby, *The Gamesman: The New Corporate Leaders* (New York: Simon and Schuster, 1976).

35. The Committee for Economic Development, *Social Responsibilities of Business Corporations*, A Statement on National Policy by the Research and Policy Committee of the Committee for Economic Development, June 1971, p. 20.

36. Clifton Garvin, "Exxon and the Arts," *The Lamp*, 1978, p. 10.

37. "Statement on Corporate Responsibility," *Business & Society: Economic, Moral an Political Foundations* (Englewood Cliffs, NJ: Prentice-Hall Inc., 1985), p. 155.

38. Paul W. MacAvoy, "The Business Lobby's Wrong Business," *The New York Times*, December 20, 1981.

39. Andrew C. Sigler, "Roundtable Reply," *The New York Times*, December 27, 1981.

40. Bruce Nussbaum and Judith H. Dobrzynski, "The Battle For Corporate Control," *Business Week*, May 18, 1987, p. 103.

41. Ibid.

42. Ibid., p. 22.

43. "Statement on Corporate Responsibility," *Business & Society: Economic, Moral and Political Foundations*, ed. Thomas G. Marx (Englewood Cliffs, NJ: Prentice-Hall Inc., 1985), p. 155.

44. The reader should note that business corporations have hardly been generous in even their charitable giving. In absolute amounts, their gifts appear large, compared to family incomes. In 1979 dollars, they provided between $1.0 billion and $2.3 billion, 1955–1980; however, as a share of their own pretex net income, they have contributed from a low of 0.86 percent in 1955 and 1956, to a high of 1.26 percent in 1969." "Lend A Helping Hand," *Public Opinion* (February/March 1982), p. 24.

45. See Earl F. Cheit, "The New Place of Business: Why Managers Cultivate Social Responsibility," *The Business Establishment*, Earl F. Cheit, ed. (New York: John Wiley & Sons, 1964), p. 157–8.

46. The Business Roundtable statement, however, mentioned plant closing as a socially difficult problem, requiring a careful balancing of various constituency interests. It did not call for the participation of constituencies in arriving at a decision, however; managers both could and should make it by themselves, in the interests of the various constituencies involved.

47. Such essential irresponsibility may provide the economy with a flexibility that is far more productive than those adversely affected realize. Compare the ease with which a business firm closes an out-of-date plant with the difficulties encountered by the Department of Defense when it attempts to close unneeded military bases, obsolete supply depots, and inefficient facilities.

48. CED, *Social Responsibilities of Business Corporations*, pp. 63–64.

49. Milton Friedman, *Capitalism and Freedom* (Chicago: The University of Chicago Press, 1963), pp. 133–134.

50. Paul W. MacAvoy, "The Business Lobby's Wrong Business," *The New York Times*, December 20, 1981.

51. Peter Drucker, "Corporate takeovers—What is to do done?", *The Public Interest*, No. 12 (Winter 1986), p. 20.

52. From George A. Stevens, *New York Typographical Union No. 6*, New York State Department of Labor, Annual Report of the Bureau of Labor Statistics (1911), Part I, pp. 239–241.

53. Quoted in Lewis Corey, *The House of Morgan* (New York: G. Howard Watt, 1930), p. 213.

54. Royal Meeker, "Employees' Representation in Management of Industry," *Monthly Labor Review*, Vol. 10, 1920, p. 7. Italics added.
55. "Taking Aim at 'Union Busters'," *Business Week*, November 12, 1979, p. 98.
56. Carey W. English, "Business Is Booming for 'Union Busters'," *U.S. News & World Report*, Vol. 94, May 16, 1983, p. 61.
57. Quoted by Earl Lathan, "The Body Politic of the Corporation," *The Corporation In Modern Society*, Edward S. Mason, ed. (Cambridge: Harvard University Press, 1959), p. 223.
58. David W. Ewing, *Freedom Inside the Organization: Bringing Civil Liberties To The Workplace* (New York: E. P. Dutton, 1977), p. 21.
59. Ian Cameron, "In Defense of Conflict?" *Unilever Magazine* (September–October 1974), p. 30.
60. Harry Levinson and Stuart Rosenthal, *CEO: Corporate Leadership in Action* (New York: Basic Books, 1984), p. 4.
61. Allen Weiss, *The Organization Guerrilla: Playing the Game to Win* (New York: Atheneum, 1975), Part III, pp. 91–124.
62. Hierarchy is so integral a part of modern business enterprises that Alfred D. Chandler, Jr., defines them as economic institutions, owning and operating a multiunit system and relying on a multilevel managerial hierarchy for administration.
63. An economy of small business units would require a great many more market exchanges than at present. Such exchanges, or transactions, are costly; about one-fifth of the labor force is presently employed in wholesale and retail trade. Although many of the workers involved store, move, and package the goods with which they deal, a sizable portion of them merely administer, carry out the exchanges, and record them.
64. See Fritz Roethlisberger, *Management and Morale* (Cambridge: Harvard University Press, 1943).
65. Mayo had reached this conclusion *before* he conducted the experiment, and without noting carefully the research findings. Two work groups were involved, men in the bank wiring room and women in the test room. The productivity of the former did not change over the course of the experiment, whereas that of the latter did. Mayo ignored the difference, focusing upon the test room outcomes as proof of his conclusion. William Foote Whyte offered another interpretation: The test room women functioned as an autonomous work group, whereas the men's group continued to work under the close supervision of the foreman. See his "Review of the Elusive Phenomena," *Human Organization*, Vol. 37, No. 4, pp. 412–420.
66. See Elton Mayo, *The Social Problems of an Industrial Civilization* (Boston: Graduate School of Business Administration, Harvard University, 1945).
67. Peter Drucker roundly condemns managers invocation of prerogatives. "This is a singularly unfortunate phrase. A prerogative is a privilege of rank. Management has no claim to any such privilege. It exists to discharge a function. Its job is to make productive the resources in its trust. A prerogative is never based on responsibility or contribution. . . . Management has authority only as long as it performs. To invoke management prerogatives undermines managerial authority." *Management: Tasks, Responsibilities, Practices* (New York: Harper & Row, 1973), p. 301.
68. See William Foote Whyte, "From Human Relations to Organizational Behavior: Reflections on the Changing Scene," *Industrial and Labor Relations Review*, Vol. 40 (July 1987), p. 492.
69. Philip H. Abelson, "Competitiveness: A Long-Enduring Problem," *Science*, May 13, 1988, p. 865.
70. William Shepherd, "Causes of Increased Competition in the U.S. Economy, 1939–1980," 64 *Review of Economics and Statistics* (November 1982), p. 613.

71. Carrie Gottlieb, "And You Thought You Had It Tough," *Fortune*, April 25, 1988, p. 83.

72. The Council of Economic Advisers have argued that "the share of value added in manufacturing has remained remarkably stable throughout the postwar years, fluctuating in a narrow range between 19 and 23 percent." *Economic Report of the President*, 1988 (Washington: Government Printing Office, 1988), p. 63. But Lawrence R. Mishel of the Economic Policy Institute concludes that the official statistics are dated, based upon an input–output model unchanged since 1977. He calculates that the decline has been one of "unprecedented magnitude." See Robert Kuttner, "U.S. industry if wasting away— But official figures don't show it," *Business Week*, May 16, 1988, p. 26.

73. See *Statistical Abstract of the United States, 1987*, (Washington: Government Printing Office, 1987), Table No. 858, p. 507.

74. *The Economist*, March 5, 1988.

75. George Gilder, "The Revitalization of Everything: The Law of the Microcosm," *Harvard Business Review*, March–April 1988, pp. 49–61.

76. Claudia H. Deutsch, "U.S. Industry's Unfinished Struggle," *The New York Times*, February 21, 1988.

77. Louis Lowenstein, "Pruning Deadwood in Hostile Takeovers: A Proposal for Legislation," 83 *Columbia Law Review* 249, pp. 297–298 (1983). He suggests that institutional investors own an even higher share of the corporations in the Standard & Poor's 500 stock index. Also see Ford S. Worthy, "What's Next for the Raiders," *Fortune*, November 11, 1986, p. 23. Peter Drucker gives a figure of 50 percent of all publicly traded common shares of large firms. "Corporate takeovers—What is to be done?", *The Public Interest*, No. 12 (Winter 1986) p. 11.

78. Bruce Nussbaum and Judith H. Dobrzynski, "The Battle For Corporate Control," *Business Week*, May 18, 1987, pp. 103–104.

79. Nearly half of the 47 million U.S. households owning stock hold it through mutual funds. The number of mutual funds has increased rapidly in recent years. Through 1985 and 1986 the number of mutual-fund shareholders increased by 2.7 million. Because households sold more stock than they bought, over the same period, for a total of $227 billion, it is probable that many are not withdrawing from the market but transferring their assets from individual accounts to mutual funds. George Russell, "Manic Market," *Time*, November 10, 1986, p. 67. Also see Kenneth R. Sheets *et al.*, "How The Market Is Rigged Against You," *U.S. News and World Report*, December 1, 1986, p. 47. Also see Nancy J. Perry, "Who Runs Your Company Anyway?" *Fortune*, September 12, 1988, p. 140. "Pension funds now own 25%, by value of all corporate shares traded in the U.S. They own 50% of the shares traded on the New York Stock Exchange and 65% of the Standard & Poor's 500 stocks." Perry presents data indicating that public funds total $576 billion, and private funds are nearly twice as large, $1,053 billion; union funds take a poor third place with $131 billion. She estimates that by 2000 pension funds assets will amount to $3.5 trillion dollars and will represent half of all corporate equity.

80. See Anthony Bianco, "American Business Has a New Kingpin: The Investment Banker," *Business Week*, November 24, 1986, p. 77. He quotes John Kenneth Galbraith, who expressed his surprise at what is happening. His earlier studies gave no hint that managers would ever have to worry about any constituency, particularly the unorganized, passive stockholders.

81. Peter C. Clapman and Richard M. Schlefer, "Recipe for a Management Autocracy," *The New York Times*, December 14, 1986.

82. For example, the California Public Employee Retirement System and the NYS Employees Retirement Fund asked for a formal long-term role in choosing Texaco directors. The New York fund holds 3 million shares and the California fund owns 783,000 shares; there

are 244.3 million shares outstanding. A number of large corporations have responded, albeit reluctantly, to the demands of institutional investors. Alcoa, General Mills, Sara Lee Corporation, and Loral Corporation have agreed to conduct board elections through secret ballot. Allanna Sullivan, "Two of Texaco's Institutional Holders to Seek a Role in Nominating Directors," *The Wall Street Journal*, August 17, 1988.

83. The share of middle managers who report favorable views of their opportunities for advancement dropped from 72 percent in 1975–1977 to 39 percent in 1983–1985. Twenty-eight percent said that merger/reorganization had changed their views. Carol Hymowitz, "Stable Cycles of Executive Careers Shattered by Upheaval in Business," *The Wall Street Journal*, May 26, 1988. Presumably most top managers arrange to bail out of a merger with a golden parachute.

84. Lipset and Schneider, p. 167. The negative opinions were consistent over four surveys, 1966–1978.

85. William Serrin, "Study Says Work Ethics Is Alive but Neglected," *The New York Times*, September 5, 1983, p. 8.

86. In 1962, over 15 percent of all the employed still worked for themselves, one-third of them in agriculture. By 1985 less than 10 percent were self-employed, and those in agriculture accounted for fewer than one out of six.

87. Claudia H. Deutsch, "U.S. Industry's Unfinished Struggle," *The New York Times*, February 21, 1988.

88. Ibid.

89. "Educational Level of U.S. Work Force Rises, Report Shows," *The Wall Street Journal*, August 30, 1988.

90. *The Wall Street Journal*, May 13, 1988.

91. *The Confidence Gap*, p. 120.

92. *Business Week*, September 12, 1988, p. 72.

93. *Business Week*, August 8, 1988, p. 46.

94. Robert H. Hayes and Ramchandran Jaikumar have also pointed out the dangers of American managers concentrating their efforts on "hardware" improvements rather than examining the adequacy of their personnel policies, attitudes, and habits of mind. "The real impediment [to productivity improvement] lies not in the inherent demands of the hardware but in the managerial infrastructure that has become embedded in most U.S. companies over the past 50 years. This includes the attitudes, policies, systems, and habits of mind that are so ingrained and pervasive within companies that they are almost invisible to those within them. . . . Traditional managerial attitudes, manifested in top-down decision making, piecemeal changes, and a 'bottom-line' mentality are incompatible with the requirements and unique capabilities of advanced manufacturing systems. . . . [We need] profound reform in the modern corporation . . . new working relationships. At a still higher level, reform means that top officers must cultivate new skills and managerial styles. It may well require a new generation of executives. "Manufacturing's Crisis: New Technologies; Obsolete Organizations," *Harvard Business Review*, September/October 1988, p. 79.

95. John T. Dunlop, "Have the 1980's changed U.S industrial relations?", *The Monthly Labor Review*, Vol. 111 (May 1988), pp. 29–34.

96. Audrey Freedman, "How the 1980's have changed industrial relations," *The Monthly Labor Review*, Vol. 111 (May 1988), pp. 35–38.

97. Elmer W. Johnson, "Management and Labor: Breaking Away," a presentation made to faculty and students at DePaul University, Chicago, Illinois, Spring 1988, pp. 5–6.

IV

PERSPECTIVES ON EDUCATION
Disciplines and Disciples

In the previous section, attention was given to such special interest groups as business, unions, and minorities. The power of vested interests is widely recognized. The power of vested ideas is less visible. Yet John Maynard Keynes, the British economist whose ideas have influenced government policies of nearly all the major nations of Western Europe, has said that, sooner or later, "it is ideas, not vested interests, which are important for good or evil."[1] Barry Schwartz has taken the Keynesian maxim so seriously that he has been impelled—if not propelled—into an in-depth analysis of the major paradigms of economics, the results of which were given in a book whose title suggests what high stakes are involved in the world of ideas. He called it The Battle for Human Nature.[2]*

Among the paradigms of neoclassical economics are the following: (1) individuals and firms seek to maximize gains and minimize losses; (2) the "invisible hand" of competition in the market disciplines sellers and buyers; (3) the effects of such disciplinary norms is to reward efficiency and punish inefficiency; and (4) the net result is increased wealth for the country as a whole. By working to promote their own self-interests, individuals wind up promoting the good of others' interests. The formula is tidy and appealing, so much so that the leaders of the scientific revolution had hailed it for its impersonalism and for its quasi-mechanical interpretations of business activity.

Not probed in the following section is the question whether neoclassical economics fails on its own terms because its theory of value is inadequate. As a professional psychologist, Schwartz wisely refrains from excursions into price theory and concentrates on the area he knows best, human behavior. From this vantage point, he moves his analysis into the fields of evolutionary biology and Skinnerian psychology. What is uncovered is an intersection of paradigms that results in narrowing our conception of the human being into something approach-

ing a mechanical robot—energized by the wires of self-interest, "manufactured" on the basis of a prototype designed in the faraway mists of time, and yet malleable in the hands of some master who knows how to make the paradigms palatable.

If such lessons are taught in some of the basic courses business students take today, do they know what they are getting? Not likely. And their ignorance could be costly, especially in light of research findings that show that the years 21 to 35 are important in shaping the moral character of individuals. Fortunately, James Glenn has undertaken to demonstrate through empirically derived data what the disciples in such disciplines believe and how they act. Glenn's findings include (1) student assessments of the inadequacy of training in business ethics; (2) perceptions of likely irresistible pressure in their future work environments to compromise personal values; and (3) reports of student cheating in their present academic environments. Implications of this research for educators—admissions, curriculum, class environment, faculty development, and future research—are offered as well as some "lessons" for business organizations in terms of their recruitment and promotion policies.

NOTES

1. John Maynard Keynes, *The General Theory of Unemployment, Interest and Money* (New York: Harcourt Brace, 1936), p. 384.
2. Barry Schwartz, *The Battle for Human Nature: Science, Morality and Modern Life* (New York: Norton, 1986).

7

King Midas in America
Science, Morality, and Modern Life

Barry Schwartz

If a man does away with his traditional way of living and throws away his good customs,
he had better first make certain that he has something of value to replace them.
                                                        —*Traditional African saying*[1]

I. INTRODUCTION

The new conservatism that captured America's fancy in this, the Reagan decade, is actually two distinct conservatisms. It is an *economic conservatism* that has tried to dismantle the welfare state and turn as many facets of life as possible over to the free-market, private sector. And it is a *moral conservatism* that has attempted to strengthen traditional values and the social institutions that foster them. These two conservatisms correspond, of course, to the economic and social agendas that have guided the policies of the Reagan administration since the president took office. The president and his supporters seem to share not only the belief that free-market economics and traditional moral values are good but that they go together, that it is possible simultaneously to strengthen both.

This is a serious mistake. The theory and practice of free-market economics have done more in the last two centuries to undermine tradi-

Barry Schwartz • Department of Psychology, Swarthmore College, Swarthmore, Pennsylvania 19081.

tional moral values than any other social force. It is not permissive parents, undisciplined teachers, prochoicers, fanatical civil libertarians, rock musicians, or drug pushers who are the primary sources of the corrosion that the moral majority is trying to repair. Instead, it is the operation of the market system itself, along with an ideology that justifies the pursuit of economic self-interest by appeal to science.

We are now engaged in what I have elsewhere called a "battle for human nature."[2] The battle is between traditional, moral conceptions and modern scientific conceptions of what it means to be a human being. The primary weapons in this battle are ideas, ideas that have their effect of helping shape the way we understand ourselves, and thus, what we expect from, and contribute to, the various social institutions and practices that surround us.

In this chapter, I am going to focus on a particular set of ideas that was born in the Enlightenment and has grown steadily in importance ever since. At present, this set of ideas forms the core of parts of the academic disciplines of economics, evolutionary biology, and behavioral psychology. Together, these disciplines share the view that significant human actions are governed not by discretion, moral evaluation, and choice, but by laws of nature. Together, these disciplines share the view that people are, by nature, self-interested, egoistic, and acquisitive without limit. Together, these disciplines provide an ideology that underwrites our current economic conservatism and simultaneously undermines any attempt to retrieve traditional moral values.

Since the writings of philosopher David Hume, 250 years ago, we have grown accustomed to the view that facts and values, is and ought, science and morality, must be kept separate. About facts it is appropriate to ask, "true or false?" About morals it is appropriate to ask, "good or bad?" But woe unto him who confuses these domains. Such a person might find himself asking questions like "Is it true or false that adultery is a sin?" or "Is it good or bad that the planets revolve around the sun?" Indeed, we are so accustomed to this view of the separation of *is* and *ought* that it is second nature to us. Facts are objective and definite; they are the province of science. Morals are subjective and individual; they are matters of opinion. It is hard to imagine carving up the world in any other way.

However, though it seems natural to carve the world into these two categories, it is not so easy to find the joints. For example, is deciding whether abortion is murder a matter of fact or a matter of opinion? Most modern Americans, I think, regard it as a matter of opinion, but does not a decision depend in part on what we think the facts are about when life begins? Or to take another example, do we routinely abridge the civil rights of children by restricting them in various ways and giving others legal authority over them? Well, does not the answer to this question depend on what we think the facts are about who is or is not a fully responsible human being? There have been times in our own national history, after all, when people who were not male, were not white, and did not own property were not regarded as fully responsible human beings.

The point is that the boundary between the domain of facts and the domain of morals is fuzzy and continually changing. And the challenge posed by economics, evolutionary biology, and behavioral psychology to our everyday conception of things is precisely that they are attempting to move aspects of human action that we have always placed squarely in the domain of morals into the domain of facts, of scientific laws. If it is a law of nature that people are self-interested and greedy, out to satisfy their preferences, then it makes no more sense to ask if they *ought* to be than it does to ask if stones ought to fall to the ground when dropped. And economics tells us that the pursuit of self-interest is a law of nature. If it is a law of nature that people are out to maximize the number of their genetically related offspring in the next generation, then it makes no more sense to ask if they *ought* to do that than it does to ask if water should boil when it is heated. And evolutionary biology tells us that it is a law of nature. Finally, if it is a law of nature that people are out to maximize the reward or reinforcement they obtain, then it makes little sense to ask whether reinforcement should be used to manipulate people—because it already does and always has. And behavioral psychology tells us that it is a law of nature. This is the view of human nature espoused many years ago by William Graham Sumner when he said, "The truth is that the social order is fixed by laws of nature precisely analogous to those of the physical order."[3]

I believe that this view is false, at least as a universal, timeless description of what it means to be a person. However, I also believe that under certain social conditions—conditions that now exist—it can be true. In short, nowadays, in modern industrial societies, people are greedy, egoistic, self-interest maximizers. But one of the reasons these conditions exist is that economics, evolutionary biology, and behavioral psychology are the living descendants of an intellectual tradition that has helped to foster these conditions and to justify them. These disciplines do provide a partly accurate description of reality, but it is of a reality that they have helped create.

Furthermore, as it becomes increasingly true of people that they are out to maximize self-interest; as human "economic" nature crowds more and more of human "moral" nature out, huge tears in the social fabric begin to appear that threaten our social and political well-being. This is why the Reagan economic agenda undercuts the social agenda. The lesson of King Midas is not so much that "money isn't everything." It is that not everything is money. And if we make everything money, we have nothing to eat, or to read, or to sleep with. But this gets us ahead of our story. Let us see what economics, evolutionary biology, and behavioral psychology tell us about people, what is wrong with what they tell us, and what are some of the unfortunate social consequences of believing it.

II.   ECONOMICS

In 1650, a Boston minister gave a sermon on immoral principles of trade. First among them was "that a man might sell as dear as he can and buy as cheap as he can."[4] Less than 200 years later, all of Europe and the United States was operating in accord with that principle, not because it had been newly adjudged to be moral but because it was human nature.

The midwife of this transformation was Adam Smith. In his famous book, *The Wealth of Nations* (1776), he put forth a conception of man's economic nature—of economic man—that has guided economics ever since. First, he said, we can look at the economy as an autonomous system, governed by natural laws and distinct from other human social institutions like the church, the family, or the state. Second, at the heart of this autonomous system is the "market," a stage on which economic men play out their propensity to "truck and barter," to exchange. And finally, the actors on this stage, the economic men, are guided by a few simple principles. They are ruled by self-interest. And they are never satisfied; they always want something. As a predecessor of Smith's, Bernard Mandeville put it:

> Men are naturally selfish; what makes them sociable is their necessity and consciousness of standing in need of others' help to make life comfortable. And what makes this assistance voluntary and lasting are the gains of profit accruing to industry for services done to others.[5]

Or as Smith himself put it, "It is not from the benevolence of the butcher, the brewer, or the baker that we expect our dinner, but from their regard to their self-interest."[6] Smith thought that if (and only if) people were left alone to exchange in the market, the market's "invisible hand" would give everyone what he wanted for an acceptable price. What assured this result was competition. The invisible hand of competition was the same kind of hand that pushes the planets around the sun; it was the hand of nature. Moreover, the system would not be stagnant. Through profit, capital accumulation, and investment, technological advance in automation and in the division of labor would increase the productivity of society, making everyone better off. The rich would get richer, but the poor would get richer too.

This was Smith's understanding of the economy and of the people who inhabited it, and it is plain that our current, conservative economic policies are Smith's direct descendants. But for Smith, economic man was not total man. He wrote another book, called *The Theory of Moral Sentiments*, in which he talked of "natural sympathy" as a part of human nature that provided a needed restraint on self-interest. He said:

> All the members of human society stand in need of each other's assistance. . . . Where the necessary assistance is reciprocally afforded from love, from gratitude, from friendship and esteem, the society flourishes and is happy. . . . Society, however, cannot subsist among those who are at all times ready to hurt and injure one another.[7]

Smith therefore understood that the economic story about people was not the whole story. However, as his ideas were developed by others, the notion of economic man was increasingly refined and formalized. Economics became *economic science*. Simultaneously, the moral side of people got crowded out. Initially, this was only a short-run, methodological strategy, an effort to keep things simple, and build up the temple of truth one brick at a time. But as so often happens in the history of science, methodological strategies were transformed in almost imperceptible stages into theoretical principles. Economic science slowly became not the science of part of man but the science of all of man. To be a person was nothing more than to be a rational economic agent. Economist Gary Becker put it thus:

> The economic approach is a comprehensive one that is applicable to all human behavior, be it behavior involving . . . emotional or mechanical ends, rich or poor persons, men or women, adults or children . . . businessmen or politicians, teachers or students.[8]

According to modern economic science, rational economic agents have the following characteristics:

1. Like young children, they make no distinction between "needs" and "wants." All desires have equal legitimacy.
2. They are never satisfied; they always want something.
3. What they want, and how much they want it, varies from person to person. Wants are individual and idiosyncratic, and interpersonal comparisons of wants are impossible. In other words, there is no way to judge whether my desire for privacy that led me to build a 12-foot high cinderblock wall around my property is greater or less than your desire for a beautiful neighborhood that led you to want to tear it down.
4. Because of this, the free market is the perfect way, perhaps the only way, to assess wants and determine value. How much you

need it is the same as how much you want it, and how much you want it becomes how much you will pay for it.

5. Rational economic men prefer more of something to less.
6. They prefer lower prices to higher.
7. They have preferences that are relatively stable over time.
8. They have preferences that are transitive (if they prefer apples to oranges, and oranges to bananas, then they prefer apples to bananas).
9. They choose with perfect information about what is available, for what price, in the market. It is as though the free market were a gigantic Chinese restaurant menu.
10. They choose always to maximize their preferences, or utilities.
11. Their choices obey the law of diminishing marginal utility; that is, the more they have of something, the less valuable each additional unit of it is.
12. Finally, rational economic men regard labor as a *disutility*, a means, a necessary evil with no intrinsic value. Rational economic men work to eat. As Adam Smith put it, "it is in the inherent interest of every man to live as much at his ease as he can."9

These are the characteristics that economists regard as the hallmark of rational, economic agents. These are the laws that people obey in their commerce with the world. And what is important, people obey these laws not in the way that they obey traffic laws but in the way that they obey laws of gravity. The pursuit of self-interest is not a matter of discretion, moral evaluation, and choice; it is a matter of natural inevitability. People need answer for their selfishness no more than planets need answer for their movement around the sun.

III. SOCIOBIOLOGY

If the economist's claims about human nature were unallied with other disciplines, we might be forgiven a certain skepticism in judging them. People live in different kinds of cultures, pass different kinds of laws, pursue widely varied interests. It seems as though people change with experience; they are influenced by the growth of knowledge about how the world works and by changing opinions about how people should conduct themselves. Why suggest then that people are *naturally* out to pursue their self-interest? Why not suggest instead that people are *taught* to pursue their self-interest? And this distinction is not merely an academic one. If people are taught to pursue self-interest as rational economic men, it is appropriate for us to ask whether this is what they *should* be taught. If the pursuit of self-interest is bred in the bone, then the question of *should* is of diminished importance.

But the economist is not without intellectual allies. Especially important allies come from the discipline of evolutionary biology, whose foundations were established in the nineteenth century by Charles Darwin. Darwin had largely developed his theory of evolution by natural selection by 1835, but he was missing the engine that drove the selection process. Then he read the Reverend Malthus and his *Essay on the Principle of Population* (1798). Malthus argued that population growth would outstrip the growth in food supply, that competition for scarce resources would result, and that only the fittest would survive the competition. Europe was in for massive starvation.

This gave Darwin the engine for natural selection—competition for scarce resources. Organisms possessing highly varied characteristics were born. Because resources were scarce, however, not all of them could survive. Natural competition for scarce resources would lead to survival—natural selection—of the fittest. As Darwin said:

> A struggle for existence inevitably follows from the high rate at which all organic beings tend to increase. . . . As more individuals are produced than could possibly survive, there must in every case be a struggle for existence. . . . It is the doctrine of Malthus applied with manifold force to the whole animal and vegetable kingdoms.[10]

An extremely influential modern descendant of Darwinian theory is *sociobiology*. It is a systematic attempt to explain the social behavior of humans and nonhumans alike by appeal to principles of natural selection. The central principle of sociobiology is that organisms are self-interested maximizers of utility. In economics, utility can be anything; it is an individual affair. In biology, utility is reproductive fitness. Nobel Prize Winner Peter Medawar says, "'fitness' is in effect a system of pricing the endowments of organisms in the currency of offspring, that is, in terms of net reproductive performance."[11]

Indeed, some argue that it is not even organisms but their *genes* that are the self-interest maximizers. Gene selfishness is the logic of biology, nature's way. The logic is roughly this. Genes are simply machines that reproduce themselves by reproducing the bodies they inhabit. Bodies that are good at staying alive and making copies will win the competition for scarce resources, and their genes will make copies more often than genes that live in less efficient bodies. And the bodies that look out for themselves and their genetic relatives will be the ones that are good at reproducing their genes. Genes living in bodies that spend time looking after other creatures, with different genes, will fare poorly. Thus the pursuit of self-interest is simply a fact of biology. To the extent that genes determine behavior, they determine behavior that is self-interested. As Michael Ghiselin says:

> The economy of nature is competitive from beginning to end. . . . No hint of genuine charity ameliorates our vision of society once sentimentalism has been laid aside. What passes for cooperation turns out to be a mixture of opportunism and exploitation. . . . Scratch an altruist and watch a hypocrite bleed.[12]

Sociobiologists use this principle of genetic selfishness to explain a wide variety of social behaviors that do not appear, on their face, to be selfish. For the most part, they study the social behavior of nonhuman animals, which they take to be genetically determined, and then argue by analogy to human behavior. The not quite syllogistic structure of such arguments is roughly this:

1. The behavior of Species X is genetically determined.
2. Species X does Behavior Y.
3. People also do Behavior Y.
4. Therefore, Behavior Y in people is also genetically determined.

From our perspective, this last step is the important one. If the pursuit of self-interest in people is genetically determined, as the biologists suggest, then the claims of economists that it is only "natural" are supported.

Let us examine an example of sociobiological analysis in action. The social activities to which sociobiologists have devoted most of their attention are sex (mating) and care of offspring, especially as regards the different and competing selfish interests of the two sexes. In species that reproduce roughly the way people do, males and females are after different things. Females are monogamous, whereas males are promiscuous; females are choosy, whereas males are indiscriminate. Sounds familiar. The sociobiological twist on this double standard is the argument that rather than being a cultural imposition, it is a biological imperative. Males have unlimited sperm, whereas females have limited eggs. Females therefore "care" about the fate of each egg. They want it fertilized by a fit male (thus their choosiness). Males, in contrast, want to spread their sperm far and wide. They know that if they waste some on an unfit female, there is still plenty more available for the next one. Once the female is fertilized, her "investment" in the egg goes up even more. She cannot produce another offspring until this one is safely born. So she wants the male to stay around, to protect her and provide for her. The male, of course, cares very little about the fate of any one particular fertilized egg. In the time it takes for the offspring to be born, the male could be fertilizing thousands more eggs.

Thus the reproductive "interests" of males and females are fundamentally incompatible. In choosing males, females look for signs of fidelity. So males evolve ways to deceive females until they are allowed to mate. Then off they run. Females in turn evolve means to read the deceptions, leading males to evolve better deceptions, and so on and on it goes, in an escalating "arms race." Its natural end point is self-deception. The male really believes that he will stay around and care for the family. He thinks he has finished sowing his wild oats. But then, much to his amazement, the wanderlust returns while the offspring are still in diapers. This vision of sex as nothing but the slavish pursuit of reproductive self-interest is captured by novelist Saul Bellow's remark that "I never yet touched a fig leaf that didn't turn into a price tag."[13] For him it was a lament; for the sociobiologist it is an anthem.

The sociobiologist's view of social behavior in nature lends support to the economist's picture of organisms as fundamentally self-interested and as self-interested by natural law. In addition, it extends the economic analysis beyond the market for goods to domains like love, marriage, and the family, domains that economists have traditionally viewed as outside the economy. We will see a little later how important this extension has become in modern society.

We surely do not like the idea that men and women are in a constant struggle to serve their individual, incompatible interests. We probably regard it as immoral for social relations to be cloaked in acts of deception and manipulation. So, probably, do most sociobiologists. But what is perhaps the deepest message of their analysis is that whether we approve of it or not is beside the point. This is the way life is. The scientific "facts" of the matter make our moral concerns essentially irrelevant. Do we blame rivers for overflowing their banks and flooding people out of their houses? Do we blame the earth for quaking? Well then we cannot blame men for their infidelities or women for their seductions.

IV.   BEHAVIOR THEORY

Though economics and sociobiology share a view of organisms as maximizers of self-interest, there is an enormous chasm between them. The sociobiologist focuses on the genetic determination of behavior. Intelligent action is the result of the machinery of natural selection and not of rational calculation on the part of individual organisms. The economist, in contrast, sees rational calculation as the heart of human activity; it is what economic rationality is all about. It is hard to think of a fly as an entrepreneur. To make the parallel between these disciplines more than superficial, we need a bridge between them, one that tells us the laws by which organisms use their past experience as a guide to successful (rational, intelligent, utility-maximizing, fitness-maximizing) future action. And this bridge is provided by the branch of modern psychology known as behavioral psychology or *behavior theory*, a discipline given its shape and direction by B. F. Skinner. Behavior theory is the crucial addition that distinguishes the modern, sophisticated twentieth-century science of self-interest from its crude nineteenth century Social Darwinist ancestor. The biology and the economics were there, albeit in rudimentary form, in the nineteenth century. But there was no companion psychology. This time around, the needed psychology was developed, with a vengeance.

The central principle of behavior theory is known as the "law of effect." What the law of effect says is that behavior is controlled by its past consequences. If something we do is followed by a good outcome—a reward or a reinforcer—we are likely to repeat it. If something we do is not followed by a good outcome, or is followed by a bad outcome—a punisher, we are unlikely to repeat it. The law of effect is the principle of natural selection applied to the life history of an individual rather than the evolutionary history of a species. Creatures start out behaving more or less at random. Those actions that produce reward are selected; all other actions drop out. Because the contingencies of reward afforded by the environment will differ from one organism to another, there is room for individual variation and plasticity in behavior. Because different cultures will reward different kinds of activities, there is room for cross-cultural variety. What the law of effect does is ensure that only those activities will be selected that actually result in outcomes that are reinforcing; that organisms like. Because in general, organisms will like only those things that do them some good, the law of effect dovetails nicely with the theory of natural selection. Because in general, the law of effect will guide organisms to allocate their time, energy, and resources in ways that maximize the satisfaction of their preferences, behavior theory dovetails nicely with the tenets of economic rationality.

By and large, behavior theorists develop general claims about the control of human behavior in the complex social environment by studying pigeons pecking at lit disks, or rats pressing on levers, for food or for water, under extremely impoverished conditions. The rat, for example, is severely deprived of food and placed in a small, soundproof box containing a light, a level protruding from a wall, and a feedtube. Presses on the level produce pellets of food through the feedtube. By manipulating such things as the number, speed, and force of presses required for food, and the amount, quality, and delay of the food provided, behavior theorists attempt to develop precise, quantitative, and general principles that describe how the law of effect controls behavior. They are confident that the semistarved rat in the box, with virtually nothing to do but press on a lever for food, captures the essence of virtually all human behavior. What is this essence? It is that behavior is a means to reinforcing ends. Bribes work. And not only do bribes work, but they are at the heart of virtually everything people do.

Armed with this simple conceptual framework and this simple methodological technique, behavior theorists have developed some very powerful principles. They have brought many of the tenets of economics into the laboratory and confirmed them with animals. Thus it is not only people who are rational economic men; pigeons and rats are, too. Furthermore, behavior theory has yielded a technology that is used effectively to control behavior in classrooms, mental hospitals, prisons, and workplaces. It is the last, crucial piece of our intellectual pie. People are biological fitness-maximizing, psychological-reinforcement-maximizing and economic-utility-maximizing organisms. Questions of right and wrong are beside the point. From conception to the grave, laws of nature guide us—no, impel us—to pursue our self-interest. And the sciences of biology, psychology, and economics are discovering those laws. Or are they?

V. LIMITS OF THE SCIENTIFIC ACCOUNT OF HUMAN NATURE

Taken together, the disciplines of economics, sociobiology, and behavior theory provide a picture of people that is truly formidable. They seem to compel the view that people are self-interested egoists through and through. As the soft focus of past romanticism is replaced by the hard, clear images of modern science, illusion must give way to fact. "Scratch an altruist and watch a hypocrite bleed."

But all is not what it seems. Despite the impressive convergence of these disciplines, they are vulnerable to serious criticism along several different lines. The one criticism I will focus on is this: It may well be true that people *can* be fitness-maximizing, reinforcement-maximizing, utility-maximizing, self-interested creatures; however, it is not true that they *must* be. Whether they are or not will depend upon how they come to think about themselves, how they are taught to act, and what social institutions like the family, the school, the church, and the state expect from them and provide for them. Under some social conditions, the claims of behavior theorists, economists, and sociobiologists may be confirmed to the tiniest detail; under others, they may not. And what social conditions people live under is subject to their own control. The planets have nothing to say about what orbits they take. People have plenty to say about what orbits they take. What this means is that the slavish pursuit of self-interest can not be regarded as a natural inevitability. It is neither natural nor inevitable; it is subject to human discretion, judgment, and choice.

In short, what economics, sociobiology, and behavior theory claim to show us is that people *must* be slaves to the maximization of self-interest. What they actually show us is that people *can* be slaves to the maximization of self-interest. This leaves open for our moral evaluation whether they *should* be slaves to the maximization of self-interest.

The critic of economics says that its picture of human nature is true only under conditions in which economic markets dominate social life. From the perspective of modern America, where practically everything is for sale, it is hard to imagine social life being organized in any other way. But economic historians and anthropologists have shown us how recent and local a contrivance the free market is, especially as an autonomous part of society that is governed by its own rules. Until the economics of Adam Smith ushered in a full-scale market economy, there was little evidence to be found that economic man existed. For example, economic historian Karl Polanyi, in *The Great Transformation*, has written:

> The outstanding discovery of recent historical and anthropological research is that man's economy, as a rule, is submerged in his social relationships. He does not act so as to safeguard his individual interest in the possession of material goods, he acts so as to safeguard his social standing, his social claims, his social assets. . . . The maintenance of social ties . . . is crucial, because by disregarding the accepted code of honor, or generosity, the individual cuts himself off from the community and becomes an outcast. . . . Such a situation must exert continuous pressure on the individual to eliminate economic self-interest from his consciousness to the point of making him unable, in many cases, even to comprehend the implications of his own actions in terms of such an interest.[14]

However, the development of a market system alters this priority of social relations. Again, here is Polanyi talking about what happens when the market takes hold:

> Instead of economy being embedded in social relations, social relations are embedded in the economic system. . . . For once the economic system is organized . . . based on specific, economic motives . . . society must be shaped in such a manner as to allow that system to function according to its own laws.[15]

In other words, economic men are made and not born. To support this argument, Polanyi, Marshall Sahlins, and others point to economic activity in nonmarket societies. In preindustrial Europe, for example, land was often inalienable (unsellable), labor (what one did, how one did it, and what one got for it) was governed by tradition, not supply and demand, and interest was illegal and immoral. Thus three of the crucial factors of production in the modern market economy—land, labor, and capital— were not open for free exchange. In many present-day agricultural societies, people produce only what they need. There is no interest in accu-mulation, in maximization. When factories get built in these societies by foreign industrialists, as wages increase, work decreases. People seem to work only as long as it takes to earn the requisite income; increasing the wage only shortens the workweek.

Just as anthropological and historical critics of economics suggest that rational economic men are made not born, critics of sociobiology argue that reproductive fitness maximizing men (and women) are made not born. If, as sociobiology claims, people are impelled to look after their genetic interests, we would expect to find that across cultures, people devote their time, energy, and resources to their genetic relatives. This should be true whether or not a given culture knows anything about genetic relatedness. But the anthropological evidence does not confirm this expectation. As a general rule, kinship is *socially*, not biologically defined. It is certainly not in one's genetic interest to look after people who are not ones genetic relatives, yet there are many cultures in which this is done routinely. Marshall Sahlins has summarized the study of kinship patterns this way:

> No system of human kinship relations is organized in accord with the genetic coefficients of relationship as known to sociobiologists. Each consists . . . of rules of marriage, residence, and descent from which are generated distinctive arrangements of kinship groups and statuses . . . that violate the natural specifi-cations of genealogy. Each kinship group has its own theory of heredity, which is never the genetic theory of modern biology. . . . Such human *conceptions* of kinship may be so far from biology as to exclude all but a fraction of a person's genealogical connections from the category of "close kin"; while at the same time including in that category . . . very distantly related people or even complete strangers.[16]

Finally, critics of behavior theory argue that reinforcement maximiz-ing people are also made, not born. Their evidence comes not from history or anthropology but from the experimental laboratory. There is now grow-ing evidence that when rewards or incentives are manipulated to control the behavior of people, the rewards change that behavior. A system of rewards can *turn people into* reinforcement-maximizing economic actors, rather than exploiting reinforcement maximization as a fundamental fea-ture of the human character.

Let me make this more concrete with an example. Nursery-school children were given the opportunity to play with special drawing pens. They loved it. Some of them were given rewards for drawing, and some were not. Later on, the drawing pens were freely available to all children without possible reward. The ones who had previously been rewarded were *less* likely to play with the pens than the ones who had not previously been rewarded. Moreover, if they did draw, their drawings were consis-tently less complex and creative than the drawings of unrewarded kids.[17]

What happened? A good guess is that the kids who were rewarded for drawing came to regard their activity simply as a means to reward. When the reward was not available at the later time, they were not interested; they had no reason to draw. In contrast, kids who were never rewarded had the same reason to draw later that they had had earlier—something intrinsic to the activity of drawing itself. It does not take a lot of imagination to see the lesson of this demonstration for the use of reward systems in schools. Very few 5-year-olds need systematic rewards to be induced to learn in school. Almost all 10-year-olds do. What is the magic transformation that our schools perform in our children's early years? Are we turning learning as an end into learning as a means? Are we turning play into work?

Now consider another example. Imagine yourself seated before a 5×5 matrix of lights with two buttons you can push. "This is a game," you are told. "By pushing the buttons, you can move around the light. If you do it right, you get a point. What I want you to do is figure out the rules of the game; figure out what you have to do to get points." What do you do? Well, you might make some exploratory moves, then formulate some hypotheses or guesses, then test them by varying your pattern of button pushes systematically from one turn at the game to the next, methodically eliminating false hypotheses until the correct one finally emerges. This game is analogous to experimental science. The game, like nature, has rules or laws. Each turn at the game is an experiment, and if you do the right experiments, you uncover the rules of the game just as good experimental science uncovers the rules of nature.

College students who were exposed to this game behaved like pretty good scientists, intelligently formulating and testing hypotheses and discovering rules. Unless, that is, they were given some prior training at the game with the instructions that every point they earned would get them a nickel. Under these circumstances, they developed high efficient, stereotyped patterns of behavior, like pigeons pecking at disks or rats pressing on levels, that persisted when the students were later asked to discover the rules. As a result, they were much less effective than students without pretraining. They took longer to find the rules and found fewer of them. Instead of approaching the game intelligently and inventively, they approached it dully and mechanically.[18]

As long as "doing science," "drawing interesting pictures," "writing novels," and the like continue to exist alongside reinforcement-maximizing, economic behavior, we need not worry that people will become efficient, stereotyped automata. And as long as some domains of life remain outside the economy, we need not worry that the "economic man" ideology will take over as the explanation and justification of everything we do. But recent developments in society suggest that we have reason to worry. The economic juggernaut will not stand still. We are faced at the moment with the prospect of an "economic imperialism." We are faced with learning anew the sad lesson that King Midas learned about the limits of gold.

VI.   ECONOMIC IMPERIALISM

King Midas was a foolish king. Granted one wish, he asked that everything he touch turn to gold. This made him the richest man in the world. But alas, he discovered that you cannot eat gold or drink it. And when he reached out and touched his daughter, he discovered that although you can love gold, it cannot love you back. The modern lesson in the Midas myth is that allowing economic considerations to dominate domains of life that ought to be noneconomic can have tragic consequences.

Adam Smith knew this. Remember that he acknowledged from the beginning that "economic man" was not all there was to man. Living alongside economic man was a person now forgotten by economists who we might call "moral man." This person possessed "natural sympathy" for his fellows and was ready to provide "necessary assistance" from "friendship and esteem," and from "the agreeable bonds of love and affection." So said Adam Smith.

And others since Adam Smith have known this. Nobel Prize-winning Economist Kenneth Arrow has said:

> We cannot mediate all our responsibilities to others through prices. . . . [It is] essential in the running of society that we have what might be called "conscience," a feeling of responsibility for the effect of one's actions on others.[19]

And William Vickrey has said:

> In any actual world there will be, for the individual, cases in which he can give free reign to his personal predilictions, and others in which it will be hoped that he will draw upon his moral resources and act in accordance with ultimate ethical values rather than indulge his own preferences. . . . One of the sins committed by the glorification of economic freedom has been precisely that it has tended to confuse individuals as to where the boundary between the two cases lies.[20]

We are now growing increasingly confused about boundaries. Partly, it is because the ideology of economic self-interest has permeated the culture to the point where acting in any other way is regarded as bizarre, or perhaps saintly, but certainly not normal. That is, we now believe that human nature is what economists tell us it is. Sociobiology, as we have seen, exacerbates the confusion by treating mating, child care, and other social activities as essentially economic. But it is not just ideology. In addition, the affluence of developed Western capitalism has created pressure on people to bring more and more of their lives into the market; to treat more and more of their activities as economic. Ideology and affluence, taken together, are a deadly combination. They are the reason why current conservative efforts to strengthen traditional moral values have failed. Markets and morals are just incompatible.

The movement of once noneconomic spheres of life into the market— what might be called *economic imperialism*—has been powerfully discussed by Economist Fred Hirsch in his book, *Social Limits to Growth*. In modern, affluent America, most people spend very little of their income on the so-called "necessities." Material needs are cared for rather easily. As a result, interest in consumption turns to other domains. And economic activity in these other domains is often what mathematicians call a "zero-sum game." Everything we get is something that someone else does not. Everything we win, someone else loses. No matter how much money we make, we cannot all have a house on a two-acre plot, in the best neighborhood, 15 minutes from the downtown area of the city. We cannot all belong to the most exclusive country club. We cannot all drive on uncrowded highways or vacation on uncrowded beaches. We cannot all send our kids to the most prestigious college. We cannot all be the boss of the company or the senior partner in the law firm. Goods like these derive some of their value from the very fact of their scarcity. The more crowded they become, the less attractive they become. But as the general level of material well-being grows, more and more people want these goods. The result is a kind of auction, in which the prices of these goods are bid to astronomical levels. And people learn a sad fact about the economic democracy of the market: What anyone can have, not everyone can have. What everyone can have, no one wants.

We are in competition, then, for certain goods, goods that will be available based upon our relative and not our absolute economic position. What this competitiveness does is put pressure on all of us to take advantage of every opportunity, to use every edge. Each act of kindness has an attached "opportunity cost." Each minute spent in social activity is a minute not spent in improving our economic position. An evening spent drinking beer with friends is an evening not spent cultivating new clients, or working on a brief, or on the next scholarly article. If we are not willing to put in 18 hours a day for the firm, we can easily be replaced by someone who is. We have to choose between social and economic activities, and once we have to choose, we must find a way to compare them. From here, it is a small step to commercializing our social time, "pricing" it to make sure we get our money's worth from each social engagement.

Furthermore, the process of commercialization of our social relations affects the product. Relations with other people become a means to the satisfaction of our own, personal ends. Just as stereos, fine dinners, cars, and the like are used to satisfy desires, so are people. Although it has surely always been appropriate to want to get satisfaction out of relations with others, to expect to benefit in some way from social activities, we have not typically set about calculating the costs and benefits of each social exchange. The reason we have not is that the character of the benefits that we normally derive from social activity is not amenable to economic calculation. In economic activity, we seek profitable exchange in each transaction. When I buy a stereo, I want my money's worth from *that* stereo. It is small comfort to know that a purchase contributes to the well-being of the market system in general, making possible many future exchanges, if this particular exchange is unsatisfactory. The situation is often quite different in the social domain. We do not analyze a marriage into a series of exchanges and ask whether each social action has been appropriately compensated. We do not have quid pro quo expectations of spouses. What matters is some assessment of satisfaction with the marriage as a whole. There is no reason to believe that this long-term, overall assessment of a marriage is just the sum of a very long and large series of particular exchanges—sex in return for doing the dishes on Tuesday, a special dessert in return for doing the marketing on Thursday, and so on.

But people certainly *can* start looking at social relations as nothing but a series of economic exchanges, and as they do, the norms that govern social relations change to reflect this economic orientation. Think, for example, about sex. What kind of "good" is sex, and what sort of stance should people adopt toward it? Clearly, sex can be regarded as a market commodity. People can purchase the services of prostitutes just as they purchase the services of plumbers. When viewed in this way, sexual activity is discrete and impersonal. Costs and benefits of an evening with a prostitute can be computed. If there are benefits to be gotten from an evening with a prostitute, they will be gotten there and then. And it matters very little, to either the customer or the prostitute, who the sexual other is. Both buyer and seller are interchangeable with other buyers and sellers. Of course some prostitutes are more skilled than others (as are plumbers), so that customers are not indifferent to the quality of the services they are buying, but it is just a collection of skills, and not a person, that the customer is evaluating. Few customers care whether their plumber is kind to his family, or votes Republican, or gives to the United Way. What matters is whether he can do his job. Customers have the same view toward prostitutes.

On the other hand, sex can be regarded as an act of spiritual as well as physical union, as an opportunity to establish intimacy. Viewed in this way, it matters a great deal who one's sexual partner is. People are not interested in being this close with just anyone. One does not become intimate with a "collection of skills." Furthermore, episodes of sexual union contribute to the building of deep and lasting personal relations. There are cumulative effects that make it important that sexual activity be with the same partner. Good prostitutes are skilled at *simulating* the care and concern for their customers that are a part of noncommercial sexual relations, or even of showing genuine concern—that ends when the night is over. But no matter how genuine the concern may be, it is money, not concern, that binds the relation.

Because prostitution is illegal almost everywhere in the United States, it seems clear which view of sexual activity is the "official" one in our society. But some feminists argue that traditional marriage is just prostitution in disguise—sexual services (and cooking and ironing) in exchange for food, shelter, and protection. And even those whose views of marriage are not this extreme have come increasingly to view the marriage "contract" as a legal, economic document and not just a spiritual, symbolic one. There is no doubt that this move helps correct many instances of serious exploitation, but it does so at a cost. In Hirsch's words, "orgasm as a consumer's right rather rules it out as an ethereal experience."[21]

Sex and marriage are not the only social relations that are taking a distinctly economic, contractual turn. The same kind of transformation is occurring in relations between doctor and patient, lawyer and client, teacher and student. Once, these relations were based upon honor, integrity, and mutual concern, and obligations were met because of fundamental moral commitments. Now, people see themselves as consumers of services, with the courts as their only guarantor against exploitation. The presumption is that only vigilance and threats of reprisal will get people their money's worth from these professionals. And "money's worth" has come, in some domains, to be taken quite literally, as when Secretary of Education Bennett wonders whether $50,000 spent on a college education will yield as high a return on investment as the same money put in Treasury bills. This is, of course, the same man who routinely excoriates educators in this country for refusing to teach "basic values," like honesty, courage, thrift, compassion, and love of country. Bennett embodies, as clearly as anyone, the lack of awareness of the corrosive character of the market. For of course, a thoroughly rational economic man has no use for these basic values; there is no profit in them.

As individuals and as a society, we do not have to allow the spread of economic imperialism to continue. There are alternatives to regarding other people as objects of desire. One such alternative, articulated by Philosopher Immanuel Kant, is to take as the first principle of morality that people always be treated as ends, never as means; always as subjects, never as objects. People are to be valued and respected in and for themselves and independent of their usefulness to others. In essence, this is a command-ment to regard other people as we regard ourselves; to be concerned for their well-being because as human beings, they are entitled to that con-cern.

Pursuing this alternative is not easy. Only saints treat all people this way. Even if we are not necessarily all greedy egoists, it is certain that we are not all saints. Adopting this Kantian moral stance toward people is hard work. It requires eternal vigilance. Indeed, without help, it may be impossible for individuals consistently to act in this way. But there is help, or at least there was help, in the form of various social institutions that functioned to make this moral stance almost automatic. The point was made by Aristotle, two millennia ago. Aristotle noted that it is hard to be good, and what makes it possible is the moral education people receive—in the home, in the school, in the temple. This is not moral education in the abstract but in the concrete. People are taught very specifically how to show respect and concern for others in the various situations they encounter in daily life. Like multiplication tables, appropriate action is drilled into people until they perform it effortlessly and automatically.

A moral education cannot cover all the situations a person may en-counter in life. Sometimes, one will have to work to be moral. Sometimes, the institutions that are the source of morality will have to struggle with changing social conditions to reach a new view of what being moral entails. But at least a moral education makes being moral easy in the most common-place situations, and it inculcates in people a standard that they can turn to and examine when difficulties arise. One of the greatest dangers of eco-nomic imperialism is that as economic considerations penetrate social institutions that once provided moral education, the education will suffer. As a result, being moral will become harder and harder, less and less automatic. Moral deliberation will be replaced by economic calculation. How can we possibly be expected to recapture traditional moral values as a society when the institutions that have always kindled those values have themselves come to substitute markets for morals?

Economic considerations can have this effect not just by penetrating social institutions but by destroying them. The accelerating death of the family farm that we are now witnessing will mean far more in the long run than economic hardship for a few people. As family farms disappear, close-knit, extended families will disappear with them. And so will the local communities that have grown up around family farms. These local communities have been as much a source of compassion, concern, and civic virtue as any institution in America. Legislation designed to save family farms, as well as legislation like the recent plant-closing bill that is designed in part to protect small, industrial communities, are steps in the right direction. I know that these measures are too little, and I fear that they may also be too late. When the next serious economic downturn comes, if people are forced to survive it without their strong, local communities of support, it will make the 1930s seem like a picnic.

VII. ECONOMIC IMPERIALISM AND THE MARKET

There is a great irony in the spread of economic imperialism to non-market aspects of life. It is the extraordinary effectiveness and productivity of the market that inspires us to take an economic view of everything. Yet taking an economic view of everything now threatens the market system itself with destruction. As Adam Smith knew, the effectiveness of the market has always depended on more than the pursuit of self-interest. It has also depended upon a set of noneconomic social and moral controls that stemmed from social norms governing appropriate conduct. Fred Hirsch put it this way:

> The payoff to religious belief was in earthly coin. The traditional concept of religion as insurance on the next world, which might or might not pay off in this one, was exactly reversed. One might or might not go to heaven for loving one's neighbor as oneself. . . . What was certain was that one would thereby get more worldly goods out of the market; provided that all ones neighbors did likewise.[22]

When Smith was writing, these social norms were firmly established and easy to take for granted. Thus he could be sanguine about the "natural sympathy" that would lubricate and cushion market activity. He could depend on people to tell the truth, to honor their contracts, and the like. What economic imperialism is now teaching us is that sympathy is not "natural." It is a social product and one that is rapidly deteriorating.

Do we need evidence that the market cannot survive the behavior of unrestrained economic men? I would suggest several modern economic phenomena that stem in part from the eclipse of moral man by economic man within the economy:

1. The "short-termism" that has chief executive officers of large corporations selling the company's future for a profitable quarter. This is what is decried in article after article as "me-first management," as if any other kind of management would make sense to a rational, economic agent. What makes the problem of short-termism especially acute is a series of developments in modern financial markets. Threats of takeover demand sustained, high levels of profit. And computer-aided, institutional trading make possible rapid shifts of large amounts of capital should any corporate weakness be detected, or even suspected.

2. The emergence of the "junk bond," the "hostile takeover," and corporate blackmail, as industrial corporations turn from making things to making money and from employing laborers to employing lawyers.

3. White-collar crime on an unprecedented scale, involving people at the highest levels of major corporations and of government. Examples include the defrauding of government by defense contractors, check kiting by a major Wall Street firm, drug money laundering by a major bank, bribery of the leaders of foreign governments by aerospace firms, violation of waste disposal laws by chemical manufacturers, and even the production of bogus food for babies. *U.S. News & World Report* concluded, a few years ago, that of America's 500 largest corporations, 115 have been convicted in the last decade of at least one major crime or paid civil penalties for serious misbehavior. And it is not just that people are being defrauded. Some of them are being seriously injured or killed. It has been estimated that dangerous products result in almost 30,000 deaths and over 100,000 injuries each year.

4. Insider trading scandals on Wall Street that are endangering the way Wall Street firms do business and leading the old veterans to wonder why the "young turks" seem so unconstrained by ethics. Interesting here is some research done by Psychologist Daniel Kahneman and several collaborators on people's conceptions of fairness in various economic transactions. Kahneman found that people had a very strong sense of fairness that acknowledged the "right" to a profit but imposed several strict constraints on that right. So, for example, 80 percent of participants in the study thought it unfair for a shopkeeper to raise the retail price of his existing stock of a commodity if its wholesale price goes up (for example, to double the price of coffee he has already purchased if the wholesale price of new coffee purchases doubles). What is interesting is that among MBA students in a very prestigious business school, only 20 percent thought this practice unfair. So it appears that unmitigated greed is an acquired taste and that our business schools are helping our future business leaders to acquire it.

5. The selling of influence by former government officials who can hardly wait until the ink is dry on their letters of resignation. "Don't ask what you can do for your country" seems to be the watchword these officials absorbed while walking the corridors of power. As Robert Reich has pointed out, this larceny on the part of public officials may once have been fairly benign, when we all believed that "what's good for General Motors is good for America." But if this little aphorism was ever true, it is certainly not true now, and larcenous public officials cost us all dearly.

When John Maynard Keynes revolutionized economics by introducing state-managed capitalism 50 years ago, he underestimated the need for government involvement in the economy because he assumed that unlike the man on the street, captains of industry had motives considerably loftier than mere self-interest. Influenced, no doubt, by the fact that the captains of British industry were largely aristocrats, as much involved in the running of the state as in the running of their companies, Keynes assumed that the leaders of the economy would show restraint in their pursuit of profit. He assumed that they would consider and act in the public interest. Keynes was guilty here of the mistake of believing that the social and moral fabrics of his society were a part of the natural order of things. He did not appreciate that the very act of participation in the market system would turn his lofty aristocrats—or if not them, their children—into self-seeking egoists no different in motive from the people they employed.

There are some who will suggest that the way to deal with problems like these is not by trying to restrain the pursuit of self-interest by individuals but by changing the rules so that when people calculate their self-interest, it will turn out that what is best for them is also best for society as a whole. This can be done by imposing a set of stiff penalties for doing the "wrong thing." I believe that a system of penalties can only be effective so long as they are not needed to control the behavior of most people. Once transgression becomes widespread, enforcement becomes almost impossible. As it becomes increasingly common for people to misrepresent themselves or their products, or to violate contracts, the legal system is overwhelmed as it attempts to catch and punish transgressors.

And even if we could afford to provide the massive legal system that would be required to police a society of completely self-interested individuals, how could we control the behavior of the enforcers? How could we stop judges and juries from selling their services to the highest bidder? Once judges were for sale, the entire system of private property on which market activity depends would collapse. As Kenneth Arrow puts it, "The definition of property rights based on the price system depends precisely on the absence of universality of private property and of the price system."[23] Once everything is for sale, nothing is sellable. But if we are all economic men, through and through, then what is to stop us from viewing everything about ourselves as a potential market commodity?

The argument I am making is, in general form, familiar. Market capitalism is in trouble; it contains the seeds of its own destruction. This is a virtual cliche. But unlike other versions of this general argument, the claim here is not that the trouble stems from conflicts of interest, either between classes or between nations. The problems I am pointing to come instead from a convergence of interests. We have learned the economic lessons of self-interest all too well and are pursuing it all too vigorously in all too many domains of life. We have failed to appreciate that rational self-interest is not enough.

VIII.   ECONOMIC IMPERIALISM AND DEMOCRACY

There is a second great irony to the spread of economic imperialism. One of the most serious moral defenses of the free market is that it is the only economic system compatible with liberal democracy. No one can be told where to live, what to wear, what to eat, what work to do. No one can be forced to buy or sell. All exchanges—of things or of labor—are free and voluntary. Any encroachment on the market system is an encroachment on individual liberty. This marriage of a free-market economic system and a liberal democratic political one seems natural enough. So natural, in fact, that it has led some political theorists to view the political domain as just another market. The result, and thus the irony, is that democracy is now under siege.

Historically, the roots of American democracy were grounded in morality. Discussions of "justice," "equality," "freedom," and "authority" derived from ideas about right and wrong and presupposed public commitment and responsibility. As citizens, people owed it to the state to be concerned for the public interest. People owed it to the state to be loyal. People owed it to the state that they would participate in public life, at least by voting. The right to vote was more than just a right; it was a responsibility. The right to vote was *inalienable*; it could not be taken away, but it could not be given away, or sold either. The preservation of democracy itself depended on this moral core.

No more. This account of democracy as grounded in moral principles has been replaced by an account grounded in economic ones. The resulting, so-called "economic theory of democracy" is rapidly becoming the standard view of what democracy is all about. According to this theory, elites (candidates) offer goods (programs) on the political market. Masses (voters) buy (vote for) the goods (programs) that best serve their individual interests. And that is all that democracy is. In the words of a former chairman of the council of economic advisors, Charles Schultze:

> Market-like arrangements . . . reduce the need for compassion, patriotism, brotherly love, and cultural solidarity as motivating forces behind social improvement. . . . Harnessing the "base" motive of material self-interest to promote the common good is perhaps the most important social invention mankind has achieved.[24]

This cynical view of what democracy and citizenship represent has now been given the official seal of approval with the award of last year's Nobel Prize in economics to "public choice" theorist James Buchanan. There is just one problem with this theory; if people really view democracy as just self-interest by another name, then this "important social invention" is a failure. In the democracy market, there is no check on aggregate demand. There are as many interest groups as there are people, everyone wants something, and the elites will promise anything to get elected. Any elite who promises to say no to certain programs will not get elected. And any elite who actually does say no after being elected will not get reelected. Elites who threaten to make people pay more for the services government provides will also be turned out of office. As a result, the elite always say "yes" to spending increases and "no" to revenue increases.

The consequence, according to some, is that we can no longer *afford* democracy. The massive deficits we now face are not fixable, at least not without a significant structural change in the way government does its business. That is, significant decisions have to be taken out of the hands of the electorate, or the country will go broke. Thus, the magnificent abdication of responsibility that was the Gramm–Rudman–Hollings bill. Either we decrease democracy, or we hope that some people will drop out of the system and stop making demands.

There is one other possibility. We can appeal to people to restrain their demand on the political system. We can appeal to their sense of justice, to their concern for the common good. That is, we can appeal to moral man rather than economic man, just the side of man that economists, sociobiologists, behavior theorists, and hard-headed, unromantic political scientists say does not exist. We better hurry. The economic theory of democracy and of citizenship has already filtered down to mass culture. People have learned that it does not "pay" to bother voting. People have learned to distrust justifications of American foreign policy initiatives, like for example, support of the Contras in Nicaragua, that are based on appeals to democratic values. Such appeals, they suspect, are just polite cover terms for the real justifications, which are based on naked self-interest. Even mass culture's current icon of traditional values, Bill Cosby, has succumbed. A few years ago, Cosby starred in a television commercial that taught everyone a lesson in "realpolitik." It featured Cosby as a Wild West sheriff. He enters a saloon full of little kids and asks them to form a posse to chase some outlaws. He knows it is dangerous, and all he can offer is a tin star, a deputy's badge. Any takers? No way, say these savvy kids; a tin star just is not enough. The kids demand something more before they will saddle up; they know the meaning of citizenship, of patriotism. Cosby manages to purchase their commitment with some instant pudding, paid in advance at the kids' insistence. John Kenneth Galbraith has said "the danger to liberty lies in the subordination of belief to the needs of the industrial system."[25] To this we might add that the danger to liberty lies in the subordination of human moral concern to the dictates of economic rationality.

IX. CONCLUSION

It is time to wrap up this long cautionary tale. The story that people are rational economic men is a fiction. But it is a powerful fiction, one that gains strength by appealing to principles of modern biology and behavioral psychology for natural support. Marshall Sahlins has said:

> So far as I am aware, we are the only society that thinks of itself as having arisen from savagery, identified with a ruthless nature. Everyone else believes they are descended from gods. . . . Judging from social behavior, this contrast may well be a fair statement of the differences between ourselves and the rest of the world. We make both a folklore and a science of our brutish origins, sometimes with precious little to distinguish between them.[26]

This "folklore" of ours becomes less and less folklore as more and more of our social institutions enter the economy and are pervaded by its assumptions. Because it is self-fulfilling in this way, we cannot expect this folklore to die of natural causes, that is, to be revealed as false in the scientific light of day. As products of the Enlightenment vision that began this folklore, we bear some responsibility for correcting it.

It is instructive that the very notion of "interest," in the economist's sense, is itself an Enlightenment invention. In the eighteenth century, the pursuit of rational economic *interest* was applauded as a much needed antidote to the reckless, capricious, *passion*-governed pursuits of kings and princes. Economic interest introduced a measure of order and predictability into an otherwise chaotic social world. It was a benign cure for a malignant social disease. Not dissimilarly, it should be noted that more recently, heroin was also introduced as a relatively benign cure for the malignant social disease of morphine addiction. We should be careful about the cures we choose. They often bring their own diseases. Some dreams come true as nightmares. Just as King Midas.

NOTES

1. Robert Ruark, *Something of Value* (New York: Random House, 1953), p. 15.
2. Barry Schwartz, *The Battle for Human Nature* (New York: Norton, 1986). This chapter is based largely on the book.
3. William Graham Sumner, *Essays of William Graham Sumner* (New Haven: Yale University Press, 1934), p. 344.
4. In R. L. Heilbroner, *The Worldly Philosophers* (New York: Simon and Schuster, 1960), p. 21.
5. Bernard Mandeville, *The Fable of the Bees*, Vol. 1, (London: Penguin, 1975), p. 42.
6. Adam Smith, *The Wealth of Nations* (New York: Random House, 1937), p. 119.
7. Adam Smith, *The Theory of Moral Sentiments* (Oxford: Clarendon Press, 1976), pp. 124–125.

8. Gary Becker, *The Economic Approach to Human Behavior* (Chicago: University of Chicago Press, 1976), p. 8.
9. Adam Smith, *The Wealth of Nations*, p. 325.
10. Charles Darwin, *The Origin of Species* (Cambridge: Harvard University Press, 1964), pp. 63–64.
11. Peter Medawar, cited in G.C. Williams, *Adaptation and Natural Selection* (Princeton: Princeton University Press, 1966), p. 158.
12. Michael Ghiselin, *The Economy of Nature and the Evolution of Sex* (Berkeley: University of California Press, 1976), p. 247.
13. Saul Bellow, cited in D. Symons, *The Evolution of Human Sexuality* (Oxford: Oxford University Press, 1979), p. 23.
14. Karl Polanyi, *The Great Transformation* (New York: Rinehart, 1944), p. 46.
15. Polanyi, p. 30.
16. Marshall Sahlins, *The Use and Abuse of Biology* (Ann Arbor, MI: University of Michigan Press, 1976), p. 68.
17. Mark Lepper, David Greene, and Richard Nisbett, "Undermining Children's Intrinsic Interest with Extrinsic Rewards: A Test of the 'overjustification' Hypothesis," *Journal of Personality and Social Psychology*, 1973, Vol. 28, pp. 129–137.
18. Barry Schwartz, "Reinforcement-induced Behavioral Stereotypy: How Not to Teach People to Discover Rules," *Journal of Experimental Psychology: General*, 1981, 111, pp. 23–59.
19. Kenneth Arrow, *The Limits of Organization* (New York: Norton, 1974), p. 27.
20. William S. Vickrey, in E. S. Phelps, ed., *Economic Justice* (Hammondsworth: Penguin, 1973), p. 60.
21. Fred Hirsch, *Social Limits to Growth* (Cambridge: Harvard University Press, 1976), p. 101.
22. Hirsch, pp. 117–118.
23. Kenneth Arrow, "Gifts and Exchanges," *Philosophy and Public Affairs*, 1972, 1, p. 357.
24. C. L. Schultze, *The Public Use of the Private Interest* (Washington, DC: Brookings Institution, 1977), p. 18.
25. John Galbraith, *The New Industrial State* (New York: Signet, 1960), p. 404.
26. Sahlins, p. 100.

8

Business Students and Ethics
Implications for Professors and Managers

James R. Glenn, Jr.

I. BACKGROUND

A. A Seminal Study

Over a quarter century ago Raymond Baumhart offered an observation that might be repeated even today when he said:

> During the past decade, much has been written about ethics in business. Most of the books and articles are based on the experiences of one man, or on a priori reasoning. Few authors have approached business ethics empirically, surveying the ideas, problems, and attitudes of a large number of businessmen.[1]

The significance of Baumhart's empirical research[2] is suggested by the fact that, in the academic community where criticism is endemic, no scholar has challenged Baumhart's findings. Two years ago Lee Preston called the study "a classic,"[3] and scholars like Gerald Cavanagh and David Fritzsche, in their 1985 review of business ethics research, noted that Baumhart's work remained "the most quoted" empirical study of business ethics."[4] Its importance continues to be recognized in widely used texts for courses in business, government and society[5] and business, environment

Note: Throughout this chapter only statistically significant data are reported. The statistical equations provided by the author have been removed; however, readers who desire to examine the data may write directly to the author.

James R. Glenn, Jr. • San Francisco State University, School of Business, San Francisco, California 94132.

and public policy.[6] In the intervening years, interest in business executives' values has increased dramatically, with scholars developing and employing a variety of research methodologies.[7]

Given the richness of Baumhart's data and the availability of his survey instrument, it is surprising that only two partial replications of his study of business executives have been published.[8] Furthermore, there has been little empirical research done in either undergraduate or graduate business schools to determine the attitudes of those who hope to lead our corporations in the future.[9] This paper reports data collected with an instrument that included Baumhart's original questions. It was administered to graduate (MBAs) and undergraduate business majors across the country in the fall of 1985.

Baumhart cited an intriguing statistic in his comments on the responses of students to a case from his questionnaire:

> At Dartmouth, Boston College, and Loyola University, 156 students completed part of the same questionnaire employed in our Project Two. The pattern of the replies was unmistakable: these collegians have a low opinion of the ethical practices and standards of businessmen. To cite a representative example: For a salesman who earns $10,000 a year to pad his expense accounts by $500 was regarded as unacceptable behavior by 85 per cent of our 1,512 business respondents, but only 17 per cent of the students thought the typical businessman would regard such padding as wrong.[10]

Given the institutions sampled, one may infer that the students were more likely to be liberal arts than business majors. Baumhart's further musing proved challenging:

> On the one hand, collegians strongly disapproved of what they perceive as the businessman's lack of integrity. On the other hand, many college students occasionally cheat on examinations. One wonders how collegians explain this apparent inconsistency. Are their temptations more severe than the businessman's? Do they regard it as less reprehensible to be unethical in academic matters than in economics? If so, why?[11]

Baumhart's "wonder" provided part of the stimulation for this research effort. In 1975 no systematic empirical research on cheating by business students was available. Although it was not clear whether it was possible to generate data to explain "this apparent inconsistency," questions were developed to establish the amount of cheating in business schools, and how students felt about the adequacy of attention to ethics in their business education, and whether they thought a separate ethics course should be included in their degree program.

Baumhart's original research produced thought-provoking results that met the second dimension of his aspirations:

> We hoped that in the process of securing and reporting the data, we would prompt top management to re-examine fruitfully its thinking and practices. In addition, we wished to give scholars the businessman's point of view, that is, what he regards as ethical problems and unethical behavior.[12]

It is the hope of this study that reporting the point of view of those aspiring to be managers will be useful to their future employers as well as to those of us trying to better prepare them for their managerial careers.

Baumhart's contributions are especially germane to current debates over business ethics because:

1. His challenge to business educators to provide clearer responses to the need for ethical education has not been met.
2. The research instrument he developed and the data he collected have been more widely *cited* than *utilized* by scholars or managers.
3. The attitudes and practices of business students about moral issues have not been systematically compared with those executives he surveyed.

This chapter focuses on research findings responsive to Baumhart's challenge. Before reporting the major findings, a brief description of the methodology will be given.

B.   Methodology

Since 1975 two data bases have been built utilizing an instrument that consisted of questions from Baumhart's original survey instrument plus 13 new questions developed by this author. For a full decade (from 1975 to 1985) this instrument was used to collect data from graduate and undergraduate business majors at six institutions in four different regions of the country; during the fall of 1985 the questionnaire was administered at 18 business schools across the country. Participating institutions were Boston University; City University of New York, Bernard Baruch College; Colorado State University; Emory University; Harvard University; Millsaps College; Northwestern University; San Francisco State University; Santa Clara University; Stanford University; University of California at Berkeley; University of Georgia; University of Maryland at College Park; University of North Carolina at Greensboro; University of Pittsburgh; University of Southern California; and The University of Texas at Austin. The national respondents' profile is (1) *institutions* (public 44 percent, private 56 percent); (2) *program level* (49 percent undergraduate, 51 percent graduate); (3) *geographic regions* (East 33 percent, Central 17 percent, South 22 percent, West 28 percent); and (4) *sex* (male 61 percent, female 39 percent).

To avoid self-selection bias, the questionnaire was used only in courses required of all students and administered in class to all students present (with one exception, where it was completed outside class and returned the next class meeting). Hence it is appropriate to view the national study as reporting population rather than sample data. There are a total of 53 questions on the Baumhart/Glenn survey instrument. The results of Baumhart questions for which comparable data are available from other studies of business executives or students have been reported elsewhere.[13] Here the primary focus will be on students' responses to six questions developed by this investigator. The results from eight of Baumhart's attitudinal questions will also be briefly reported, and the responses of the executives he surveyed will be compared with the responses made by students in this study.

II. RESULTS

A. Ethics in the Business Curriculum

Ethics and the business curriculum is a hot topic these days. A legion of studies have been conducted to establish how widely ethics has penetrated the curriculum.[14] A review of these surveys and the methodological questions they provoke invites further analysis, but it does appear that more schools are reporting that ethics is being included in their curricula. Unfortunately, one is left with the troubling suspicion that less is actually going on than has been reported. In this study, the majority of the 18 institutions had no ethics course. Only three undergraduate programs and four graduate programs had an elective ethics course; two undergraduate programs had a required ethics course, and no graduate programs had a required ethics course. There may indeed be substantive differences between institutional claims and institutional performance that, if true, poses an intriguing ethical question to members of the academic community itself.

The students participating in the national study were asked:

Do you feel that ethics has been adequately stressed in your business education?
Yes/No

Fifty-eight percent of the respondents answered negatively. Without further analysis such a response might be viewed as a source for optimism or pessimism in the classic story of the glass being half-full or half-empty. A more fine-grained analysis of the results reveals a much more complex and less tractable picture. The aggregation of the data masks dramatic differences among the respondents, depending upon the school attended, educational level, sex, type of institutional support, and geographical region. The range of the responses when viewed by school was from 20 percent to 72 percent, depending on which school the student was attending. With one exception, the responses of students attending institutions that offered an elective or required course in business ethics did not significantly vary from the rest: Having an ethics course in the curriculum did not reduce the perceived need for more stress on ethics in their business education. But this finding, important in itself, raises more questions than it answers. To illustrate: Because a free-standing course in business ethics is perceived by students as not meeting their need, should such courses be dropped from the curriculum? Or should they be substantially strengthened? If strengthening is needed, should we go from three- to four- or six-credit courses? Or—and this is a more provocative interpretation of the finding—should a free-standing course be used only as one of several advanced electives in the field of business ethics? Clearly a dilemma is in the making, somewhat like the dilemmas that confronted educators a quarter century ago when the computer demanded greater student sophistication in quantitative methods. So far as I know, no business faculty has seriously examined students' request for better instruction in moral reasoning.

Additional statistically significant differences exist when other ways of categorizing the respondents are reviewed. 64 percent of the respondents attending public institutions were not satisfied with the instruction given in ethics, and this compares with 52 percent of their private institution peers. Dissatisfaction by respondents' geographic region was: Central 64 percent, South 60 percent, East 57 percent, and West 53 percent. Fifty-five percent of the graduate students gave negative responses, whereas 58 percent of the undergraduates did; many more women students (62 percent) felt unhappy with the ethics curriculum than did their male classmates.

In an attempt to measure the perceived importance of attention to ethics within the business curriculum as a whole, the students were asked to respond to the following statement:

A separate ethics course should be included in my degree program. Yes/No

Fifty-three percent of the students thought that a separate ethics course should be included in their degree program. As with the previous question, the range of the responses, when viewed by school of the respondents, was dramatic: from 30 percent to 81 percent. There were no significant differences between respondents attending public or private schools or between undergraduate and graduate responses, but there were statistically significant differences by the region and sex of the respondents who answered the question affirmatively. The following numbers tell the regional story: Central 59 percent, South 63 percent, East 56 percent, and West 42 percent; the breakdown by sex was 51 percent for males and 58 percent for females.

When these numbers are compared with results of other surveys of business executives, business deans, and business faculties as well as students, a consistent pattern emerges: *Future managers and their teachers view ethics as much less relevant in their curriculum than do current practicing managers, especially CEOs.*[15] To illustrate: When Judith Briles surveyed *Fortune* 500 CEOs, she found that 81 percent disagreed with the statement that "ethics is being adequately stressed in business education today"; and 79 percent answered "yes" to the question, "Should a separate ethics course be required in university degree programs?" for undergraduates; and 87.5 percent answered "yes" for graduate/professional programs.[16] LaRue Hosmer concludes his analysis on why a majority of business schools do not offer a course in business ethics in this way: "In the past, we have often spoken about the need to sensitize business students to the presence of ethical problems in management; I am suggesting the prior need to sensitize business faculty to the importance of those problems."[17] Pogo revisited?

It seems clear, however, that most professors in business schools are either indifferent or hostile to the teaching of business ethics. If true, then those scholars committed to the field face a formidable challenge in trying to get a fair hearing for their work. Memory of other major education reforms (such as Harvard's case method for its law and business schools, or Columbia's early use of undergraduate study in contemporary civilization) suggest that unless a flagship university is willing to make a major commitment to the field of business ethics, less prestigious institutions will move timidly. So the committed ethicist and the committed executive are left with Hosmer's question: How can business faculties be made aware of, and sympathetic to, the need for moral instruction in business schools?

Nevertheless, much as we intuitively want to believe that what we are doing—or want to do—is efficacious, the empirical jury is still out on the late Ted Purcell's question, "Do courses in business ethics pay off?"[18] Using several of Baumhart's questions with graduate business students in 1961 and again in 1971, Purcell concluded that his data read affirmative. But others have reached quite opposite conclusions,[19] so we again are faced with uncertainties about the efficaciousness of what we are doing. This researcher has been using the Baumhart/Glenn instrument in a pre–post experiment for several years to see if it would measure effects of student exposure to ethics material. Unfortunately, at this writing, the analysis is not completed.

B. Perceptions of Ethics Challenges in Business Careers

To establish future managers' perceptions of possible pressure to compromise their personal values in business, and their ability to resist that pressure, the students were asked what they thought about two statements.

Statement I   A person can be both financially successful and uncompromisingly honest.

Five-point scale: Agree (1)—Disagree (5)

A resounding 92 percent of the students agreed (73 percent) or partly agreed (19 percent) with this statement. There were no statistically significant differences by type of institution or geographical region. There were differences by educational level: Seventy-seven percent of the graduate students agreed with the statement and 67 percent of the undergraduates agreed; 75 percent of the men agreed, whereas only 70 percent of the women did.

It is difficult to reconcile the apparent optimism reflected in this response with the pessimism/realism of their responses to the next statement. One might hypothesize that they recognize the way the world is but are confident that they will be able to resist the pressure; incidentally, this parallels the perceptions of Baumhart's executives that they were more virtuous than their peers. Student perceptions of their moral superiority over businessmen were confirmed by other studies completed in the seventies.[20]

Statement II   A person in business is forced to do things that conflict with his/her personal values.

Five-point scale: Agree (1)—Disagree (5)

A majority (54 percent) of the respondents agreed (12 percent) or partly agreed (42 percent) with this statement. Fortunately, this is one question where the student perceptions can be compared with practitioner responses to similar questions. In 1961 Baumhart reported that 76 percent of the executives agreed with a similar statement and 15 years later Archie Carroll reported that 65 percent of the executives in his study agreed with a statement like this. The range of his responses is informative: Fifty percent of the top managers, 65 percent of the middle managers, and 84 percent of the lower managers agreed with the statement. Carroll concluded: "This suggests that the greatest pressure is perceived in the lower ranks."[21] One of the most recent studies reported a pattern of responses that support Carroll's conclusion.[22] There is one sobering thought: The ranks reporting the greatest pressure are the very ranks into which our future managers will be entering!

C. Actual Behavior during Academic Career

Certainly, expressed attitudes are important. Never to be neglected, however, is actual behavior. Baumhart's comment about student cheating was the stimulus for adding several questions to the survey to see if it would be possible, through an anonymous questionnaire, to get useful information about actual behavior—either on observations about other's behavior or one's own behavior. Students were asked two questions. The first was:

Question: How many cases of cheating have you observed in the College of Business?

Responses:	None	One–Three	Four–Six	Seven–Nine	Ten +
	41%	27%	13%	4%	14%

Once again the national aggregation masks some dramatic differences among the respondents. Among the 18 schools the range of responses for those observing no cases of cheating ranged from 8 percent to 85 percent. Public-school students were more likely to have observed cheating (30 percent had observed "none") than students attending private schools (52 percent reported observing "none"). The regional variation was: Central 33 percent, South 38 percent, East 43 percent, and West 48 percent. The greatest difference was between the graduate students who had observed no cheating (64 percent) and the undergraduates who had observed no cheating (18 percent). There was no statistically significant difference in the responses of the men and women to this question. It would be tempting to speculate on reasons for the difference between graduates and undergraduates. Do students improve their moral behavior as they advance in their studies? Or have bad apples been dropped? Or does peer pressure begin to work as the student becomes more aware of the sophisticated nature of the business system? Put another way, does knowledge of business complexities not only induce student perplexities but also student awareness that the mills may grind slowly—but they grind?

The second question was:

Question: Have you cheated since you've been a student at the university?

Responses:	Never	1–3 times	4–6	7–9	10 or more
	69%	25%	4%	1%	1%

Of the 1,633 participants in this study who answered this question, 31 percent reported that they had. There is a statistically significant difference between student responses as to the percentage in each school reporting they had cheated, and the range of reported cheaters by school is dramatic (from 6 percent to 52 percent). Fourteen institutions in the national study had graduate programs. Of the 840 graduate respondents, 14 percent reported having cheated. There was a statistically significant difference between student responses at the different schools and the range of the percentage of self-reported cheaters was from 3 percent to 32 percent. Among the graduate student respondents, there was a statistically significant difference between those respondents attending public universities (18 percent reported having cheated) and those attending private universities (12 percent reported having cheated).

Eleven institutions had undergraduate business programs. Forty-nine percent of the 793 undergraduate respondents reported having cheated. There was a statistically significant difference between the responses among the different undergraduate business schools. The range of the percentage of undergraduate cheaters was from 28 percent to 69 percent. Locating each of the eighteen institutions in one of four geographical regions uncovers some interesting differences (Figure 1). Among the 975 male respondents, there is a statistically significant difference in the percentage of reporting cheaters between the four regions (East 25 percent, South 38 percent, Central 35 percent, and West 30 percent). Yet there was no significant regional differences among the female respondents. Among the 793 undergraduate respondents there is a statistically significant difference in the percentage of reported cheaters among the four regions: East 41 percent, South 52 percent, Central 48 percent, and West 56 percent. There were no significant regional differences among the graduate respondents. The West had the highest ratio of cheaters to noncheaters (1.3) and the East had the lowest ratio (.68). Among the 759 public institution respondents, there is a statistically significant difference in the percentage of reporting cheaters among the four regions: East 23 percent, South 38 percent, Central 43 percent, and West 38 percent. And finally, among the 874 respondents attending private institutions, there is a significant difference in the percentage of reporting cheaters between the four regions: East 26 percent, South 30 percent, Central 7 percent, and West 24 percent.

These percentages, if they are as reliable as those collected in other large surveys, suggest that business students may cheat less than their peers in other academic disciplines. In one large study ($N = 2926$) of an entire campus at an eastern university, the investigator found that 85 percent of the juniors, 79 percent of the seniors, and 35 percent of the graduate students reported having cheated. The only solace that comes

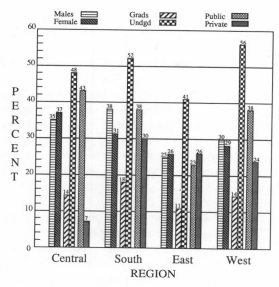

Figure 1. Percentage of Cheaters by Region.

from the numbers is the fact that only 15 percent of the sample were from business and economics.[23] The data provided some new insights into the richness and complexity of studying this problem. To illustrate; some activities that might be viewed as cheating were identified, and students were then asked whether the matter was cheating and if they had engaged in that activity. Between 30 and 40 percent did not regard the following activities as cheating: plagiarism, getting an exam from someone who took it earlier, padding a bibliography, working on an assignment with another student when they were not allowed, and doing a homework assignment for someone else. "Twice as many people in this group reported having engaged in these activities as those who regarded them as cheating. They also engaged in them more frequently."[24]

It is difficult to account for the differences in the percentage of cheaters among our surveyed schools. At least three variables might have some impact upon the observed/reported behavior: the people, the environment, and/or the technology. It might be hypothesized that different people go to different schools, (e.g., old folk tales have the wealthy going to private universities and the hard-working/honest going to public institutions). But the data do not support the assumption. It might be hypothesized that the same kind of people go to all schools and that it is the school environments that shape the behavior of the students. It is a widely held belief that graduate school places more pressure on the students than undergraduate programs, and the temptation to cheat is consequently more severe. Others claim that it is the very pressure to acquire the grades necessary to get into graduate school that tempt good students to cheat. Others hypothesize that it is the academic environment (technology) that invites good people, in otherwise good environments, to engage in cheating. Multiple-guess quizzes, papers prepared outside of class, and take-home exams beg for abuse. It is reasonable to assume that these variables and their complex parameters are interactive and interdependent.

D.   Behavior and Attitudes

Do the attitudes and judgments of students who report having cheated differ from those who say that they have not? The respondents were divided into two groups, and the four attitudinal questions already considered were reviewed in order to see if there were any significant differences in the responses of the two groups. There were no significant differences between the two groups in their answers to the two questions concerning the teaching of ethics in the business curriculum. However, the responses agreeing with the statement that "a person can be both financially successful and uncompromisingly honest" were statistically significant between the cheaters (67 percent) and those reporting that they had never cheated (76 percent); the differences in the responses of the two groups to the statement that "a person in business is forced to do things which conflict with personal values" were statistically significant: Among those that agree—cheaters (17 percent), noncheaters (9 percent), and those that disagree—cheaters (14 percent), noncheaters (18 percent).

It is important at this point to make a brief excursion into autobiography. Thirteen years of using this survey instrument has made me increasingly convinced that collecting attitudinal data was of marginal utility to those concerned with actual behavior. The history of attempts to connect behavior to stated attitudes has been less than glorious. However, preliminary analysis of this data using Logit (logistic regression) appears to suggest that it may be possible to predict which students (employees) will report having cheated by analyzing their responses to other items on the Baumhart/Glenn questionnaire. If this should prove to be accurate, a whole new set of questions concerning research ethics will need to be addressed. For example, if such a technology were possible, should it be used? By whom? Under what circumstances? What error rate would be acceptable?

III.   IMPLICATIONS FOR EDUCATORS

These findings have a number of implications for educators in such areas as admissions policies, curriculum, school environment, faculty development and research needs.

A.   Admissions

With the amount of cheating reported today in secondary education and the amount reported in higher education, there is need to look at university admissions practices at both the undergraduate and graduate level.[25] What do we currently communicate about our priorities through the admissions process? If we were to decide that we value students with character and strong personal integrity, how might we best communicate this to prospective applicants? Two schools in this study with the lowest reported rates of cheating require admission applicants to write essays on ethics. Although writing an essay is more symbol than solution, ignoring the subject of ethics in the admissions process is itself a message.

B.   Curriculum

The majority of the students in this study felt that instruction in ethics has been inadequately stressed in their business education, and a majority favored a separate ethics course in their degree program. Since these findings were collected, there has been a surge of interest in talk about the desirability of integrating ethics into all of the functional areas of the business curriculum. Faculty at the Wharton School have made efforts in this direction and the Arthur Andersen accounting firm has committed $5 million for a project to improve the teaching of ethics in the business schools functional areas. Although findings reported here cannot directly respond to the debate between those favoring a separate course and those favoring the integration of ethics throughout the curriculum, it is clear that students feel that ethics needs to be given more serious attention. The faculty and administrators' responses remain to be observed.

C.   Environment

Although unable to establish reasons for cheating, the search for a plausible explanation of why some schools in the study have such low reported rates of cheating was instructive. When the author asked a graduate of one of the participating schools how the apparent virtue of his school's students could be explained, he replied: "Virtue is probably not an issue since there is little or no opportunity to cheat." Providing minimal opportunity is certainly counterpoint to those evaluation technologies that provide the opportunity (and some say the invitation) for student abuse. It is a sad commentary on our times that one of the classic learning technologies of higher education—the research paper—has stimulated an industry to supply products to students who want someone else to do their work—for cash. And surrogate exam takers are readily available in the academic marketplace. Alternative evaluation technologies that are creative and effective include in-class evaluation of a student's understanding of the implications and the applications of an out-of-class research assignment; projects and presentations that require a level of personal intellectual involvement and accountability that cannot be delegated to someone else outside of class; and writing exercises that focus on the rigor of analysis, the quality of thought, and the effectiveness and humanity of solutions rather than on information storage and retrieval. All such possibilities are faculty intensive.

D.   Faculty Development

Our students' relatively modest enthusiasm for ethics in the curriculum is closer to the level of business school faculty support than the substantial level of enthusiasm reported by CEOs. If Hosmer and the other critics are correct, then we have a substantial faculty development opportunity before us. Fortunately, leaders in the business community have recognized the problem and are beginning to provide support. Arthur Andersen's commitment has already been noted. Hopefully, others may follow. Perhaps we really can disprove Pogo.

E.   Research

Teachers in this domain have a stake in better understanding the empirical reality within which they work. If unwilling to do the work themselves, then they should, at a minimum, make extra efforts to encourage and cooperate with those willing to do more rigorous empirical work. Certainly this study illustrates the primitive level of behavioral research in this area and the need for more rigorous and sophisticated data collection and analysis.

IV.   COMPARISON OF ATTITUDES FOR BUSINESS

It may be useful to consider briefly some of the data that compare the reactions of managers and students to eight of Baumhart's attitudinal questions. For each question or statement, the 1961 percentages are those reported by business executives, whereas the 1985 percentages show student reactions to the same question or statement. The results literally beg for more research—or at least, more sophisticated levels of speculation.

I. From your experience, how would you rank each of the factors listed according to the influence it exerts on an executive to make decisions which are ethical?

	1961	1985
Formal company policy	2.8*	2.8
One's personal code of behavior	1.5	1.9
The behavior of one's equals in the company	4.0	3.4
Ethical climate of the industry	3.8	3.5
The behavior of one's superiors	2.8	2.6

*The rankings given are weighted averages of respondent's rankings of each item (1, 2, 3, 4, or 5), with most influential equal to 1 and least influential equal to 5.

In spite of the differences in age, work experience, education, and twenty-five intervening years, it is remarkable how little difference there is in the businessmen's responses of 1961 and the responses of the business students in 1985. Both future and practicing managers rank one's personal code of behavior as the most influential factor in making ethical decisions. The businessmen had two factors tied for second ranking: formal company policy and the behavior of one's superiors. The business students clearly ranked the behavior of one's superiors second and formal company policy third. There is a slight tendency for students to give greater weight to people (superiors and peers) than to abstractions (company policy and industry climate) in their rankings than do the businessmen.

II. Which of the following two statements better describes your feelings about the ethical problems you have had to face?

	1961	1985
"It is easier to know what is right than it is to do it."	57%	73%
"It is more difficult to know what is right than it is to do it."	43%	27%

The differences between the responses appear to be explained by the differences in work experience or age or the passage of twenty-five years.

III. How often do you find yourself in the following situation: "I had to make a decision so quickly that there was no time to consider its ethical implications."

	1961	1985
Never	23%	13%
Rarely	56%	47%
Occasionally	19%	39%
Regularly	1%	4%
Very frequently	1%	1%

A few observations are in order. It should first be noted that 10 percent fewer students had "never" found themselves having to make a decision so quickly that there was no time to consider its ethical implications and that 9 percent fewer business students than businessmen "rarely" found themselves in such a situation.

IV. Listed are a number of business practices that occur from time to time. Please indicate which best approximates your opinion about each of these practices.

	1961	1985
An executive owns stock in a company with which his own company does business regularly	Always ethical 2%	17%
An executive arranges for a "call girl" at the request of a purchasing agent with whom he regularly does business	Always unethical 88%	75%
An executive exchanges price information with a counterpart in other companies in his industry	Always ethical 4%	5%

One might arouse an intergenerational debate by simply noting that the results suggest that the young play closer to the ethical margins than do their elders. Questions arise: Do people become more virtuous with age? Through peer influence? By degree of accountability and responsibility?

V. "For corporation executives to act in the interest of shareholders alone, and not also in the interest of employees and consumers is unethical."

	Agree	
	1961	1985
	83%	73%

The answers bear significantly on the debate over corporate social responsibility (CSR). At this point it is well to recall Kuhn's perceptive treatment of the issue: Are socially responsible corporate executives arrogant in exercising the role of allocators of the firm's profits without specific stockholder approval? Or are they behaving ethically? Our data suggest support for an affirmative response to the second question. Nevertheless, one must wonder why that support declined by 10 percent between 1961 and 1985.

VI. How do you feel about efforts to develop a code of ethics for business? How would you react if a group of experienced executives in business tried to draw up such a code?

Feeling	1961	1985
Favor strongly	50%	20%
Favor somewhat	21%	41%
Neutral	19%	20%
Oppose somewhat	6%	13%
Oppose strongly	4%	6%

The differences are dramatic. Only 20 percent of the business students registered strong positive feelings about the proposal. But a caveat is in order. Given the ambiguity of the question, one cannot be confident that the students understood that the question was referring to industrywide codes rather than codes in individual companies. If they did interpret the question in the way Baumhart intended—and were aware that in the intervening 25 years no industrywide codes have been adopted—then their lack of enthusiasm is easily understood. If, on the other hand, students thought that the question was referring to individual company codes and they were aware of the substantial increase in the number of company codes without any noticeable accompanying decrease in unethical behavior, then their lack of enthusiasm is also readily understood.

VII. Assume that an ethical practices code has been drawn up for business by experienced executives. What do you think such a code (and its reasonable enforcement) would accomplish? Please indicate your opinion of each of the possible consequences listed.

A. The code would raise the ethical level of business		
	1961	1985
Agree	36%	12%
Partly agree	35%	45%
Neutral	12%	18%
Partly disagree	7%	16%
Disagree	10%	9%

Before jumping to conclusions, it is worth noting that when a 1976 survey was conducted, businessmen's agreement with the statement had dropped from 36 to 19 percent. The difference between practitioners and students is 8 percent, not the hefty 24 percent that the 1961/1985 comparison showed.

Baumhart's final question on codes of ethics dealt with the appropriate enforcement entity. He asked respondents to assume that a businesswide code of ethics had been drawn up and then asked:

VIII. Which one of the following groups would you choose to enforce the code?

	1961	1985
A group of executives selected from various companies	28%	11%
A government agency	4%	13%
The management of each company	40%	28%
A group composed of executives from the industry plus other community members	28%	48%

The businessmen clearly prefer self-enforcement, but again a caveat is required. By 1976 the strength of that preference had decreased, and support is now greater for a group of executives and community members that is the same group favored by students.

V. POLICY IMPLICATIONS FOR BUSINESS

A. Recruitment

As educators face challenges to improve their admissions techniques, so, too, do managers face challenges to improve their recruitment policies. For too long the dominant criteria have been two measurements: class standing and school reputation. Only a few comments need be made. Bright people have been escorted from Wall Street investment houses to federal jails. Competence, of course, is needed. But so is character. We need to develop techniques that discern the applicant's sense of moral propriety and do not, at the same time, invade the applicant's privacy. For example, the job interview process may require changes. The widespread practice of lying on application forms may be stopped only by severe sanctions, including a willingness to share such information when other potential employers seek such information. We need new ideas to help resolve conflicting rights and obligations.

B. Promotions

Job appraisals have proved to be essential instruments for determining rewards. Yet how often are appraisals conducted with care and rigor? So far as divisional cooperation is concerned, how often do division heads write glowing recommendations for subordinates they intended to "dump"? Some companies—Gannett, Levi-Strauss—now take into account a manager's performance in hiring and promoting minorities and women. If bad examples come from the top, how severely should miscreants be handled by the directors? Too often the mischiefmakers are provided with legal advice at company expense and given generous separation benefits. If companies want morally tough employees, they must get tough with the ethical "softies" at the top.

Finally, if CEOs really believe that moral training should be a fundamental part of professional preparation, then they are in the ideal position to translate conviction into reality by providing leadership and resources to those individuals and institutions who are trying to meet this need as well as to encourage others to join in these research and teaching efforts.

NOTES

1. Raymond C. Baumhart, "How Ethical Are Businessmen?" *Harvard Business Review*, 39 (July–August 1961), p. 7.
2. Raymond C. Baumhart, *Ethics in Business* (New York: Holt, Rinehart & Winston, 1968), p. 19.
3. Lee E. Preston, *Social Issues and Public Policy in Business and Management: Retrospect and Prospect* (College Park, MD: Center for Business and Public Policy, 1986), p. 29.
4. Gerald F. Cavanagh and David J. Fritzsche, "Using Vignettes in Business Ethics Research," in Lee E. Preston, ed., *Research in Corporate Social Performance and Policy* (Greenwich, CT: JAI Press Inc., 1985), p. 284.
5. George A. Steiner and John F. Steiner, *Business, Government, and Society*. 5th ed. (New York: Random House, 1988).
6. Rogene A. Buchholz, *Business Environment and Public Policy*. 2nd ed. (Englewood Cliffs, NJ: Prentice-Hall, 1986).
7. See, for example, the following: John W. Clark, *Religion and the Moral Standards of American Businessmen* (Cincinnati: South-Western Publishing, 1966); Roger Ricklefs, "Executives Apply Stiffer Standards Than Public to Ethical Dilemmas," *The Wall Street Journal* (November 3, 1983); Milton Rokeach, *The Nature of Human Values* (New York: The Free Press, 1973); Warren H. Schmidt and Barry Z. Posner, *Managerial Values and Expectations: The Silent Power of Personal and Organizational Life* (New York: American Management Associations, 1982); Archie B. Carroll, "Managerial Ethics: A Post-Watergate View," *Business Horizons*, Vol. 18 (April 1975). pp. 75–80; George W. England, *The Manager and His Values* (Cambridge, MA: Ballinger, 1975); David J. Fritzsche and Helmut Becker, "Linking Management Behavior to Ethical Philosophy—An Empirical Investigation," *Journal of the Academy of Management Journal*, Vol. 27 (March 1984), pp. 166–175; Barry Z. Posner and Warren H. Schmidt, "Ethics in American Companies: A Managerial Perspective," *Journal of Business Ethics*, Vol. 6 (1987), pp. 383–391; and John W. Newstrom and William A. Ruch, "Managerial Values Underlying Intraorganizational Ethics," *Atlanta Economic Review*, Vol. 26 (May–June 1976), pp. 12–15.
8. See Helmut Becker and David J. Fritzsche, "Business Ethics: A Cross-Cultural Comparison of Manager's Attitudes, *Journal of Business Ethics*, Vol. 6 (1987), pp. 289–295 and Steven N. Brenner and Earl A. Molander, "Is the Ethics of Business Changing?", *Harvard Business Review*, Vol. 57 (January–February 1977), pp. 57–71.
9. Theodore V. Purcell, "Do Courses in Business Ethics Pay Off?", *California Management Review*, Vol. 19 (Summer 1977), pp. 50–58; and Robert M. Fulmer, "Business Ethics: Present and Future," *Personnel Administration*, Vol. 34 (September–October 1971), pp. 48–56.
10. Raymond C. Baumhart, *Ethics in Business*, 19.
11. Ibid.
12. Baumhart, p. 7.
13. James R. Glenn, Jr. "Comparing Future and Practicing Managers' Ethical Attitudes." San Francisco State University, School of Business Working Paper, 1986, and James R. Glenn, Jr. and M. Frances Van Loo, "Business Students' and Practitioners' Ethical Decisions Over Time" (Berkeley: University of California, Berkeley Business School, Working Paper, No. BPP–34, 1988).
14. Representatives of research in this area include: Thomas McMahon, "Classroom Ethics—A Survey of Business School Courses," *Business and Society Review*, No. 14 (Summer 1975), pp. 21–24; Michael Hoffman and Jennifer Mills Moore. "Results of a Business Ethics Curriculum Survey Conducted by the Center of Business Ethics," *Journal*

of Business Ethics, Vol. 1 (May 1982), pp. 81–84; Rogene A. Buchholz, *Business Environment and Public Policy: A Study of Teaching and Research in Schools of Business and Management* (Saint Louis: Washington University, 1979); Richard DeGeorge, "Teaching Business Ethics: Is There a Gap between Rhetoric and Reality?", *Journal of Business Ethics*, Vol. 6 (1987), pp. 513–518; Lynn Sharp Paine, *Ethics Education in American Business Schools* (Washington, DC: Ethics Resource Center, Inc., 1988); and Audrey Sullivan Jacob and Kimerer L. LaMothe, *Teaching and Research Initiatives in Business Ethics at Leading American Business Schools* (Boston: Harvard Graduate School of Business Administration, 1987).

15. Roger L. Jenkins, Richard C. Reizenstein, and F. G. Rogers, "Report Cards on the MBA," Vol. 62, *Harvard Business Review* (September–October 1984), pp. 20–30; and McFeely Wackerle Jett, *The McFeely Wackerle Jett Survey on Ethics* (Chicago: McFeely Wackerle Jett, 1987).

16. Judith Briles, "Fortune 500 CEO Ethics Survey." Unpublished data for forthcoming book.

17. LaRue T. Hosmer, "The Other 338: Why a Majority of Our Schools of Business Administration Do Not Offer a Course in Business Ethics," *Journal of Business Ethics*, Vol. 4 (1985), p. 22. Other studies have supported Hosmer's conclusion. See Charles J. Hollon and Thomas A. Ulrich, "Personal Business Ethics: Managers vs Managers-To-Be," *Southern Business Review*, Vol. 5 (1977), pp. 17–22; and J. Siegel, "Machiavellianism M.B.A.'s and Manager's Leadership Correlates and Socialization Effects," Vol. 16, *Academy of Management Journal* (1973), pp. 404–411.

18. Purcell, *op. cit.*, pp. 48–50.

19. David P. Boyd, "Improving Ethical Awareness through the Business and Society Course," *Business and Society*, 20/21 (Winter 1981/Spring 1982), pp. 27–31; T. R. Martin, "Do Courses in Ethics Improve the Ethical Judgment of Students?", *Business and Society*, 20/21 (Winter 1981/Spring 1982), pp. 17–26; and Peter Arlow and Thomas A. Ulrich, "Business Ethics and Business Students: A Longitudinal Study." *Akron Business and Economic Review*, Vol. 16 (Spring 1985), pp. 13–17.

20. See John W. Newstrom and William A. Ruch, "Managerial Values Underlying Intra-organizational Ethics," *Atlanta Economic Review*, Vol. 26 (May–June 1976), pp. 12–15, and Steven N. Brenner and Earl A. Molander, "Is the Ethics of Business Changing?", *Harvard Business Review* (January–February 1977), pp. 57–71.

21. Archie B. Carroll, "Managerial Ethics: A Post-Watergate View," *Business Horizons*, Vol. 17 (April 1975), p. 77.

22. Barry Z. Posner and Warren H. Schmidt, "Ethics in American Companies: A Managerial Perspective." *Journal of Business Ethics*, Vol. 4 (1987), pp. 383–391.

23. Carol Pemberton, *Results from the Spring 1983 Student and Faculty Surveys on Academic Honesty at the University of Delaware* (Newark, DE: The University of Delaware, 1983).

24. Ibid, p. 2.

25. See Diane Curtis, "Cheating, 'Epidemic' Worrying Educators," *San Francisco Chronicle* (February 24, 1987), p. 6; Claudia H. Deutsch, "Students Cheating Even More," *San Francisco Chronicle* (April 15, 1988), p. B3; and Michael Norman, "Lessons," *New York Times* (April 20, 1988), p. B10.

V

A SPECIAL PERSPECTIVE
The AIDS Crisis

Nothing has hit the United States and, indeed the entire world, with the ferocity of the AIDS pandemic. During World War I when suddenly influenza struck military and civilian personnel, people were frightened. With the emergence of AIDS as a national and international problem, people are terrified. The only thing that dwarfs it is the Black Plague that began in 1347 when a merchant ship, loaded with infected rats, arrived in Italy from Tana in the Crimea. In some places on the Continent, one of every two persons perished. Lack of knowledge permitted the devastation in Europe to continue for two centuries. Clarence Gibbs feels strongly that today's policymakers in both the public and private sectors need to have something more than superficial knowledge of the disease to make proper decisions. For that reason he uses his long experience in scientific research to give lay readers a precise scientific account of what AIDS is, according to the latest findings.

Even now, however, experts are confessing to uncertainties. Gordon Nary, the executive director of both the AIDS Medical Research Center and the Physicians' Association for AIDS Care in Chicago, has said that the "nature of the disease is changing so rapidly that as soon as physicians begin to think they understand it, more variables arise."[1] Agreement seems to converge on one fact: Only the tip of the iceberg is visible, and the tip projects a rise in AIDS deaths of 100,000 each year after 1992. Costs for drugs alone have been estimated to run as high as $20,000 for each patient. And despite progress in treating the disease through such drugs as AZT, marketed under the name Retrovir, therapeutic breakthroughs in curing AIDS victims are not anticipated in the near future. Because an infected 35-year-old male can live for 10 or 11 years, what he does with his life and what society allows him to do with his life are questions of great moral significance.

Adding to the moral complexities related to AIDS is the relationship of the disease to homosexual behavior. Before 1987, courts and legislatures turned their backs on Gays' repeated calls for protection against discriminatory actions taken because of their sexual orientation. Efforts to win support from the Equal Employment Opportunity Commission (EEOC), which Gays thought would lend a sympathetic ear, failed on several occasions. To the Commission, adverse employment actions that were undertaken because of a person's sexual preference did not constitute discrimination. Neither were the courts inclined to support the Gays. In the 1978 case of Smith v. Liberty Mutual Insurance Company, *the Fifth Circuit Court of Appeals affirmed a lower court ruling that discrimination because of a person's sexual orientation did not violate the law. The issue was interesting because Liberty Mutual stated very openly that Smith was not hired because the company's interviewer found him to be very "effeminate." It was the court's view that when Congress proscribed sex discrimination it intended only to assure equal opportunity to men and women.[2] Slowly the courts gave ground. In 1984 a male pilot with nearly 12 years' experience on Eastern Airlines was fired when surgery turned him into her.[3] The trial court, distinguishing between* preference and identity, *ruled in favor of the plaintiff. But the story did not end here because the decision was reversed.*

It seems clear that the position of judges and lawmakers reflected a public opinion caught in an historic struggle whether to maintain a taboo, modify it, or drop it altogether. Recognizing Gay rights under the law meant, at least by implication, recognizing society's obligation not only to protect such rights but to assist those who incurred a disease because they indulged in sexual behavior related to those rights. Funding for AIDS research came slowly. It would be unfair, however, to ascribe the tardiness to public hostility alone. Budgetary constraints, plus the need to respond to other "killers" such as heart disease and cancer also played a factor. As Gibbs's analysis unfolds, ethicists will begin to ask new questions—not only about the decision itself and public attitudes toward it but about the legal reasoning used by courts to explain a person's identity on the basis of a sex factor.

NOTES

1. Carol Van Houten, "AIDS Claim: Startling Statistics," *Best's Review* (April 1989), p. 113.
2. Essentially the same reasoning was used the following year in *DeSantis v. Pacific Telephone and Telegraph*. The plaintiffs had argued that Congress's definition of the term *sex* did include protection for those whose sexual orientation was different.
3. *Ulane v. Eastern Airlines* (7th Circuit Court, 1984).

9

Acquired Immune Deficiency Syndrome
The Biological, Ethical, and Moral Dilemmas
of This Twentieth-Century Plague

Clarence J. Gibbs, Jr.

In the life of society, as in the lives of individuals, there are events of significance and moments of indecision. Today our society is experiencing a significant event and a decisive moment: the ominous presence of the disease known as acquired immunodeficiency syndrome (AIDS).

Whether this infection exists as an unrecognized human immunodeficiency virus (HIV) in a pregnant woman or in a newborn child; whether it weakens the body of a person with AIDS-related complex (ARC); or whether it comes as the likelihood of a more imminent death from the disease itself, AIDS is a reality which we must all face.

—The Many Faces of AIDS: A Gospel Response, *Origins*, USCC, Vol. 17: December 24, 1987

The etiology of this deadly pandemic, its treatment, prevention, and cure, the responsibilities of society toward those afflicted, and the care of those stricken present scientists, executives, and society at large with serious scientific, moral, and ethical decisions. Such decisions require more than a

Clarence J. Gibbs, Jr. • Laboratory of Central Nervous System Studies, National Institute of Neurological Disorders and Stroke, National Institutes of Health, Bethesda, Maryland 20892.

casual knowledge of the problem if policymakers in both the public and private sectors are to make right judgments—scientifically right and morally right. The two cannot be separated.

The first part of this chapter concentrates on the scientific aspects of AIDS, perhaps to the degree that lay readers might not like—but likely need. It presents information on the disease, its etiology and epidemiology; current methods of treatment, and prospects for effective immunoprophylactic measures (vaccines). The second part touches on the significance of the disease's psychosociologic and moral impacts on the patients, society, and, less specifically but importantly, on business organizations within the society. Here, however, a caveat must be entered. Because of long research experience, there is self-assurance that the scientific data in this chapter are accurate. The second part, however, is more tentative. Business students, corporate managers, the moralists and ethicists, will therefore have to draw on their own expertise and ultimately they must provide guidance to others in their field of expertise.

I. INCIDENCE AND PREVALENCE OF HIV INFECTION IN THE UNITED STATES

The United States is currently facing the most critical and devastating epidemic of a fatal disease in recent history. The acquired immune deficiency syndrome (AIDS), more commonly referred to as the human immunodeficiency virus (HIV) infection, and the clinical complications that follow are already placing a heavy strain on medical and social services in both the public and private sectors. Since 1981, when the causative virus was first isolated and identified, nearly 68,000 persons with AIDS have been reported in the United States alone, with over 38,000 deaths by July, 1988. Over 30,000 AIDS cases are expected to have been reported in the United States for 1988 alone, and the total number of infected individuals in the United States is estimated by the Public Health Service to be 1 to 1.5 million.

The Public Health Service projects that by the end of 1992, the cumulative number of diagnosed AIDS cases meeting the current definition will total nearly 365,000 with 263,000 cumulative deaths. In 1992 alone, 80,000 cases of AIDS are expected to be diagnosed with 68,000 deaths. During 1992, 172,000 AIDS patients will require medical care, at a cost expected to range from 5 to 13 billion dollars.

The global scope of the pandemic indicates that more than 110 countries have reported AIDS cases and it is unlikely that any part of the world will remain unaffected much longer. Most countries in the Western hemisphere besides the United States are experiencing growing numbers of

AIDS cases, as are Australia and most countries in Western and Eastern Europe. The Arab states have reported few cases to date, and most Asian countries are sparsely involved thus far. However, the presence of even a few cases of AIDS strongly suggests future trouble, given the silent incubation interval of up to 10 years between acquisition of HIV and onset of recognizable disease.

The most intensive foci of epidemic activity are in sub-Saharan Africa: In Central African nations, there are regions where as much as 5 percent of the adult population is now infected. Some urban centers in East Africa are heavily involved, and spread to Southern and Western Africa has begun at variable rates. Recently, in a vivid summary of the African situation, Dr. I. S. Okware, Health Office of Uganda, focused on his own country's experience.[1] He commented that, whereas only 4,000 cases of AIDS had been reported by a total of 25 African countries, this was surely a gross understatement of the extent of HIV-related disease, and it was merely a question of time until all had felt "the full, uncompromising ferocity of the epidemic." Okware noted that AIDS was first suspected in Uganda in 1982, that between 1983 and 1986 there were 1,138 cumulative cases recorded, and that 85 percent of cases were in the most sexually active groups in Uganda, strongly implicating heterosexual transmission. This conclusion was reinforced by data from a serologic survey of 114 Ugandan households in which cases of AIDS had occurred and in which no serologic evidence was found for HIV transmission other than sexual contacts. Thus, although blood transfusions and needle transmission were clearly important in individual cases, heterosexual transmission appears to be the dominant mode of spread. As a final point of ominous significance in terms of social impact, Okware pointed out that HIV disease still affects urban populations primarily, with relative sparing thus far of rural groups. Despite the fact that 90% of the Ugandan population falls in the latter category, the pattern of urban concentration means that the most economically productive members of the society are hardest hit by the epidemic.

In our own country, the prevalence of HIV disease in blacks and Hispanics has occurred at twice their proportion in the general population.[2] Although all primary modes of transmission are found in these populations, intravenous (IV) drug abusers and their sexual partners are overrepresented. Case reports are increasing at alarming rates among Puerto Ricans. The rates of HIV infection and AIDS in Asian/Pacific Islanders and both Native American Indians and Alaskans are reportedly low but may be underestimated.

The sense of real and potential disaster invoked by the epidemiologic data has been only somewhat relieved by findings throughout the world that reaffirmed the highly specific and restricted modes of HIV transmission HIV. Studies of prostitutes in both the United States and Africa often showed high rates of antibody positivity for HIV, but commonly the risk of infection was strongly associated with IV drug use and an alarmingly high practice of sexual promiscuity.[3,4] The rates of sexual promiscuity and drug abuse experienced in the United States have been the underlying cause of the more rapid spread of AIDS in the heterosexual community, including the occurrence of the disease in a number of our higher socioeconomic class of professionals and college and university students.[2]

In contrast, the risk of infection of health care workers who have not engaged in high-risk behaviors continues to be remarkably low, and the few breakthrough cases would appear to be due to the failure to follow recommended safety techniques. It should be noted in this respect that protective precautions appropriate to the avoidance of hepatitis B virus offer substantially extra protection against the more fragile AIDS virus.

II.   NATURAL HISTORY OF HIV INFECTION

The natural history of HIV infection and its progression to disease continues to be a major focus of intensive research.[5] In particular, determining the likelihood that an individual will develop AIDS or other illnesses once infected is a matter of profound importance, both for infected persons and in predicting the scope of future pandemic impact. Past studies had indicated that between 15 percent and 40 percent of HIV antibody-positive individuals would develop AIDS within a 5-year period.[6] These findings were extended by several reports that confirmed those data and indicated that additional risk of disease occurrence, even following a single sexual encounter with an infected individual, extended well beyond the 50-year figure. As mentioned earlier in this chapter, the long-term asymptomatic period is currently listed as 9 to 10 years before clinical signs of disease become apparent. This extraordinarily long incubation period is not as surprising as it might be, for it is a uniform characteristic of other members of the lentivirus subgroup of retroviruses, to which HIV belongs. In the studies I have been conducting over the past 30 years on the "transmissible dementias"—kuru, a heredofamilial disease of the Fore people of Papua, New Guinea, and Creutzfeldt-Jakob disease, a presenile dementia that occurs throughout the world—the incubation period between the time the virus enters the body and the symptoms of the disease appear can be as long as 30 years. Although the long-term incubation periods of AIDS and the transmissible dementias are similar, unlike AIDS, the transmissible dementias do *not* appear to be contagious.

Thus, AIDS is a virus-induced "slow infection" with incubations of months to years. This is quite important, for these data not only increase the estimate of the mean incubation period between initial infection and onset of disease, but they also indicate, as earlier noted, *that there is sure to be a marked increase in the needs for health care over the next decade or more among young and middle-aged adults who normally do not tax the resources of the health care system appreciably.* Indeed, if one extrapolates such data to 1 to 1.5 million people estimated to be infected in the United States, it becomes clearly evident that urgent steps are necessary to prepare the U.S. health care system to care for this large number of clinically ill people. Clearly, other countries will be stressed as well, and the problem is at its most awesome in Africa, where the paucity of resources in hard-hit areas means that the rest of the world must be ready and willing to provide resources and manpower to help.

III. CLINICAL AND LABORATORY FEATURES OF HIV INFECTION

Patients with illnesses that, in retrospect, were manifestations of AIDS, were first described in the summer of 1981. As the AIDS epidemic continues to spread, primary care physicians, psychiatrists, psychologists, clergy, social workers, and families will see more and more patients with indications of HIV. Primary care physicians can recognize the clinical signs in patients with AIDS and AIDS-related syndromes, guided, when necessary, by specialists in infectious disease, neurology, oncology, and pulmonary medicine. They will require the support of allied medical personnel in providing hands-on care, and psychiatrists, psychologists, social workers, religious, and community leaders to meet the needs of their patients, the patients' families and members of the community in which the patients live. In all too many instances, medicine has failed to face the issue of disease impact on the family and society in general.

A. Case Definitions

The clinical features of HIV infection form a spectrum.[7] It ranges from those individuals who are infected but in apparent good health to those with rapid disease progression and mortality from a complicating infection or malignancy. Within this spectrum of clinical manifestations, several syndromes have been defined: persistent generalized lymphadenopathy, AIDS-related complex, and AIDS itself.[8]

Because the areas on the spectrum tend to overlap, definitions of AIDS-related syndromes can be arbitrary and occasionally misleading. In addition, definitions do not fully reflect the morbidity caused by HIV infection. For example, some patients are incapacitated by the anxiety of knowing they are infected with the virus, even though they are healthy by all objective standards. And although some patients that are antibody-positive experience a rapidly fatal disease course, others live in reasonably good health more than 5 years after the diagnosis of an AIDS-related malignancy.[5]

However, HIV infection is so complex that definitions are essential to understanding the illness. Although imperfect, surveillance definitions enable the monitoring of the progression of the pandemic through different risk groups.

B. Subclinical HIV Infection

With only rare exceptions, all subclinically infected individuals are HIV-antibody positive. Although people in this group are clinically well, laboratory abnormalities are common. It was hoped that individuals could remain fully immune-competent with HIV infections, but it appears this is not the case. In one recent study, more than 90 percent of subjects followed for more than 2 years after HIV infection showed evidence of T-helper cell (the cells concerned with immunity) depletion. Although the long-term health consequences of HIV infection in subclinical subjects are not fully known, the near universal finding of T-helper cell depletion is a cause for grave concern. Although the long-term health consequences of subclinical HIV infections are unknown, current estimates range from 30 to 50 percent or more for developing AIDS over a 5-year period.

C. Persistent Generalized Lymphadenopathy

Although there is no uniform consensus in this area, it seems reasonable to differentiate patients who are otherwise asymptomatic with the exception of diffuse lymphadenopathy from those with AIDS-related complex. Nevertheless, functionally, many patients with lymphadenopathy might also be diagnosed with mild AIDS-related complex. Persistent generalized lymphadenopathy is defined as (1) lymphadenopathy of at least 3-month duration involving two or more extrainguinal sites and confirmed by physical examination; (2) absence of any current illness or drug use known to cause lymphadenopathy; and (3) reactive hyperplasia in a lymph node, if a biopsy was performed.[9,10]

D. AIDS-Related Complex (ARC)

This syndrome has recently been reclassified by the Centers for Disease Control (CDC) and has been designated AIDS. It nevertheless is presented in this chapter to note the complexity involved in diagnosis. Even before HIV was isolated and antibody testing became available, it became clear to physicians that many other individuals in AIDS high-risk groups suffered clinical illness that suggested immune deficiency yet did not meet the CDC surveillance definition of AIDS. As the spectrum of immune deficiency clinical symptoms has become clearer, the system complexes have variably been called ARC or symptomatic HIV infection. Although the definition is not precise, ARC can be diagnosed when an individual infected with HIV demonstrates persistent clinical abnormalities not within the CDC surveillance definition of AIDS. Some of the more common symptoms are (1) fever, > 100°F, intermittent or continuous ≥3 months, in the absence of other identifiable cause; (2) weight loss, 10 percent of normal body weight or ≥15 pounds; (3) lymphadenopathy, persistent ≥3 months in the absence of other identifiable cause(s); (4) fatigue, to the point of decreased physical or mental function; (5) night sweats, intermittent or continuous ≥3 months, in the absence of other identifiable causes.

To these clinical symptoms must be added one or more of the following laboratory abnormalities: (1) depressed helper T-cells; (2) depressed helper/suppressor ratio; (3) at least one of the following: leukopenia, thrombocytopenia, absolute lymphophenia or anemia; (4) elevated serum globulins; (5) depressed blastogenesis; and (6) abnormal intradermal tests for delayed cutaneous hypersensitivity.[11]

E.   Acquired Immune Deficiency Syndrome (AIDS)

According to the CDC surveillance definition, AIDS can be diagnosed when an unusual opportunistic infection or rare malignancy occurs in an otherwise healthy individual. The infection or malignancy must suggest a relationship to underlying cellular immune deficiency, and the individual must have no prior illness or medication use that would independently increase risk for these clinical manifestations.

Most AIDS diagnostic infections and cancers do not require laboratory confirmation of HIV infection, although in greater than 95 percent of the cases this is now required. Currently, for example, histoplasmosis or diffuse B-cell lymphomas are considered as AIDS in an individual who has independent confirmation of HIV infection whether by antibody or direct viral isolation.

Although the case definition of AIDS is straightforward, occasional problems rise. For example, Kaposi's sarcoma is considered diagnostic when seen in an individual less than 60 years old. Yet, cases of Kaposi's sarcoma have been reported in homosexual men older than 60, but this does not meet CDC criteria for AIDS even though the risk group membership and subsequent course indicate the presence of AIDS. Therefore, surveillance definitions, such as that of the CDC for AIDS, must be used cautiously in specific instances.

Recently the CDC proposed a revised system of classification for HIV, and this system now includes definitions for the spectrum of HIV-related clinical manifestations as shown in the following:

Group I. Acute infection
Group II. Asymptomatic infection
Group III. Persistent generalized lymphadenopathy
Group IV. Secondary infectious diseases
   Subgroup A. Constitutional disease
   Subgroup B. Neurologic disease
   Subgroup C. Secondary infectious disease
      Category C-1. Specified secondary infections listed in the CDC surveillance definition for AIDS
      Category C-2. Other specified secondary infectious diseases
   Subgroup D. Secondary cancers
   Subgroup E. Other conditions

IV.   EFFECTS OF HIV ON THE NERVOUS SYSTEM

Shortly after AIDS was first described, mental disturbances were noted to be a common feature of the disease. Initially these disturbances were attributed to psychiatric or systemic complications as well as to the direct effects of tumors or opportunistic infections within the peripheral (PNS) and central nervous systems (CNS). Psychiatrists and psychologists identified the profound psychosocial stressors of this stigmatizing and contagious illness. Virologists noted that HIV had a preference for both the PNS and CNS and classified the virus as neurovirulent. Evidence shows that the virus infects the nervous system in a matter of days following entrance into the body.

The difficulties in establishing the frequency of HIV-induced dementia become readily apparent from the numerous reviews and case reports of mental disturbances in patients with AIDS.[12,13] HIV infection can mimic almost any neurologic or psychiatric disorder including Alzheimer's disease, insidious depressive withdrawal, seizures, acute florid psychotic delirium, and mania with grandiose delusions. The signs and symptoms include forgetfulness, loss of concentration, disorientation, delirium, slowness of thought, aphasia, apraxia, deterioration of handwriting, apathy, social withdrawal, organic psychosis, and sociopathic behavior. Added to this list are the cognitive deficits and psychosocial developmental lags noted in perinatally infected children in whom dementia develops in more than 75 percent of patients during the late stages of their disease. The prominence of neurologic disease in HIV-infected individuals has resulted in the identification of a new neurologic disease referred to as AIDS Dementia Complex (ADS) that is characterized by cognitive, motor, sensory, and behavioral disturbances. Although the CNS may also be affected by a wide variety of opportunistic conditions including herpes viruses, toxoplasmosis, papova viruses, infections, and neoplasms, ADC is by far the most frequent and most important cause of neurologic morbidity in patients with AIDS.

Emerging studies of altered brain function accompanying ADC support the idea that the syndrome is a subcortical dementia. As in other disorders tentatively described as subcortical dementias, clinical and neuropsychologic evaluation of patients with ADC reveals psychomotor slowing, impaired problem solving, reduced spontaneity, and poor fine motor control as the early and most prominent features; the frank aphasia, amnesias, or parietal lobe syndromes, mentioned in this chapter, are not observed until later in the disease. In many instances, it is the PNS that becomes affected such that patients with peripheral neuropathies, Guillain-Barré syndrome, and the like should be tested for HIV infection.

The evolving evidence that ADS is partly or wholly caused by direct HIV brain infection, in concert with the frequency of CNS infection very early in the course of systemic HIV infection, provides strong rationale for seeking antiviral drugs capable of penetrating the blood–brain barrier for treatment of ADC and perhaps HIV infection in general.[14] In this regard, preliminary data suggest that the antiviral drug idovudine induced improvement in symptoms and neuropsychological test performance. AZT, the drug of choice for prolongation of the life of AIDS patients, has also been reported as effective in reversing temporarily the symptoms of AIDS encephalopathy, including dementia. But it should be understood that AZT is extremely toxic and capable of causing brain dysfunction. At present, it is uncertain whether viral suppression will provide substantial restoration of functional capacity or only stabilization.

One could ask why I have given so much consideration to the devastating effects HIV and AIDS have on the nervous system. Until 1981, when AIDS was first recognized, the single most importance cause of acute brain infection was the herpes virus, and about 65 percent of all patients with dementia were diagnosed as having Alzheimer's disease. And, because the United States is experiencing a linear increase in the life span of its population, we had predicted an increase in the number of aged people with dementia for which the health care system of this country was not and still is not prepared to provide care. Today the single most important cause of dementia is HIV. Superimposing the number of AIDS cases with dementia on those with Alzheimer's disease, we can expect by 1992 that the demands on the health care delivery system, families of the patients, and the economy will become even more significant in their impact on society in general.

V. BIOLOGY AND PATHOGENESIS OF HIV

HIV is a human retrovirus that has been isolated from peripheral blood mononuclear cells (white blood cells), autopsy tissues, and a variety of body fluids, including urine, saliva, tears, semen, vaginal/cervical secretions, cerebrospinal fluid, and blood of ARC and AIDS patients. These isolates have been recovered from individuals of widely disparate ethnic groups, living in different parts of the world, and from all socioeconomic levels. The previous isolation by Gallo and his colleagues of a virus as the etiology of adult T-cell leukemia and called the human T-lymphotrophic retrovirus type I (HTLV-I) with a trophism for a receptor on cells known as the CD-4 receptor had focused attention on the possible causal role of a retrovirus replicating in T-cells as a cause of AIDS.[15] In May 1983, reports were published of an association between AIDS and HTLV-I both by viral isolation and serology. An additional paper from Montagnier's laboratory at the Pasteur Institute in Paris described the isolation of a unique T-lymphocyte-trophic retrovirus that appeared to be only distantly related to HTLV-I.[16] This retrovirus was initially considered to be a member of the HTLV family, and Gallo designated it HTLV-III. Subsequently, the Pasteur virus was named lymphadenopathy-associated virus (LAV). In both laboratories, the virus isolated from AIDS patients produced a lytic infection of proliferating lymphocytes in culture in contrast to the transformation and immortalization of T-lymphocytes infected with HTLV-I.

HIV contains three structural genes typical of all retroviral genomes and designated *gag*, *pol*, and *env*. Replication of the viral ribonucleic acid (RNA) is by a deoxyribonucleic acid (DNA) intermediate termed the DNA provirus, utilizing the virus-encoded RNA-directed DNA polymerase called reverse transcriptase.[17,18,19,20]

Retroviruses are classified by morphology, clinical diseases they induce, and their genomic structure into three groups:

1. *Spumarviruses*. These occur in cats and primates, and induce vacuolation (foamy cells) in culture but are not currently associated with any recognizable disease.

2. *Oncoviruses*. These are animal and tumor viruses, frequently with ability to transform (immortalize) cells as well as nononcogenic endogenous strains. Oncoviruses are further subdivided by electron microscopic morphology into B-type (mammary tumor viruses), C-type (leukemia viruses, including HTLV-I), and D-type (Mason-Pfizer monkey virus) forms.

3. *Lentiviruses*. These cause slow degenerative neurologic diseases in animals, such as visna/maedi in sheep and caprine arthritis/encephalitis virus in goats. Lentiviruses now include HIV, the newly recognized feline T-lymphotropic virus, bovine lentivirus (BLV), and simian lentiviruses (SIVs). Equine infectious anemia virus also belongs to this group.

AIDS is the end stage of HIV infection and is simply defined as an irreversible breakdown in the cellular immune system marked clinically by a profound decrease in the number of and function of peripheral blood CD4+ lymphocytes. Although only a small proportion of circulating T-cells are infected by HIV in AIDS patients, perhaps only 1 in 10^5 cells, there exists some paradox between the number of directly infected cells and the number of affected cells. There are numerous theories proposed to explain the pathogenesis of the disease caused by HIV: (1) direct HIV killing; (2) HIV-induced alteration of cell membranes resulting in the fusion of cells (syncytia formation); (3) secreted viral envelope induced fusion; (4) antilymphocytic antibodies/cytotoxic T-cells; and (5) secreted antilymphocytic factors.

None of these theories has yet been fully substantiated. The evidence for a direct role of HIV cytopathic effect in cells is supported from aspects of tissue culture studies *in vitro*, where HIV can directly cause cell death, without necessarily causing cell fusion (syncytia). It has been suggested that the *gag* gene, or one of the regulatory genes, contains a sequence whose expression causes premature cell senility. The development of large multinucleated giant cells (syncytia) by the fusion of HIV-infected cells with receptor-bearing cells is a marked property of HIV, in common with many other retroviruses. Were the resulting syncytia induction to occur *in vitro*, then this could be a mechanism for HIV pathogenesis. However, giant cell formation has rarely been observed in the peripheral blood of AIDS or ARC patients, and this theory does not seem to be easily associated with the low expression of HIV-infected cells in the blood. Thus the pathogenesis of HIV in AIDS and the underlying mechanisms leading to the development of this fatal disease remain essentially unknown in spite of the extensive knowledge that scientists have of the molecular biology of the virus.

VI.   EVOLUTION OF THE RETROVIRUSES

In his keynote lecture for the meeting on human retroviruses, cancer, and AIDS, held in Keystone, Colorado, in April 1987, the Nobel Laureate in Medicine, Howard Temin, addressed one of the most frequently asked questions about AIDS and HIV: Where did HIV come from? Similar questions had been raised for HTLV and adult T-cell leukemia. Obviously the answers to these questions are important in understanding and controlling the epidemics caused by these viruses. Temin pointed out that three answers have been proposed to the question of HIV origin: (1) HIV has existed for a long time in isolated villages in Africa, but it was only recognized recently when it was transmitted into urban populations; (2) HIV was created in a genetic engineering laboratory, probably in the United States but possibly in Haiti; and (3) HIV is a newly appearing virus derived from some viral precursor, probably from infected nonhuman primates who have their own types of retroviruses.[21]

Because, in the history of Africa, there is considerable evidence of wide diffusion of cultural artifacts and villages were not isolated from one another, the first theory can be ruled out. The molecular structure and organization of the HIV genome are much more complex than that of any previously known retrovirus, and thus, as Temin concluded, no earthly scientist could have constructed HIV before the time it first appeared—the technology and knowledge were simply not available. These facts exclude the second theory. Thus, as Temin pointed out, we are left with the only statement that now can be definitively made—that retroviruses and some movable genetic elements are evolutionarily homologous, that is, the similarities between retroviruses and some cellular movable genetic elements represent an evolutionary relationship that has resulted in the emergence of a new virus.[21]

VII.   ETHICAL AND LEGAL ISSUES ASSOCIATED WITH HIV INFECTION

The ethical and legal issues associated with the recognition of AIDS and the isolation of HIV as the etiologic agent were simply but emphatically stated by Jonathan Mann of the World Health Organization in his keynote address to participants in the Third International Congress on AIDS, held in 1987 in Washington, DC. He stated: "A global epidemic has entered a stage in which prejudice about race, about religion, about social class, and about nationality is spreading as fast as the virus itself."[22]

The number one issue confronting the health care field today is: How can we control the pandemic, prevent the further spread of the disease, and control the psychologic, economic, and social harm that it causes without unjustly discriminating against particular social groups and without unnecessarily infringing on the freedom of individuals? Walters, in his paper on the ethical issues in the prevention and treatment of HIV infection and AIDS, points out that the formulation of the question accepts the importance of halting the transmission of HIV infection but recognizes that achieving that goal may at times conflict with moral constraints, constraints based on justice or respect for autonomy.[23] It is obvious to the reader of this chapter that I subscribe to the basic tenet that any effective response to the problem must be based primarily on an understanding of the disease and the lessons we have learned from epidemiologic surveillance. It thus follows that the proper knowledge of the goals of both public and health policies intended to reduce the risk of exposure should be consistent with the historical mission of health care providers. These goals should enable medical facilitators and other providers (i.e., nursing homes, hospices, etc.) to deliver *high quality* and *compassionate* care that is respectful of the interests of the patients. Further, actions to prevent transmission of HIV infection should *not* interfere, unless absolutely necessary, with the interests of HIV-infected patients, particularly their interest in maintaining the confidentiality of sensitive medical information and in receiving the same care and consideration provided other patients. At the same time, the concerns and fears of health care providers and their staffs require careful *attention* and a *commitment* to the *development* and *implementation* of policies, procedures, and techniques that can be effective in preventing transmission of HIV in the health care and community settings. Finally, and most important, is the urgent need for *an informed society*. The only currently available effective means of controlling the spread of HIV infection is *education* of the general public, members of high-risk groups, employers and employees, and primary, secondary, and college/university students.

If the biologic challenge of HIV were not enough, the social context of the HIV epidemic presents at least as great a challenge to control.[24] Spread of the virus is largely among social groups whose sexual activities were until recent years illegal (i.e., homosexuals) and among groups both legally and socially marginal (i.e., IV drug users).[25] In the lay press and early in the scientific recognition of the disease AIDS remained largely presented as a "gay plague" or homosexual disease, respectively. Although the prevalence of the disease is overrepresented in this group, particularly among blacks and Hispanics, education on the mode of spread of HIV has actually resulted in a dramatic decline of the disease in the gay population in San Francisco. In homosexual sexually transmitted disease centers in London, there has been a significant reduction in the incidence of new HIV infection, a fall in gonorrhea rates, and marked changes in homosexual behavior. There can be little doubt that the effectiveness of these educational strategies owes a lot to the ability of the gay community to mobilize its own resources and to carry out its campaigns through gay clubs, bath houses, and other social networks.

Perhaps the most distinguishing feature of the AIDS epidemic in the context of the ethical and legal issues is the sensitivity of our social institutions to the human dimensions of the disease. We must be concerned that fundamental rights are not trampled in the process of coming to terms with the disease.[26] In the case of health care professionals and allied medical personnel, as well as in the research laboratory working on HIV, two approaches to minimize the risk of HIV transmission have received considerable public debate and discussion: the use of protective barriers for all patients (*universal precautions*) and testing for HIV.[27] Because it is often not possible to know when an individual may be infected with HIV, consistent use of a barrier to reduce the chances of direct contact with potentially infected blood and body substances is the best way to avoid accidental exposure to HIV infection. Accordingly, universal precautions have been recommended by CDC and the Occupational Safety and Health Administration for all health care workers, public safety personnel (police, fire, emergency medical, etc.), and relatives caring for AIDS patients, whose functions could bring them into contact with blood and body substances.

The second important, and yet very controversial approach, is *HIV testing*. The general issue posed by HIV testing concerns the appropriate circumstances under which such a test should be performed. For the military, the Secretary of Defense has prescribed the policy and procedures to be followed on "identification, surveillance and administration of personnel infected with HIV." The policy is intended to address the risks to the infected individual incident to military service, the risk of transmission of disease to noninfected personnel, the effect of infected personnel on the function of the unit, and the safety of the blood supply. However, there are rather strict limitations on the use of generated information, for example, information obtained from a service member during—or as a result of—an epidemiologic assessment interview may not be used against the service member in a court martial, nonjudicial punishment, involuntary separation other than for medical reasons, administrative or punitive reduction in grade, denial of promotion, or unfavorable entry in a personnel record. Results obtained from laboratory tests for HIV performed may not be used as the basis for separation of the service member except for separation based upon physical disability.

In the health care sector (hospitals), the chief debate has centered on whether routine testing of patients or employees is necessary to reduce the risk of HIV infection.[27] In order to assess the value of routine testing, it is important to evaluate why testing would be performed and what actions would result from "knowing" an individual's status. If no different action would be taken, or if the actions taken would not lessen the risks of transmission, then testing serves no purpose. The American Hospital Association, St. Clare's Hospital and Health Center in New York, advisory committee on AIDS, addressed this problem and concluded that HIV testing is appropriately performed for the purposes of making a diagnosis of AIDS; answering a patient's questions about whether he or she is infected; screening blood, organs, or other body substances prior to donation; or conducting follow-up after a potential exposure to HIV has occurred. However, they also felt that routine testing of either patients or staff is not necessary to reduce the risk of exposure to HIV and should not be substituted for rigorous adherence to universal precautions.

In any circumstance in which HIV testing is done, the testing agency must recognize the extreme sensitivities associated with these tests by adopting policies that address the use of informed consent, the standards for using an HIV test as a screening device, notification of patients or volunteers of results, the need for counseling patients, volunteers, and their families, and the strict maintenance of confidentiality of information about HIV status.

Perhaps the most controversial issue for hospitals involves the suggestion by some that HIV test results are appropriately used as the basis for refusal to perform certain procedures on infected individuals. The American Hospital Association again states that HIV test results will be used by physicians or hospital staff to conduct or direct a patient's medical care.[27] However, if a hospital allows its physicians and other staff to use test results for the purpose of refusing to treat HIV-infected patients, its ability to fulfill its mission and legal obligations may be jeopardized. The obligation to insure the provision of appropriate care is shared by hospitals and their medical staffs. The development of policies to insure the ability to meet that obligation should be a joint effort. Employees and medical staff have a right to be made aware of the need for, and content of, such policies so that they will understand the consequences of their actions should they refuse to provide care because of a patient's HIV status.

It should be noted that, as a general rule, there is no legal support for mandatory testing in civilian health care settings at this time in the absence of compelling circumstances.[28] Advisory and professional organizations do not presently support mandatory testing as a condition of treatment. Indeed, requiring antibody tests prior to treatment may result in actions alleging invasion of privacy, lack of informed consent, abandonment, and failure to treat. Constance Baker, legal counsel to the American Hospital Association, has addressed the question: "Is there an existent rule entitled 'Duty to Treat'?" As a general rule, private physicians, dentists, and other licensed health care providers are not required to accept any particular individual as a new patient. The Council on Ethical and Judicial Affairs of the American Medical Association has stated that physicians competent to treat AIDS patients may refuse to treat an individual solely because the individual tests positive for antibodies to the HIV virus (Report of the Council on Ethical and Judicial Affairs, Ethical Issues Involved in the Growing AIDS Crisis, Report: A [1–87], November 12, 1987).

Once the patient–physician relationship has been established, a physician or dentist has a duty to continue treatment until the patient's condition has stabilized or the patient has transferred to another health care provider. Failure to continue treatment may result in charges of abandonment and disciplinary action.

In the United States, nearly all states require each case of AIDS to be reported to the state health department. Although still controversial, several states have also established systems for reporting antibody-positive test results. Traditionally, public health authorities have been empowered to impose various forms of control in preventing the spread of contagious notifiable diseases such as smallpox, yellow fever, measles, poliomyelitis, typhoid, diphtheria, plague, cholera, tuberculosis, anthrax, and so forth. This has included forms of quarantine. The latter may be a reasonable control measure where person-to-person spread occurs through casual contact, the period of infectiveness is limited to a few weeks, and effective means of treatment are available. For HIV, such quarantine is clearly both impractical and inappropriate because casual spread does not occur and infectiousness may be lifelong. Legislative procedures have been used to consider quarantine procedures for persons spreading HIV through irresponsible sexual behavior (i.e., prisons in the United States). Lawsuits have occurred to close bathhouses on the basis that they represented a public health nuisance. However, a recent case failed on the basis that health officials could not prove that closing such establishments would reduce the spread of HIV.

Instructions governing the confidentiality of reporting systems and legislation have been passed to control the use of antibody testing and the disclosure of results. The issue of confidentiality in "contact tracing" remains unresolved. Increasingly, legal cases have been brought forth concerning employment, housing (including neighborhood hospices), and insurance discrimination. Legislation in this field is heavily controversial and is still evolving and includes discussions of antidiscrimination legislation to restrict the use of antibody testing by insurance companies, and so on. The field is moving fast, and our attitudes to testing and control might change quickly if drugs become available that either reduce infectivity or slow progression of the disease.

If we address the problem only from the public health and legalistic point and fail to include the very significant moral issues, we remain on the horns of a dilemma. In his recent address to scientists at a recent meeting in Rome, Pope John Paul II stated: "Compared with many other diseases known by mankind in the course of history, AIDS has by far many more *profound repercussions* of a moral, social, economic, juridical and structural nature not only on individual families and on neighborhood communities, but also on Nations and on the entire community of peoples."[29] In meeting the crises, the federal government has rapidly provided additional funding to research, treatment, and to a more limited degree for the case of those infected who do not have health insurance. More needs to be done, especially in providing financial support for those impoverished by their illness. We need much greater efforts on the part of the federal government, industry, and all levels of educational institutions to provide more effective educational media programs to help reduce fear, prejudice, and discrimination against persons infected and those perceived to be in high-risk groups. Current programs and services need to be expanded to assist the families of those with AIDS while they are alive and to insure that there is a continuity of health care and pastoral services available to families and patients in response to the unique setting of psychologic, social and spiritual issues that arise during the illness. Again quoting Pope John Paul II:

> The threatening spread of AIDS hurls at all men a *double-edged challenge* which the Church also wants to meet in fulfilling her due share: I am referring to the *prevention of the disease* and to the *health care offered to those who suffer from it*. A truly effective action in these two areas cannot be developed without looking to sustain a common effort which results from a constructive vision of the dignity of the human person and his transcendent destiny.[29]

As an individual, I oppose the approach of "safe sex" because it compromises human sexuality and makes it safe to be promiscuous and misleading. Prevention methods that instead promote egotistic interests, deriving from considerations that are incompatible with the fundamental values of life and love, can only end up being contradictory as well as illicit, merely circling the problem without resolving it at its roots.[29] As pointed out by most religious leaders, it is long overdue to once again teach that "human sexuality is to be genitally expressed only in a monogamous heterosexual relationship of lasting fidelity in marriage" (USOC Administrative Board—The Many Faces of AIDS: A Gospel Response; December 24, 1987, Volume 17, No. 28). AIDS prevention to be *worthy of the human person* and at the same time truly effective must propose two objectives: *to inform* adequately and *to educate* for responsible maturity. Personal human dignity demands that each person be helped to grow in effective maturity by means of a specific educational process.[29]

Finally, my work on HIV, its mode of spread, and the physical, biological, and biochemical properties convinces me that most people infected with the virus are able to continue working for long periods without further risk to themselves or others. Such people are entitled to the same treatment with regard to employment and insurance as other persons. Those unable to continue working because of their physical deterioration should continue to receive health and other benefits available to other employees, but, because of the expense, the response to this need should in all probability be shared by the federal and local governments, industry, and charitable organizations.

To address more specifically the moral problems facing business organizations requires insights from the moralists. For it is obvious that my primary concern has been with the *is* issue: What *is* AIDS? How *is* it gotten? How *is* it developed? How *is* it transmitted? The limits of one's expertise, however, can too easily be used as a defense for intellectual retreat. My moral perspectives persuade me that primary emphasis on the "safe sex" approach is ethically flawed because it demeans the human significance of sex and encourages promiscuity. Hedonism has enough going for it in contemporary society, and further inducements to self-indulgences will be counterproductive. Responsibility for engaging in activities whose threat to well-being are known rests primarily on the individual. Should, for example, employers be asked to help an employee whose illness is totally unrelated to the work environment? Is it the government's job? Although a case can be made for negative answers, it seems that an authentic moral response requires employers to do more than wring their hands. After all, employees are human, not angels; the knowledge about AIDS is not without missing elements; prejudice often displaces prudence; possibility of prohibitive costs can frighten even the most sensitive manager. Because the disease has been linked to promiscuous homosexuality, attempts to deal with the former have been stalled by legal indecision regarding the latter. For this reason, it is well to review briefly the judicial attitude toward homosexuality, remembering all the while that AIDS is not restricted to the homosexual population. Certainly business cannot be blamed; as late as 1986, the courts and legislatures had virtually ignored the Gay Rights movement. The gays' attempts to assert legal rights were largely unsuccessful. Even the Equal Employment Opportunity Commission (EEOC) was unsympathetic, and it issued several decisions to the effect that adverse employment actions against individuals because of their sexual orientation did not constitute discrimination under Title VII. The case history is worth reviewing.

In 1978 (*Smith vs. Liberty Mutual Insurance Company*), the Fifth Circuit Court of Appeals upheld a lower court's dismissal of race and sex discrimination claims brought by a job applicant who asserted that he was not hired because of his sexual orientation. Liberty Mutual admitted that it had refused to hire the plaintiff solely because its interviewer concluded that the plaintiff was "effeminate." The district court dismissed the action. A year later (*DeSantis vs. Pacific Telephone and Telegraph Company*), several male and female employees brought suit alleging discrimination based on their sexual orientation. The district court dismissed the plaintiffs' claims, concluding that it lacked jurisdiction. On appeal, the employees argued for a broad definition of the term *sex*, saying that Congress intended to include discrimination on the basis of sexual orientation. This led the EEOC to distinguish between sexual identity and sexual conduct. One of the first cases to attempt a distinction was *Ulane vs. Eastern Airlines*. Ulane was a male pilot for Eastern Airlines nearly 12 years before her sex reassignment surgery. Terminated, she brought suit in the Illinois district court alleging that her dismissal was based on her transsexuality and prompted by her surgery. During the trial, the judge declared: "I find that sex is not a cut-and-dried matter of chromosomes, and that . . . the evidence in this record satisfies me that the term, *sex*, as used in the statute can be and should be reasonably interpreted to include among its denotations the question of sexual identity and that, therefore, transsexuals are protected by Title VII" (p. 424). A more generous interpretation of the statute was hailed as a great victory by many. The liberal perspective of the district court was, however, reversed.

Recently, the Ninth Circuit decided a case with potentially far-reaching implications for discrimination on the basis of homosexuality. Sergeant Perry Watkins was a career Army man with an impeccable military record. From the day he enlisted, he openly admitted his homosexuality; he had, in fact, with the permission of his superiors, performed as a female impersonator on occasions (*Watkins vs. U.S. Army*). In 1981, 14 years after Watkins enlisted, the Army issued new regulations requiring that all homosexuals be disqualified from service regardless of the term of character of that service. When Watkins was discharged, he brought suit in the California Federal District Court challenging the constitutionality of the Army's regulations. Watkins advanced a sophisticated legal theory. Unlike predecessors who had challenged laws that discriminated against Gays on the basis of deprivation of property, right to privacy, or rights to due process, Watkins challenged the regulations on the basis of equal protection, characterizing the rules as "invidious discrimination based on sexual orientation."

According to Watkins, the regulations illegally burdened homosexuals not because they engaged in homosexual conduct but simply because they admitted they were homosexuals. The plaintiff's theory provided the court with an opportunity to use a legal analysis that required it to look at homosexuals at a distinct minority deserving special protection.

Under the equal protection analysis, a court must initially review whether the group alleging discrimination is a "suspect class" for purposes of constitutional protection. In applying this analysis, the Watkins court found that (1) as a group, homosexuals had a history of suffering from purposeful discrimination; (2) the discrimination arose from a characteristic that had no relation to the homosexual's ability to contribute or perform and was a result of prejudice; and (3) the homosexual traits were immutable, that is, they "were so central to a person's identity that it would be abhorrent for the government to penalize a person for refusing to change them." In his dissent, Judge Reinhardt argued reluctantly, but persuasively, that the Supreme Court's decision in *Bowers vs. Hardwick* effectively precluded the majority's conclusion that homosexuals constitute a suspect class.

In *Hardwick*, the Supreme Court had held that the constitutional right of privacy does not extend to homosexual sodomy and, thus, such a conduct could be outlawed by the states. According to Judge Reinhardt, the Supreme Court's emphasis on the homosexual nature of the illegal conduct is a clear indication that it will not extend constitutional protection on the basis of homosexuality. Meanwhile, however, it is well to remember that in the current climate *all* people, as well as all institutions, have a responsibility and those with power and resources have greater responsibility. Employers, for example, can take a few practical steps among which are, of course, the development and promulgation of a policy that deals with AIDS-affected employees. Among the positive elements of such a policy are the following:

- Provisions of testing services on a voluntary, cost-free basis
- Guarantees of total confidentiality
- Assurances to working colleagues that termination of AIDS personnel will occur once doctors tell the employer and its infected employee that termination is warranted
- Severance on an unpublicized basis—even through the grapevine—can never be cut
- Generous severance payments
- Counseling services to victims and shared costs with public agencies to help their families
- Continuing education programs

Insurance poses especially severe problems to business. Developing fairly reliable actuarial figures is a *sine qua non* for the industry, and such numbers are related to risk assessments of potential customers. Horror stories exist. There is, for example, the story of a severely ill AIDS patient who bought term insurance of $500,000 from each of three companies. His heirs collected $1.5 million on the man's modest investment. When insurance companies try to protect themselves, public criticism swells. The simple fact is that, from the moral standpoint of justice and the business standpoint of profitability, AIDS victims will be best protected when insurers are protected. And this note becomes the theme: Help and protection are needed by patients, health providers, employers, and insurers. Recognizing this interdependence is probably the first sensible step toward reaching a solution.

Listed later are examples of tough decisions associated with AIDS; the reader can certainly add to these examples. From these, I put major emphasis on the family, the patient, and society. Parents are morally and ethically responsible for providing the first and most effective program of prevention of sexually related diseases by supplying correct information for the formation of life's responsibilities in all its aspects. Parents must prepare their children for responsible choice of appropriate behavioral patterns that are both individual and social. Families who are living with AIDS have a very difficult mission. The loss of family unity and concern causes a loss of psychological and spiritual state of immunity that at times is as important as physical immunity in sustaining the individual's capacity of reaction. They have the mission to offer support and affection—not abandonment but rather attentive care and affectionate presence.[29]

As noted, society has a major role in combating AIDS. Society must not reject the patient and must not fear the disease. As a community, it must respond to the needs of the affected individual and provide the support necessary for the patient to maintain self-respect, dignity, self-support, and a feeling of belonging. Society must meet the challenge with timeliness and courage, with clear ideas and upright initiatives for prevention, treatment, and rehabilitation.

Above all, the patient must strive to prevent the development of despair and recrimination. Recognizing that scientists throughout the world are tirelessly striving to overcome the disease, the patient must protect society from spread of the disease, and must face the disease with courage and determination to remain a productive and contributing member of society insofar as health will permit. The patient must also be compassionate, aware of his burden but possessing dignity and moral strength that will be of particular help for those who are tempted to despair.

VIII.   TOUGH DECISIONS ASSOCIATED WITH AIDS

Employers must balance the rights of the affected employee with the concerns of frightened co-workers or face the possibility of a lawsuit.

Insurers must confront the potentially enormous cost of health care and death benefits for persons with AIDS.

Attorneys must press for swift resolution of legal disputes over hiring and firing practices, discrimination based on sexual orientation and handicap, testing and screening, public health policies, and other AIDS-related issues.

Public officials must walk the line between the rights of the individual and their responsibility to protect the public health.

The family must not reject but must provide the love, care, and physical, mental, and moral support; the gospel of the prodigal son.

Society must not reject and must not fear. As a community it must respond to the needs of the affected individual and provide the means for the patient to maintain self-respect, dignity, and a feeling of belonging.

Patients must protect the public health of the community from spread of the disease and must learn to accept and balance life with care, concern, dignity and moral strength.

ACKNOWLEDGMENTS

I wish to acknowledge the reference value of *The AIDS Manual: A Guide for Health Care Administrators*, edited by J. A. DeHovitz and T. J. Altimont, with legal contributions by Venable, Baetjer, and Howard, National Health Publishing, Williams and Wilkins, Owings Mills, Maryland, 1988, and the Abbot Diagnostics Educational Services, Diagnostics Division, Abbott Laboratories, Abbott Park, Illinois.

NOTES

1. Pinching, A. J., Weiss, R. A., Miller, D. (eds.). (1988). AIDS and HIV infection: The wider perspective. *British Medical Journal, 44* (1) (January).
2. Wiley, J. A., Samuel, M.C. (1989). Prevalence of HIV infection in the USA. *AIDS, 3* (Suppl. 1), S71–S78.
3. Turner, C. F. (1989). Research on sexual behaviors that transmit HIV: Progress and problems. *AIDS, 3*(Suppl. 1), S63–S69.
4. Day, S. (1988). Prostitute women and AIDS: Anthropology. *AIDS, 2*, 421–428.
5. Moss, A. R., Bacchetti, P. (1989). Natural history of HIV infection. *AIDS, 3*, 55–61.
6. Polk, B. F., Fo, R., Brookmeyer, R., *et al.* (1987). Predictors of the acquired immunodeficiency syndrome developing in a cohort of homosexual men. *New England Journal of Medicine, 316*, 61–66.
7. The case definition of AIDS used by CDC for national reporting (CDC Reportable AIDS). Document No. 03125, August 1, 1985, Centers for Disease Control, Atlanta, Georgia.

8. CDC Classification System for HIV Infections (1986). *Morbidity and Mortality Weekly Report, 35*, 334–339.
9. Abrams, D. I. (1986). Lymphadenopathy related to the acquired immune deficiency syndrome in homosexual men. *Medical Clinics of North America, 70*, 693–706.
10. Gottlieb, M. S., Wolf, P., Hardy, D., *et al.* (1985). Persistent generalized lymphadenopathy: The UCLA experience. In S. Gupta (Ed.), *AIDS associated syndromes* (pp. 85–92). New York: Plenum Press.
11. Cooper, D., MacLean, P., Finlayson, R., *et al.* (1985). Acute AIDS retrovirus infection definition of a clinical illness associated with seroconversion. *Lancet, II*, 537–540.
12. Elder, G. A., Sever, J. L. (1988). AIDS and neurological disorders. An overview. *Annals of Neurology, 23*(Suppl.), S4–S6.
13. Janssen, R. S., Saykin, A. J., Kaplan, J. E., *et al.* (1988). Neurological symptoms and neuropsychological abnormalities in lymphadenopathy syndrome. *Annals of Neurology, 23*(Suppl.), S17–S18.
14. Fischl, M. A. (1989). State of antiretroviral therapy with aldovudine. *AIDS, 3*(Suppl. 1), S137–S143.
15. Gallo, R. C., Sarin, P. S., Gelmann, E. P., *et al.* (1983). Isolation of human T-cell leukemia virus in Acquired Immune Deficiency Syndrome (AIDS). *Science, 220*, 865–867.
16. Barré-Sinoussi, F., Chermann, J. C., Nugeyre, M. T., *et al.* (1983). Isolation of a T-lymphotropic retrovirus from a patient at risk for Acquired Immune Deficiency Sydrome (AIDS). *Science, 220*, 868–871.
17. Martin, M., & Weiss, E. A. (1989). Virology overview. *AIDS 3*(Suppl. 1), S3–S4.
18. Fenyo, E. M., Albert, J., & Asjö, B. (1989). Replicative capacity, cytopathic effect, and cell tropism of HIV. *AIDS 3*(suppl. 1):S5–S12.
19. Wain-Hobson, S. 1989. HIV genome variability in vivo. *AIDS 3*(suppl. 1):S13–15.
20. Cann, A. J. and Korn, J. 1989. Molecular biology of HIV: New insights into the virus life cycle. *AIDS 3*(suppl. 1):S19–S34.
21. Temin, H. M. 1988. Evolution of retroviruses and other retrotranscripts. In: D. Bolognesi, ed. *Human Retroviruses, Cancer, and AIDS: Approaches to Prevention and Therapy*. UCLA Symposia on Molecular and Cellular Biology, New Series, Volume 71, Alan R. Liss, Inc., New York, pp. 1–28.
22. Wann, Jr. 1987. Summary Report. IIIrd International Conference on AIDs, sponsored by the U.S. Department of Health and Human Services, Public Health Service, and the World Health Organization (Washington D.C., June 1–5).
23. Walter, L. 1988. Ethical issues in the prevention and treatment of HIV infection and AIDS. *Science* 239:597–603.
24. Mann, J. M., Carballo, M. (1989). Social, cultural and political aspects: Overview. *AIDS 3*(Suppl. 1), S221–S223.
25. Turner, C. F. (1989). Research on sexual behaviors that transmit HIV: Progress and problems. *AIDS 3*(Suppl. 1), S63–S69.
26. Somerville, M. A., & Orkin, A. J. (1989). Human rights, discrimination and AIDS: Concepts and issues. *AIDS 3*(Suppl. 1), S283–S287.
27. DeHovitz, J. A., & Altimont, T. J. (Eds.). (1988). *The AIDS Manual: A guide for health care administrators*. Owings Mill, MD: National Health Publishing, Division of Williams and Wilkins.
28. Dickens, B. N. (1988). Legal rights and duties in the AIDS epidemic. *Science, 239*, 580–586.
29. Address of Pope John Paul II (1989). *To live, why*. Fourth International Conference, sponsored by the Pontifical Council for Pastoral Assistance to Health Care Workers, Vatican City State, Italy, 12–15 November 1989.

VI
CONCLUSION

10
Retrospection

Clarence C. Walton

In presenting these essays, the editor's primary purpose was to encourage the expansion of dialogue between business ethicians and scholars working in cognate fields. An early, albeit modest, step has been taken. Yet even at this early stage, business ethicians have opportunity to review (for possible incorporation into their own analyses) a set of important conclusions, and it is salutary to identify some of them.

I. RELIGION

Because theology and philosophy deal with the world of *oughts*, ethics—even though its mode of reasoning is independent of religious dogma—needs to be aware of the belief systems represented by the major religious traditions. The symbiosis was captured in a remark made by one very well-known ethicist, Daniel Callahan, who said that although he "ceased to be a religious believer nearly twenty years ago," he found it difficult to "lead a full and satisfying life . . . and a fairly rich philosophical life . . . without some sense of the religious issues and possibilities."[1] Called to provide this "sense of religious issues and possibilities," were Gordon Tucker, Paul Camenisch, and Dennis McCann, each of whom has had substantial practical and scholarly experiences with a major creed. From them may be learned, or relearned, how certain Jewish, Protestant, and Catholic traditions have retained their relevance for the business world. An examination of their common elements shows the following:

Clarence C. Walton • The American College, Bryn Mawr, Pennsylvania 19010.

- Work is a calling or a vocation to be followed according to the individual's perception of the Divine will.
- All social institutions rest on trust.
- The responsible person uses his/her gifts not only for personal fulfillment but also for the common good.
- Only by searching for the common good is the vitality of the communal life preserved.
- Viable organizations are "caring" organizations that, in turn, contribute to a caring community.
- Everyone has a responsibility to be "additive," that is, to increase the stock of resources.

The relevance of religious principles to business practices was given by Rabbi Gordon Tucker in the examples of foreign bribery and insider trading. It is interesting, however, to explore how these respective religions look at another fundamental concept, namely, the right to work—a critical point where intersections between religions and economic principles have intriguing implications for public policy. To be noted, of course, is the fact that the science of economics is necessary but not determinative for the formulation of economic policy. In terms of the policies designed to guarantee the right to work, convinced Jews and Christians might subscribe to Keynesian or supply-side theories. The Keynesian would advocate a policy of demand management in order to achieve a targeted employment rate; the neoclassicist, on the other hand, might argue that the right to work is better promoted by restrictions on unemployment benefits, curtailment of corporate and union monopolies, and abolition of the minimum wage.

Whether churches have anything definitive to say on public policies regarding a right to work, however, is precisely the one that intrigues most spiritual leaders because it touches on the spirit and need for human fulfillment through work. This religious view runs counter to the position taken by some of the most distinguished economists who insist that "mere existence cannot confer a right or a moral claim on anyone or any other."[2] To insist otherwise leads churches to see the next step as inevitable, that is, to tell how such claims must be facilitated through political and economic policies. Under the banner of rights, church leaders often, say their critics, use their gospel to create a "mirage of social justice," the most extreme expression of which is liberation theology and Christian socialism. Even the social encyclicals of the Pope and the policy statements coming from Anglican synods, Presbyterian General Assemblies, and the National Council of Christian Churches, strike critics as examples of unctuous welfarism. Despite the criticism that blankets Jewish, Protestant and Catholic perspectives under one cover are differences among them, the identity of which becomes an intriguing exercise.

In the Jewish view, justice means that every person be guaranteed a right to work. Even a cursory economic examination of Jewish sources shows a clear support for the concept of the nonprofit corporation as the solution for problems of unemployment. This has been, in fact, the cornerstone of economic and fiscal policy in contemporary Israel. Firms were subsidized by public funding if they promised to increase work opportunities; public sector bailouts of successful firms that had encountered difficulties have been common; and tariff protection has been given to those enterprises that have promise of expanding work opportunities. In short, the concept of the right to work has been translated by the government most influenced by the Jewish tradition into actions where rewards and punishments of the market have often been removed in the government's search for full employment.

Prominent Israelis are now asking whether such a policy is economically and *morally* desirable. Rampant inflation, declining productivity, protectionism, and a somewhat smug work force have taken their toll. Maier Tamari, the well-known director of the Jerusalem Institute for Ethics, Economics and Management, and an employee of the Bank of Israel, has recently asked whether the policy made sense. The obligation of justice rests on the shoulders of every person regardless of the individual's preferences. But here is the interesting point: Whereas giving is meritorious and praiseworthy, receiving is not. Tamari noted how the Hebrew word for charity (*tzedakah*) is the same root word for justice: The public is obligated only to provide the minimum standards of living, and charity is not a way to equalize incomes. If justice means the right to work, it also means the duty to work at something productive. If, however, the duty cannot be translated into possibility then charity remains. The state might provide the unemployed with cash grants with the clear understanding that shame is attached to the recipients. If "unnecessary" work is provided, it would be through nonprofit organizations recognized by everyone as inefficient ones. Those given make-work nonproductive jobs would be absorbed in sheltered workshops, and there would be no delusions on the part of anyone that the recipients must carry a burden of shame.[3]

The idea of shame is muted in the Protestant tradition and largely rejected in the Catholic perspective. Particularly for the Calvinists, the doctrine of predestination did not mean that work itself guaranteed salvation; however, it did imply that the worker who achieved financial success in his or her calling (or vocation) had reasonable assurances that God was showing a favor on earth that strongly indicated favor in the hereafter. The sense of shame for any unemployed person was little discussed, but a strong inference can be made that the unemployed and the unsuccessful were not to be considered among the chosen ones. Those who were successful had a solemn obligation to give to the unfortunate, the unlucky, the unskilled. Andrew Carnegie is the classic example. He followed this religious summons but also was quick to point out how much better it was to provide a poor person with a fishing rod than with a fish.

The Catholic tradition was, if anything, more emphatic in holding that the dignity of the human person brought a natural right to a decent job, a decent livelihood, and a living wage. Back in 1906, when John A. Ryan of Catholic University found that 6 of every 10 American workers were receiving wages below minimum living needs, he made the then-revolutionary recommendation that the state should intervene in the market to force employers to pay a living wage.[4] But what of the unemployed poor? Unlike the Jewish tradition that placed on the heads of the subsidized poor a Hester Prynne mark of shame, or the Calvinist tradition that strongly hinted that the poor were among the nonelect, Catholic theorists have always seen poverty as a blessing—a view drawn from Christ's Sermon on the Mount.

In the early tradition, emphasis was on distributive justice: One should get a fair wage for a fair day's work. More recently, however, a subtle expansion of this view was revealed—first in a little publicized talk of Pope John Paul and, second, in the widely publicized Bishops' pastoral letter of 1986, *Economic Justice for All*.[5] A note on the Pontiff's and the hierarchy's view is instructive. On June 9, 1979, John Paul II, referring to his title as Pope in the third person, told listeners at Nowa Hota:

> Christianity and the Church have no fear of the world of work. They have no fear of a system based on work. The Pope has no fear of men of work. They have always been particularly close to him. He has come from their midst. He has come from the quarries of Zakrzowek, from the Solvay furnaces in Borek Falecki, and then from Nowa Huta. Through all these surroundings, through his own experience of work, I make bold to say that the Pope learned the Gospel anew. He noticed and became convinced that the problems being raised today about human labor are deeply engraved in the Gospel and cannot be fully solved without the Gospel. The problems raised today about human labor . . . do not come down in the last analysis—either to technology or even to economics, but to a fundamental category: the category of the dignity of work, that is to say, of the dignity of man.[6]

Linking honorable work to an individual's fulfillment means that where such work is denied, there is a denial of human rights. This view harmonizes with the Jewish religious outlook. But there is in the Pope's expression no hint that shame attaches to one because a job is not available. Nor is shame hinted in the Bishops' pastoral letter on social teaching and the economy. If shame attaches itself to anything, it is to social institutions that fail in their duty to provide work for willing and able people, certainly not to the individual. On this point the Bishops' language is quite forthright: "When people are without a chance to make a living, and must go hungry and homeless, they are being denied basic rights and society as a whole, acting through public and private institutions, has the moral responsibility to enhance human dignity and protect human rights."[7] Unlike present Israeli policy, the bishops did not place primary responsibility on the government, but rather held that the state must act only when intermediary institutions in the private sector fail their duty![8] When failures occur, the best solution to the problem of unemployment is cooperative effort by state and industry."[9]

Preoccupation with religious theory—Jewish, Protestant, and Catholic—may lead, however, to a certain blandness, if not blindness toward present realities. Dennis McCann noted that "devotional Catholicism" (individualism, sobriety, sacrifice, and loyalty) was not only " compatible with, but actually helped support, the middle-class mentality of Calvinism." And with the death of the immigrant Church came the death of the "devotional Catholicism." The new Americanist version is no longer critical of capitalism, only of its failings. Increasing productivity (the additive factor) is now seen by the Bishops in quite the same way as seen by recent Jewish critics of Israeli policy. Furthermore, a renewed emphasis on "industriousness" suggests a close affinity to the Protestant work ethic. And while churches differ less from one another on attitudes toward business, each is experiencing internally ideological wars between so called conservatives and liberals.

To summarize: In Jewish, Catholic, and Protestant ethics the common view is that this world is prelude to another, that God's will calls everyone to respect the rights of others, and that there is an ongoing dialogue between Creator and created. Economists most critical of church claims about the inherent job rights of individuals—F. A. Hayek comes to mind—readily admit that societies simply cannot exist if people have no sense of obligation.[10] Because obligations may be strengthened or weakened by the relationship of the duty bearer to the rights carrier (e.g., obligations toward others in the immediate family are easier to recognize than duties toward friendly neighbors or toward unknown strangers), the "language of interaction" in any extended social order uses a vocabulary of obligations provided mainly by religion.[11] *Duty* is so common a word in ethical enquiry—Kant made it central to his analysis—that business philosophers literally have a vested interest in knowing what the churches say on this and related matters.

II.   LAW, SOCIOLOGY, AND LABOR RELATIONS

The move from the so-called "sacred" science of religion represented in the previous section to the secular sciences of law and sociology, labor, and economics handled in the second part is taken possibly more frequently, by executives than by scholars who represent a post-Enlightenment tradition that emphasizes reason over religion, fact over faith. Corporate executives, on the other hand, are not inhibited by the lines of demarcation found in the disciplines. By the nature of their work, executives are called upon to be generalists who see the totality of their markets and their organizations. A fairly typical view was expressed by the chairman and CEO of the California-based Olga Company, John Jan Erteszek, when he said that "the paradigm in economic science of self-interest is inadequate and that a new vision can be supplied in Judeo-Christian virtues."[12] Former CEO Donald Siebert of Penney's spoke to a large audience when he noted the importance of the Ten Commandments to all members of the business community.[13] Aside from their religious convictions, both executives felt that the very survival of the free market depended on the ability of business leaders to integrate the system of Western moral values into the world of practical affairs.

A. Law

In a religiously diverse society, however, conscientious people may believe that imperatives from religion are either inappropriate or too hard to apply to the complexities of contemporary business. Laws must be crafted or revised to meet the exigencies of new situations, and Lynn Paine's formula provides an exciting ethical base on which such laws can be drafted. She has used in a very effective way the practice of intelligence gathering (when knowledge is the most valuable sort of property) to show how new forms of competition require new forms of law.

Business ethicians will, of course, want to explore other areas. Of the many available, one is especially interesting because it relates to the hallowed concept of fiduciary responsibility. The classic case on this point occurred in 1742 (*The Charitable Corporation v. Sir Robert Sulton*) in which directors of the company were held personally responsible for failing to monitor the behavior of managers whose embezzlements and faked receipts led to the company's bankruptcy. Today focus is on the 1985 landmark case, *Smith v. Gorkum*, wherein the Delaware supreme court held that the directors of Trans Union Corporation failed to use information available and relevant to their decision to recommend a cash-out merger proposal by the Marmon Group. The Trans Union's directors had breached their fiduciary responsibilities to the shareholders.[14] A blending of religious and legal values is often seen in discussions on organizational loyalty, disclosure, policies, and the like. Paine's essay, although not addressing the "blending" process directly, makes clear inferences that such processes do occur.

B. Sociology

By its very nature, law is mainly reactive not proactive. But significant social movements require a proactive stance by everyone, especially by policymakers who struggle with questions such as these:

- Should a "foreign" language be made an official second language alongside English?
- Should gays be allowed to marry? Adopt children?
- Should public schools be privatized so that entrepreneurs can start institutions that meet the special needs of special students?
- Should big city mayors provide multilingual street signs?
- Should nonregistered aliens be deported as soon after their arrival as possible?

Questions multiply in the light of Ivar Berg's findings. In introducing his essay, mention was made of the influence Crevecoeur and Tocqueville have had on American thought. It is, therefore, appropriate to close the circle on Berg's provocative thoughts by recalling another French visitor, Jean-François Revel. Revel visited the United States during the tumultuous days of the late 1960s when campuses exploded with student unrest, when anti-Vietnam War protesters clogged the streets of the country's major cities, and where buildings in urban ghettos erupted in flames. Recalling these things, Revel concluded that America was a country of revolutionary change.[15] He observed that enduring revolutions never came from a single source. Essential to their nature are those multidimensional factors introduced by diverse groups who have different grievances or goals—economic, political, and cultural. Why the revolution would come into the United States, explained Revel, was because this country had all the necessary prerequisites. These included:

- High economic growth
- High levels of technological and research competence
- A future-oriented culture
- A break by youth from the behavioral standards that had guided their elders
- A constitutional system and political philosophy that allow all subcultures to coexist alongside the main culture.

The diversity of cultures, coupled to the existence of contradictory moral systems, is bound to generate a collective and individual crisis with increasing intensity.[16] These crises—and those who precipitate them—are not repressed by the American legal system but are, rather, safeguarded under Constitutional guarantees. Because each subculture can "do its own thing," the result is a "creative revolution" that moves the United States ahead of other countries in the drive for the 1789 revolutionary ideals of liberty, fraternity, and equality. In the past, it was assumed that extremists on the Left or the Right would carry the revolution forward. But the Left is handicapped because it is more interested in its own triumphs than it is in destroying injustices; the Right is hobbled because the wall of separation between church and state is used to make them appear as religious zealots.[17]

With subtle strokes, Berg has painted the cultural landscape of contemporary America: a new wave of immigrants who study English as a second language and speak pridefully of their Asian culture; churches burdened by ideological conflicts over public policy and yet united in many of their most fundamental beliefs; blacks increasingly (especially if they are of the urban poor) seceding from the union. In their search for identity, each group seems to the American majority to be perversely committed or committed perversely. Yet their commitments have to be taken seriously. The long and short of it is that, although Berg is too careful to predict an inevitable revolution, he is too wise not to see the multiple forces that may make one happen. Like the coming of Social Darwinism in the nineteenth century, the coming of social pluralism in the twentieth may lead to new ideologies that reshape the nature of the American culture. Thus far, each group has accepted a kind of moratorium where no decisive decision must be made. Yet those who will benefit from a moratorium (either by acquiescence or activism), will eventually force a decision for themselves, for their identity, and for the identity of the United States.

C. Labor

The second section is concluded by James Kuhn's assessment of the future needs in labor–management relations. Traditionalists may argue that facts will overtake Kuhn's prophesy. The perception of labor as a wounded animal was gotten from the serious setbacks unions experienced in the 1980s. Beginning in 1981 when Ronald Reagan fired 11,500 striking air traffic controllers who refused to modify their wage demands, unions lost one after another strike—from the Phelps Dodge strike by copper miners to the strike by the burly athletes of the National Football League and to the highly publicized strike by workers of the National Broadcasting Company. Compared to 1955, the year the AFL-CIO merged, public approval of the unions had dropped from 76 to 55 percent in 1988.

But the wounded animal is roaring back. Disgruntled workers saw real wages (adjusted for inflation) fall by 15 percent from 1973 to 1988. They point out that Nissan auto workers in Japan averaged about $38,000 a year—$14,000 more than the average American worker. In the past, union leaders justified their willingness to accept wage concessions by pointing out how global competition was hurting the bottom lines of corporate America. But corporate profits have run nearly 15 percent in 1988 over the previous year and the steel industry, which lost over $12 billion from 1982 to 1986, posted more than $3 billion in profits from 1987 to 1988. Before the 1989 negotiations over the future contract had ever begun, workers had geared up to fight contract-out policies and to seek meaningful job security, better pensions (still stuck at the 1980 levels), and, most particularly, wage increases. Further, one union (the United Auto Workers) had developed a $4 million ad campaign that blames Wall Street financiers for the country's slow rate of productivity growth—an obvious effort to shift responsibility for America's noncompetitiveness in global markets from manufacturers to investment bankers.

It is well to reemphasize the significance of the UAW strategy. Their enemy is not so much the boss but those junk bond specialists who made money simply by moving money. This reflects, at least in part, Kuhn's theory that management and labor have more to gain by sticking together than by falling apart. One way to stay together is to learn lessons from UAW head Douglas Fraser's experiences on the General Motors board of directors. Another learner has been the McDonald–Douglas Corporation that, in 1989, named to a vice presidential position Joel Smith, a former UAW staff member who, 6 years earlier, had picketed company headquarters during a mean 4-month strike against the airplane company. If the examples are followed, companies will get valuable information on how— and what—their workers think. The power of those midlevel managers who control vital information essential to the decision maker can be greatly weakened by ex-labor leaders who had learned how to break information bottlenecks.[18] On its part, workers might well remember the Knights of Labor that fell apart for a variety of reasons, one of which was "unscrupulous rascals and the most infamous damn liars and tricksters" who "feasted on the carcass of the movement that had once tried to hold them at bay."[19] Labor itself needs internal discipline. So Kuhn's historical survey may, despite the resurgence of union power at the close of the 1980s, provide lessons for the future. If both management and labor read the history books carefully, they might bring to reality the dream of Samuel Gompers, founder of the American Federation of Labor, who said in 1883 that labor's goals were simple:

> We want more school houses and less jails; more books and less arsenals; more learning and less vice; more constant work and less crime; more leisure and less greed; more justice and less revenge."[20]

Gompers's dream continues to be expressed on contemporary tongues. And it is one that has more chance to succeed today, suggested Kuhn, than

in the nineteenth century when a savage form of Social Darwinism prevailed.

III. DISCIPLINES AND DISCIPLES

Having concentrated on what the major religions had to say about
business and what scholars from three major areas of study had to say
about the future of society, corporations and labor, it was quite logical to
move the exploration into analyses of certain basic assumptions that under-
gird subjects most business students take in the course of their degree
programs: economics, organization theory, and human resource management. Each is influenced by assumptions made about human nature and
human society by philosophers, evolutionary biologists, and Skinnerian
psychologists. Barry Schwartz has provided several interesting propositions that converge on one disturbing theme: Liberty is possibly more
chimera than reality. It is well to take a second look at the conclusion.

So far as economic theory is concerned, one clarification is needed:
Adam Smith, the man generally acclaimed as father of the field, did not
seek to provide a justification for acquisitive egoism. To see him in that
light is to suggest that his *Wealth of Nations* has a life independent of his
earlier work, *The Theory of Moral Sentiments*.[21] Admittedly, there is a surface
contradiction between the morality of the first book and the self-interest of
the second. It would, however, be unfair to Smith to ignore his oft-repeated
stress on the relationship of self-interest to sympathy and benevolence in
human nature. This point emerges quite clearly from his observation that
"how selfish soever man may be supposed, there are evidently some
principles in his nature which interest him in the fortunes of others, and
render their happiness necessary to him, though he derives nothing from it
except the pleasure of seeing it."[22] This insight, reinforced on separate
occasions, has impressed moral philosophers as the "true" Adam Smith
and the view of one ethicist, C. D. Broad, is the common property of many
other ethicists: Every human is "a complex whole of various propensities
arranged in a hierarchy, [and the trick is to] distinguish between the actual
relative strength of our various propensities and that which they ought to
have."[23] The latter may be called their "moral authority."

If any single lesson emerges from Schwartz's analysis of neoclassical
economic theory it is this: Business moral philosophers owe it to themselves and to their students to reexamine the paradigms of economic
theory as they have been attributed to Adam Smith. It is a healthy sign that
distinguished economists like Herbert Simon, Harvey Leibenstein, and

Thomas Schelling have offered new paradigms to macroeconomics, each of which also requires careful analysis by moral philosophers.

The second interest of Schwartz dealt with the theory of evolutionary biology, especially as it has been expounded by Edmund Wilson. It was Wilson's brave—and bold—claim (sociobiology is destined to become the new discipline that would combine the paradigms of the social and biological sciences in ways that explain the fundamental patterns of human beings through neo-Darwinian principles) that raised the hackles. Two assertions from sociobiology are worth repeating: (1) Biology (particularly genetics) could explain some fundamental constants of human behavior such as mating patterns, territoriality, and aggression in the chain of evolving species and (2) that aspects of the theory could be applied to human social behavior in terms of long evolutionary perspectives.

The expansive claims can be best appreciated by comparing Wilson to Ruth Benedict, one of the most distinguished anthropologists of a half-century ago. Writing in 1934, Benedict expressed the view that although there are societies where behavior is predetermined, these are societies of social insects, not people.

> Not one item of his tribal social organization, of his language, of his local religion, is carried in his germ-cell. . . . Man is not committed in detail by his biological constitution to any particular variety of behavior. The great diversity of social solutions that man has worked out in different cultures in regard to mating, for example, or trade, are all equally possible on the basis of his original endowment. . . . We must accept all the implications of our human inheritance, *one of the most important of which is the small scope of biologically transmitted behavior*, and the enormous role of the cultural process of the transmission of tradition.[24]

Although the clash between the old anthropological and the new sociobiological views is likely to be hotly debated, it is also clear that the relationships of biology to the social sciences will become increasingly close. Schwartz warns ethicists to be wary of such intimacy. The warning applies with particular force to organizational theory. If, for example, Wilson is right about territoriality, there arises almost inevitably the issue of a *tribal* versus a *universal* ethic; if he is right about human aggression, there arises the problem of justice and benevolence, as well as specter of the manager's conflict between the organization's self-interest and the workers' needs. The problem was well stated by Neil Chamberlain, the well-known industrial relations scholar, in these words:

> Employees are being paid to produce, not to make themselves into better people. Corporations are purchasing employee time to make a return on it, not investing in employees to enrich their lives. Employees are human capital, and when capital is hired or leased, the objective is not to embellish it for its own sake but to use it for financial advantage. But somewhere in this philosophy

there is an inconsistency with the notion of a society of self-governing individuals. The large corporation has become an organizer of people, a user of people, a molder of identities, according to criteria that it has evolved, without regard to the effect on those people except at this is registered on the balance sheet.[25]

One clear inference from Chamberlain's comment is that liberty and justice—what Americans consider as fundamental to their fulfillment as humans—are not seen in the dominant management creed as inalienable rights but as instrumental values used to improve the organization's performance.[26]

The third implicit challenge Schwartz poses for business ethics comes from Skinnerian psychology's tool kit for control. That managers must revert to control mechanisms if the work of the organization is to be fulfilled is the premise of almost all organization theorists. The real question pertains to the nature of control. Because management's practices are based on the psychologists' theories, their view of human nature becomes critical. One of the most prominent expositors of management theory was the late Douglas McGregor with his famous theories X and Y.[27] Although Theory Y has a more tolerant view of human nature, McGregor's aim is to control employees by shaping them to the employer's will. Even when due process practices are introduced, they are designed less to promote justice and more to advance the organization's goals. As a result, critics say that management has never really departed from the ideology underpinning Theory X: "The major difference between modern management and the past lies in the method of implementation," not the rights of people.[28] At this juncture, Skinner's theory of *operant conditioning* adds a new gun to management's arsenal, and Schwartz is troubled by a theory that makes it easier to turn human beings into instruments for another's use. Kantian ethicists would, of course, rebel at the notion. So would others. The point is that whatever social scientists say of human nature is germane to the work of business ethicists.

If basic paradigms in certain disciplines significantly influence the student, can the "disciples" significantly influence the disciplines? Probably not. But they can influence the curricular contours of business schools. Such influence is particularly important at this time when the most important accrediting agency for business schools, the American Assembly of Collegiate Schools of Business (AACSB), is calling for reform of curricula that have been only moderately altered since the late 1950s when the Ford and the Carnegie Foundations successfully brought about change. Even the AACSB itself has become the object of so much criticism that splinter groups are coming into existence.

For the foregoing reasons, James Glenn's data have taken on a new urgency. Findings from his surveys result not so much in an intellectual as a practical challenge, namely, how to introduce more ethics and, implicitly, better teaching, in the field of business ethics. In the eyes of some professors, student opinions on these subjects are suspect. Their suspicions are not without some merit, especially at the undergraduate level where faculty effectiveness was closely correlated to the professor's "entertaining" ability or on skill in getting students to "fantasize."

Glenn's work, however, has focused not on student reactions to teachers but on student expressions of their educational needs. When 58 percent of them said that ethics had not been adequately stressed in their business education, neither deans nor faculties can shrug off the report as quickly as they might dismiss student views on particular teachers. When Glenn says that his findings show that "having an ethics course in the curriculum did not reduce the perceived need for more stress in ethics in their business education," those teaching such courses have important questions to ponder: Is the course in business ethics poorly taught? Should ethical instruction be incorporated into such functional areas of marketing, production, accounting, and finance—as the Wharton program seeks to do? Is a single course an invitation to so much generality that only advanced courses in business ethics can meet the need?

Finally, Glenn noted an irony in one brief sentence: "Future managers [the students] and their teachers view ethics as much less relevant in their curriculum than do current practicing managers, especially the CEOs." More questions are raised: Should the gap between academic life and business be closed? If so, how? What role is appropriate for professors of business ethics? What strategies are available to them? Although Glenn reports his findings in a matter-of-fact fashion and although he is careful in warning readers not to jump to conclusions based only on statistics, the "numbers game" will be played by somebody, and "somebodies" ought to include a fair number of professors who know ethics best. Speaking of executive MBA programs, Bernard Keys and Joseph Wolfe wrote that there was "a mismatch between theory based management education and the practical preferences of managers."[29] If senior and midmanagers feel that enough is not being done in business ethics, perhaps the mismatch extends beyond executive programs. There are already signs that the humanities— and ethics particularly—will have a greater role in business education than ever before. Glenn's findings can be used to accelerate the process.

IV. PERSPECTIVES ON A SPECIAL PROBLEM: AIDS

Looking back at Clarence Gibbs's essay, philosophers recognize how closely they are tied to the scientist's enterprise. It is axiomatic that every breakthrough in science brings sets of new moral problems over which philosophers will wrestle. AIDS-related research is obviously not on the grand scale of Copernicus, Darwin, Freud, Crick, and Watson. But its side effect has been to spur interest in different questions faced by policymakers and judges. It is indeed a profitable exercise for ethicists to ask themselves a few questions that have already confronted those charged with making policy in government and business. Among them are the following:

- Would they support public policies (such as the one adopted by the District of Columbia in 1986) that prohibit testing for life, health, and disability income insurance without regard to the face value of the policy?
- Or should support be given to the Congress when, in 1980, it determined to withhold its annual appropriations to the District unless it repealed its policy? (*Note*: In 1988 courts in Massachusetts and New York invalidated regulations prohibiting AIDS testing for insurers.)
- Who has the better moral case—the employer who refuses to hire any AIDS victim when union leaders express grave concern for the safety of their workers, OR the employer who, listening to Gibbs's statement that AIDS workers can do the job, rejects labor's request?
- Does an employer have a right to do random testing on the firm's employees so long as informed consent and confidentiality are respected? (*Note*: In 1988, 12 states passed laws requiring informed consent, an end to discriminatory employment policies based on a person's sexual preference, and assurances of confidentiality before any test could be administered.)
- When an employee with AIDS requires hospitalization, do employers and insurors have a right to explore home-care and sub-acute-care centers as substitutes for treatment in a hospital setting?
- Should governments prohibit what is alleged to be the usual 200 to 300 percent markup on drugs charged in physicians' offices and home-care facilities?

Business ethicists are wary about getting involved in debates over specific government or employment policies toward AIDS victims. Certainly, no blanket approvals or disapprovals can be prudently given on generalized statements. The caution of the philosophers is matched by the caution of the scientists, and Gibbs is in good company when he mainly restricts his analysis to the scientific questions. Policymakers have no such protections. They need help. They want help. The way business ethicists respond may set examples for their responses to other ethics-laden issues such as employee privacy, retirement benefits, rights of healthy workers, obligations of society to the ill as well as obligations to the victims themselves, and so on.

V. EPILOGUE

In this preliminary endeavor what has their widened lens brought to business ethicists? Self-interest prompts the writer to say "lots." Disinterested persons may have different answers. From his perspective, however, it is fair to suggest that ethical inquiry into business issues is sharpened by taking into account the modes of reasoning used by scholars in other disciplines, the latest findings of these scholars, and the moral problems such findings may raise. One thing is as certain of business philosophers as it is with all who deal with applied ethics: Moral theory cannot be divorced from temporal reality. In the interest of efficiency it seems prudent to let experts from other fields produce their results, while encouraging business philosophers to exploit what they offer.

NOTES

1. Daniel Callahan, "Tension Between Religion and Philosophy," *Daedalus*, Vol. 117 (Spring 1988), pp. 151–152.
2. F. A. Hayek, *The Fatal Conceit: The Errors of Socialism* (Chicago: University of Chicago Press, 1988), p. 152.
3. Maier Tamari, "Employment Is a Moral Issue." Paper to be published in 1990.
4. John A. Ryan, *A Living Wage* (New York: Macmillan, 1906), pp. 288–290.
5. *Economic Justice for All: Pastoral Letter on Catholic Social Teachings of the U.S. Economy* (Washington: National Conference of Catholic Bishops, 1986).
6. Quoted by Jan P. Schotte, "The Social Teaching of the Church: *Laborem Exercens*, A New Challenge," *The Review of Social Economy*, Vol. 40 (December 1982), p. 340.
7. *Economic Justice For All*, p xi.
8. Ibid., pp. 155 and 314.
9. Ibid., pp. 137 and 281.
10. Hayek, *The Fatal Conceit*, Chapter 9.
11. Lon Fuller, *The Principles of Social Order* (Durham, NC: Duke University Press, 1981), pp. 239–241.
12. John Jan Erteszek, "Corporate Enterprise and Christian Ethics," *Review of Social Economy*, Vol. 40 (December 1982), p. 323.
13. Donald Siebert, "Time to Revive Commitment to Ethics," *New York Times*, (December 25, 1983).
14. An exciting book on this and other cases related to corporate directors has been written by Arthur Fleischer, Jr., Geoffrey Hazard, Jr., and Miriam Klipper, *Board Games: The Changing Shape of Corporate Power* (Boston: Little, Brown, 1988).
15. Jean-François Revel, *Without Marx or Christ* (Garden City, NY: Doubleday, 1971), pp. 183–184.

16. Ibid., pp. 262.
17. Jean Jacques Servan-Screiber, *The American Challenge* (New York: Atheneum, 1968).
18. Paul Milgrom and John Roberts, "An Economic Approach to Influence Activities in Organizations," *The American Journal of Sociology*, Vol. 94, (1988), Supplement.
19. Leon Fink, "The New Labor History," *The Journal of American History*, Vol. 75 (June 1988), p. 127.
20. Quoted by John P. Diggins, "The Misuses of Gramsci," *The Journal of American History*, Vol. 75 (June 1988), p. 141.
21. Adam Smith, *Theory of Moral Sentiments* (Indianapolis: Liberty Classics, 1982). Reprint. Edited by D. D. Raphaela and A. L. Macfee.
22. *Moral Sentiments*, p. 9.
23. C. D. Broad, *Five Types of Ethical Theory.* (New York: Harcourt Brace, 1930), p. 56.
24. Ruth Benedict, *Patterns of Culture* (Boston: Houghton Mifflin, 1964), pp. 14–16.
25. Neil Chamberlain, *The Limits of Corporate Responsibility* (New York: Basic Books, 1973), p. 92.
26. W. G. Scott and T. R. Mitchell, "The Universal Barnard: His Macro-Theory of Organization," *Public Administration Quarterly*, Vol. 11 (1987), pp. 34–58.
27. Douglas McGregor, *The Human Side of Enterprise* (New York: McGraw-Hill), 1959. For a sharp critique of McGregor's postulates, see David K. Hart, "Management and Benevolence: The Fatal Flaw of Theory Y," in Konstantin Kolenda, ed., *Organizations and Ethical Individualism* (New York: Praeger, 1988), Chapter 4.
28. W. G. Scott, "The Management Governance Theories of Justice and Liberty," *Journal of Management*, Vol. 14 (June 1988), p. 281.
29. Bernard Keys and Joseph Wolfe, "Management Education and Development: Current Issues and Emerging Trends," *The Journal of Management*, Vol. 14 (June 1988), p. 222.

Index

Achenbaum, A. A., 8
Acquired immune deficiency syndrome. *See* AIDS
Advertising, 101-102. *See also* Media; Public relations
Affirmative action programs, 121, 129, 133
AFL. *See* American Federation of Labor (AFL)
AFL-CIO. *See* American Federation of Labor-Congress of Industrial Organizations (AFL-CIO)
AIDS, 29-33, 233-258, 273-275
  biology/pathogenesis of HIV infection, 244-245
  clinical/laboratory features of, 239-242
  culture and, 131
  epidemiology of, 236-238
  ethical/legal implications of, 31-33, 246-256
  impact of, 233-234
  insurance and, 255
  natural history of HIV infection, 238-239
  nervous system and, 242-244
  retrovirus evolution, 246
AIDS-related complex (ARC), 240-241
AIDS-related moral problems, 32, 252-258
Alcohol abuse. *See* Substance abuse
American Civil Liberties Union (ACLU), 32
American Federation of Labor (AFL), 21, 151
American Federation of Labor-Congress of Industrial Organizations (AFL-CIO), 153, 164, 268
American Manufacturing Association, 21

American Medical Association, 32
American Telephone and Telegraph Company, 157
"Americanist" Catholicism. *See* "Republican" Catholicism
"Americanist" heresy, 75
Antitrust law, 93, 140
Aquinas, Saint Thomas, 26
Aristotle, 7, 20, 26
Aron, H. J., 33
Arrow, Kenneth, 201, 208
Arts, 129
Asceticism, 72-73
Attitudes
  business school students, 223
  competition and, 107-109
Auchincloss, Louis, 27
Authoritarianism, 163-166, 167-168
Authority, 73-74

Baal Shem Tov, 10
Baby Boom. *See* Demography
Baer, George F., 163
Baker, Constance, 250
Ball, George, 51
Barton, Bruce, 66-67
Baumhart, Raymond, 213-215, 218
Beard, Robin, 132
Becker, Gary, 28, 137, 191
Behavior theory, 195-197. *See also* Human nature
Bell, Daniel, 131-132, 133, 142
Benedict, Ruth, 271